The Heinemann
English Grammar

Digby Beaumont & Colin Granger

HEINEMANN INTERNATIONAL

A division of Heinemann Educational Books Ltd
Halley Court, Jordan Hill, Oxford OX2 8EJ

OXFORD   LONDON   EDINBURGH
MELBOURNE   SYDNEY   AUCKLAND
MADRID   ATHENS   BOLOGNA
SINGAPORE   IBADAN   NAIROBI
GABORONE   KINGSTON   PORTSMOUTH (NH)

ISBN 0 435 28365 0 (with answers)
0 435 28364 2 (without answers)

Designed by Mike Brain

Acknowledgements

The authors would like to thank all those people whose
suggestions and comments have helped with this book,
especially Gibson Ferguson at the University of
Edinburgh's Institute of Applied Language Studies, Hazel
Barker at the English Language Centre, Hove, Sussex,
and Michèle Cronick at Heinemann International,
Oxford.

Phototypeset by Advanced Filmsetters (Glasgow) Ltd
Printed in Great Britain
by Butler and Tanner Ltd, Frome and London

89 90 91 92 93 94 10 9 8 7 6 5 4 3 2 1

Contents

Contents

Introduction

The Heinemann English Grammar is written for students who want to study and practise using English grammar. It is intended mainly for students working on their own, but the material is also suitable for use in class. The book is written for students at an intermediate level, but more advanced students will also find it useful for revision and consolidation.

EXPLANATIONS

The grammatical explanations are made as clear and simple as possible. In general, the language used is ordinary everyday English. However, some grammatical terms (eg adjective, noun, subject) have been used where this is necessary. These terms are explained in the *Glossary* on pages 295–297.

HOW THE BOOK IS ORGANIZED

- There are 190 units in the book. Generally, each unit deals with a particular point of grammar (eg the present continuous, *will*, or the articles *a, an* and *the*). The units begin with explanations and examples, followed by one or more exercises.
- In addition, some units contrast grammar points from previous units (eg Unit 2 contrasts the present continuous and present simple, and Unit 18 contrasts *will* and *going to*).
- Also, there are some general 'review' units which bring together and practise a number of points from previous units (eg Unit 28 has general practice in the present and past tenses). These review units contain exercises only and no extra explanations.
- A few units (eg Unit 35, Unit 67, Unit 75) are for reference only and contain no exercises.
- There is a list of *Contents* on pages iii–v.
- The *Index* on pages 298–303 gives a detailed list of grammatical structures (eg articles, present continuous, reported speech) and key words (eg *a/an, enough, for, will*). It also includes headings which are concerned with the way language is used (eg ability, obligation, requests, suggestions).
- There is also an *Appendix* on page 294 which gives some information about American English.

HOW TO USE THE BOOK

Some general suggestions   Use the *Index* or *Contents* list to find the unit(s) which deal with the particular point you want to study. Study the explanations and examples, then do the exercise(s).

You can, of course, also use the book simply for reference, by studying the explanations and examples and not doing the exercises.

1 Present continuous

Form

We form the present continuous with *be* + ...*-ing*.

AFFIRMATIVE

I	am	
you	are	
he she it	is	working
we you they	are	

NEGATIVE

I	am not	
you	are not	
he she it	is not	working
we you they	are not	

QUESTION

am	I	
are	you	
is	he she it	working?
are	we you they	

This form is sometimes called the 'present progressive'.

CONTRACTIONS

'm = am
're = are   *aren't = are not*
's = is   *isn't = is not*

When we add *-ing* to verbs, there are sometimes changes in spelling
eg *have* → *having*. See 188.3–6.

2   Use

a

We use the present continuous to talk about something which is in progress at the
moment of speaking.

'Where are the children?'   'They're playing in the garden.'
'What are you doing at the moment?'   'I'm writing a letter.'
You can switch off the TV. I'm not watching it.
Look, there's Sally. Who is she talking to?
We're leaving now. Goodbye.

b We also use the present continuous to talk about something which is in progress around the present, but not necessarily exactly at the moment of speaking.

You're spending a lot of money these days.
Sue is looking for a job at the moment.

We use the present continuous to talk about something which is in progress for a limited period around the present.

Robert is on holiday this week. He's staying with his sister in Bournemouth.

We use the present continuous to talk about situations which are changing or developing around the present.

Your English is improving.
The population of the world is increasing very rapidly.

EXERCISE 1A

What are the people in the pictures doing? Make sentences.

1 2 3 4 5

Example:

1 *He's reading a newspaper.*

EXERCISE 1B

Complete the sentences. Use the verbs in brackets in the present continuous.

Example:

'Where are Ken and Kate?'   'They*'re waiting* (wait) outside.'

1 '____ (Sally | have) a shower?'   'No, she ____ (wash) her hair.'
2 You ____ (not | watch) the TV at the moment. Why don't you switch it off?
3 '____ (you | enjoy) yourself?'   'Yes, I ____ (have) a great time.'
4 'What ____ (Maria | do) these days?'   'She ____ (study) English at a school in London.'
5 Ben and Patty are in London on holiday. They ____ (stay) at a small hotel near Hyde Park.
6 Prices ____ (rise) all the time. Everything ____ (get) more and more expensive.

Note

–See also 3. Present continuous and present simple.
–Some verbs eg *like, know* are not normally used in the continuous forms. See 27.
–We can use *always* with the continuous forms to mean 'too often' eg *He's always saying stupid things.* See 26.
–We also use the present continuous to talk about the future eg *I'm meeting Sue on Saturday evening.* See 19.

2 Present simple

1 Form

AFFIRMATIVE		NEGATIVE		QUESTION		
I you	work	I you	do not work	do	I you	
he she it	works	he she it	does not work	does	he she it	work?
we you they	work	we you they	do not work	do	we you they	

CONTRACTIONS

don't = do not
doesn't = does not

After *he*, *she* and *it*, verbs in the affirmative end in *-s/-es* eg *I work* ⟶ *he works; you play* ⟶ *she plays; we finish* ⟶ *it finishes.*

When we add *-s/-es* to verbs, there are sometimes changes in spelling eg *study/ studies.* See 188.1,4. For the pronunciation of *-s/-es*, see 187.1.

2 Use

a

We use the present simple to talk about repeated actions or habits.
*I **get** up at 6.30 every day.*
*Most evenings my parents **stay** at home and **watch** TV.*
***Do** you **go** to the cinema very often?*
*What time **does** Kate **finish** work?*

b

We use the present simple to talk about situations which are permanent (continuing for a long time).
*Mr and Mrs Shaw **live** in Bristol.* (That is their permanent home.)

9

c | We also use the present simple to talk about general truths.
*The River Amazon **flows** into the Atlantic Ocean.*
*Vegetarians **don't eat** meat or fish.*

EXERCISE 2A

Complete the sentences. Use the present simple of the verbs in brackets.

Examples:

The President of the USA *lives* (live) in the White House.
I *don't go* (not | go) to the theatre very often.

1 Jet engines ____ (make) a lot of noise.
2 I ____ (not | live) in London. I ____ (live) in Brighton.
3 The sea ____ (cover) two thirds of the world.
4 Loud music ____ (give) me a headache.
5 We ____ (not | come) from Canada. We ____ (come) from the USA.
6 She ____ (work) from Mondays to Fridays. She ____ (not | work) at weekends.

EXERCISE 2B

Complete the questions in the present simple.

Example:

'What time *do you get up* every morning?'   'I normally get up at 7 o'clock.'

1 '____ to the radio every morning?'   'I listen to it most mornings.'
2 '____ in Manchester?'   'No, he lives in Newcastle.'
3 'What time ____ work every day?'   'She usually finishes at 5.30.'
4 'How often ____ to the cinema?'   'I go about once a week.'
5 '____ TV every evening?'   'They watch it most evenings.'
6 '____ the guitar?'   'Yes, she plays the guitar and the piano.'

Note

–See also 3 Present continuous and present simple.
–*What do you do?* is a question about someone's occupation. eg **'What do you do?'** *'I'm a doctor.'*
–When *who, what,* or *which* is the subject of a present simple question, we do not use *do/does.* eg **Who lives** in that flat? See 144.
–We often use words such as *usually, often, every day* with the present simple to say how often things happen. eg *I **usually get** up at 6.30 every day.* See 135.
–We also use the present simple to talk about the future. eg *The train **leaves** at 7.30 tomorrow morning.* See 21.
–For the present tense of *be (am, are, is),* see 31.

3 Present continuous and present simple

Compare:

PRESENT CONTINUOUS

PRESENT SIMPLE

We use the present continuous to talk about something that is in progress at or around the moment of speaking.	We use the present simple to talk about repeated actions or habits, and things which are generally true.
*Are you **working** now?* *The water **is boiling**. Can you make the tea?*	*Do you **work** every Saturday afternoon?* *Water **boils** at 100 degrees centigrade.*

We use the present continuous for temporary situations and the present simple for permanent situations. Compare:

*He's **living** in a friend's flat at the moment.*	*She **lives** in Paris. She's lived there all her life.*

EXERCISE 3A

Choose the correct form.

Examples:

~~*It's raining*~~/*It rains* a lot in Britain in March and April.

1 'I'm going shopping.' 'Don't forget your umbrella. *It's raining/It rains* outside.'
2 *I'm going/I go* to bed now. Goodnight.
3 Normally, *I'm going/I go* to bed at around 11.30 every night.
4 'Where's Simon?' '*He's cooking/He cooks* the dinner.'
5 There is something wrong with Lynne's car at the moment so *she's going/she goes* to work by bus this week.
6 The River Thames *is flowing/flows* through London.

Note

–Some verbs eg *like, want* are not normally used in the continuous forms. For example, we cannot say ~~*I'm liking this music*~~. See 27.
–We also use the present continuous and present simple to talk about the future. See 19, 21.

4 Past simple

1 Form

The form of the past simple is the same for all persons (*I, you, he, she*, etc).

AFFIRMATIVE

I you he she it we you they	worked came

NEGATIVE

I you he she it we you they	did not	work come

QUESTION

did	I you he she it we you they	work? come?

CONTRACTION

didn't = did not

Some verbs are 'regular', other verbs are 'irregular':

- The affirmative past simple of regular verbs ends in *-ed* eg *work* —> *worked*; *play* —> *played*; *live* —> *lived*. When we add *-ed* to verbs, there are sometimes changes in spelling eg *stop* —> *stopped*. See 188.3,4,6. For the pronunciation of *-ed*, see 187.2.

- Irregular verbs have different affirmative past simple forms eg *come* —> **came**; *see* —> **saw**; *go* —> **went**. See 190.

2 Use

We use the past simple to talk about actions and situations in the past.

*I **played** football yesterday.*
*He **lived** in London from 1970 to 1973. Then he **moved** to Manchester.*
*'**Did** you **see** Sarah yesterday?' 'No, I didn't.'*
*We **didn't go** out last night. We **stayed** at home and **watched** TV.*
*They **went** to Italy on holiday last summer.*
*Marie and Pierre Curie **discovered** radium.*

EXERCISE 4A

(i) What are the past simple forms of the verbs in the box?

Example:

1 paint   *painted*

| 1 paint   2 make   3 end   4 invent |
| 5 discover   6 die   7 win |

(ii) Complete the sentences using the past simple of the verbs in the box in (i).

Example:

Ferdinand Magellan *made* the first voyage around the world in 1519.

1 The First World War ____ in 1918.
2 Marie and Pierre Curie ____ the Nobel Prize for physics in 1903.
3 Marconi ____ the radio.
4 Elvis Presley was born in 1935 and ____ in 1977.
5 Leonardo da Vinci ____ *The Mona Lisa (La Gioconda).*
6 Alexander Fleming ____ penicillin in 1928.

EXERCISE 4B

Complete the questions in the past simple.

Examples:

'I went to the cinema last night.'   'Which film *did you see?*' (see)
'She went to London last weekend.'   '*Did she go* on her own?' (go)

1 'What ____ last night?' (do)   'I stayed at home and watched TV.'
2 'Why ____ so early on Saturday morning?' (get up)   'Because she had a lot of things to do.'
3 '____ shopping yesterday?' (go)   'Yes, I bought some new clothes.'
4 'He went to the party on Saturday.'   '____ himself?' (enjoy)
5 'They went out a few minutes ago.'   'Where ____?' (go)
6 'We stayed at home last night.'   '____ TV?' (watch)

EXERCISE 4C

Complete the sentences. Use the past simple of the verbs in brackets.

Example:

We *didn't play* (not | play) tennis last Monday because it *rained* (rain) all day.

1 I ____ (not | feel) very well last night so I ____ (stay) at home.
2 They ____ (not | go) to Portugal on holiday, they ____ (go) to Spain.
3 He ____ (not | write) to me because he ____ (not | have) my address.
4 I ____ (invite) her to the party, but she ____ (not | come).

Note

–See also 5 Past continuous; 12 Present perfect and past simple.
–When *who*, *what* or *which* is the subject of a past simple question, we do not use *did* eg **Who discovered** radium? See 144.
–For the past tense of the verb *be (was, were)*, see 31.

5 Past continuous

1 Form

We form the past continuous with *was/were + ...-ing*.

AFFIRMATIVE

I	was	
you	were	
he she it	was	working
we you they	were	

NEGATIVE

I	was not	
you	were not	
he she it	was not	working
we you they	were not	

QUESTION

was	I	
were	you	
was	he she it	working?
were	we you they	

This form is sometimes called the 'past progressive'.

CONTRACTIONS

wasn't = was not
weren't = were not

When we add *-ing* to verbs, there are sometimes changes in spelling
eg *write* → *writing*. See 188.3–6.

2 Use

a

We use the past continuous to talk about something which was in progress at a past time. The action or situation had started but it had not finished at that time.

'What **were** you **doing** at 8 o'clock last night?'   'I **was watching** TV.'

More examples:
*I saw you last night. You **were waiting** for a bus.*
*She **was working** at 10 o'clock yesterday morning.*

Compare the uses of the past continuous and past simple:

PAST CONTINUOUS	PAST SIMPLE
*I **was writing** a letter.* (= I was in the middle of writing it.)	*I **wrote** a letter.* (= I started and finished it.)

14

b   We often use the past continuous and past simple together in a sentence. Notice what happens in sentences like these:

PAST CONTINUOUS	PAST SIMPLE
I **was driving** along	when suddenly a child **ran** across the road.
When Kate **was watching** TV	the telephone **rang**.
We **were walking** in the park	when it **started** to rain.

The past continuous describes a longer action or situation which was in progress at a past time; the past simple describes a shorter action which happened in the middle of the longer action, or interrupted it.

But to say that one thing happened after another, we can use the past simple.

*When the telephone **rang**, Kate **answered** it.*
*We **sheltered** under a tree when it **started** to rain.*

Compare:

| *When Peter arrived we **were having** dinner. (Peter arrived in the middle of dinner; when = at the time that.)* | *When Peter arrived we **had** dinner. (Peter arrived, then we had dinner; when = after.)* |

c   When we tell a story, we often use the past continuous to describe a background scene and the past simple for events and actions.

PAST CONTINUOUS	PAST SIMPLE
I **was standing** outside the bus station. It **was getting** late and I **was feeling** tired. I **was waiting** for a man called Johnny Mars.	Suddenly, a woman **came** round the corner and **walked** right up to me. 'Are you Mr Marlowe?' she **asked**.

EXERCISE 5A

Join each idea in **A** with the most suitable idea in **B**. Make sentences using *when* and the past continuous or past simple of the verbs in brackets.

Example:

1 *I burnt myself when I was cooking the dinner.*

A
1 I (burn) myself
2 I (break) a cup
3 My car (break down)
4 I (see) a shark
5 My clothes (get) dirty
6 I (break) a tooth

B
I (drive) to work
I (eat) a sandwich
I (cook) the dinner
I (do) the washing up
I (swim) in the sea
I (clean) the attic

EXERCISE 5B

Put the verbs in brackets into the correct form: the past continuous or the past simple.

Examples:
When she *came* (come) into the room I *was writing* (write) a letter.
When my car *broke down* (break down) I *phoned* (phone) a garage.

1 We ____ (go) down in the lift when suddenly it ____ (stop).
2 ____ (they | have) dinner when you ____ (call) to see them?
3 When the doorbell ____ (ring) I ____ (get) up and ____ (answer) it.
4 When I ____ (open) the door, a friend ____ (stand) there.
5 'When I ____ (arrive) back at the car park, my car wasn't there!'   'Oh, no!
   What ____ (you | do)?'   'I ____ (report) it to the police.'

EXERCISE 5C

These paragraphs begin three stories: a love story, a western and a horror story.

1 Complete the paragraphs using the past continuous or the past simple of the
   verbs in brackets.

  (i) It was midnight and I was alone in the house. Outside it *was raining* (rain) very
      hard. I __1__ (get) ready to go to bed when I suddenly heard a strange noise
      outside my room in the corridor. Then, when I looked at the door, I noticed
      that someone __2__ (turn) the handle! I __3__ (rush) over to the door and
      quickly __4__ (turn) the key in the lock. Then I __5__ (ask) in a trembling
      voice, 'Who is it?'

 (ii) It was early evening and it __1__ (begin) to get dark in the surgery of Doctor
      Nigel Harris. The young, handsome doctor __2__ (stand) looking sadly out of
      the window when there was a quiet knock at the surgery door. The door
      __3__ (open) and Dr Harris __4__ (turn) round to see the young girl who
      had just entered the room. She was very beautiful. With a sad smile the doctor
      __5__ (ask), 'Are you the new nurse?'

(iii) I __1__ (sit) in the big chair in Henry's barber's shop at the time. Henry
      __2__ (cut) my hair with his big pair of scissors when we heard the sound of
      horses outside. The noise was so loud that we __3__ (go) over to the window
      to look. Through the window we could see at least twenty gunmen riding into
      town. Henry immediately __4__ (go) over to his desk and __5__ (put) on his
      gun and Sheriff's badge.

2 Which paragraph begins which story?

Note

–Some verbs eg *like, own* are not normally used in the continuous forms. For
 example, we cannot say, ~~I was liking the film~~. See 27.
–We can use the continuous forms with *always* to mean 'too often'. See 26.

6 Present perfect simple

1 Form

We form the present perfect simple with *have/has* + past participle.

AFFIRMATIVE

I you	have	worked
he she it	has	gone
we you they	have	

NEGATIVE

I you	have not	worked
he she it	has not	gone
we you they	have not	

QUESTION

have	I you	worked?
has	he she it	gone?
have	we you they	

CONTRACTIONS

've = have   *haven't = have not*
's = has   *hasn't = has not*

Some verbs are 'regular'; other verbs are 'irregular':

- The past participle of regular verbs ends in *-ed* eg *work* → *worked; live* → *lived*.
  When we add *-ed* to verbs, there are sometimes changes in spelling
  eg *stop* → *stopped*. See 188.3,4,6. For the pronunciation of *-ed*, see 187.2.

- Irregular verbs have different past participle forms eg *go* → *gone; be* → *been*.
  See 190.

2 Use

Sentences with the present perfect always connect the past and the present:

a We use the present perfect to talk about something which started in the past and
continues up to the present.

I **was** here at 3.00.   I **am** still here now – at 4.00.

Past ————————————————————— Present

Present Perfect

I've been here for an hour.

More examples:

She has worked in London for six months. (= She still works in London now.)
How long have you lived here? (= You still live here now.)
Kate and Ken have been married for 20 years. (= They are still married now.)

For *for* and *since*, see 11.

b We also use the present perfect for things which have happened during a period of time that continues up to the present.

I've been to Africa and India. (= in my life, up to now)
Have you ever eaten Chinese food? (= in your life, up to now)

We often use the present perfect in this way with 'indefinite' time words eg *ever* (= at any time up to now), *never* (= at no time up to now), *yet* (see 8) and *before*.

What's the best film you've ever seen?
I've never seen a ghost.
She's been there before.

We do not use the present perfect with 'definite' past time words (*yesterday, last night, in 1985*, etc). For example, we cannot say ~~She's been there yesterday~~.

We use the present perfect with *today, this morning, this afternoon*, etc when these periods of time are not finished at the time of speaking.

I've written six letters this morning. (It is still 'this morning'.)

c We also use the present perfect when the result of a past action is connected to the present.

Someone has broken the window. (= The window is now broken.)

More examples:

The taxi has arrived. (= The taxi is now here.)
We've cleaned the flat. (= The flat is now clean.)

We often use the present perfect in this way to announce 'news'.

My brother has grown a beard.
I've found a new job.

EXERCISE 6A

Complete the sentences using the present perfect simple of the verbs in brackets.

My name is Lynne Carter. I work for a travel company called Timeways Travel. I*'ve been* (be) a travel agent for six years now. I'm the manager of Timeways Travel London office. I __1__ (have) this job for three years. I've got a new flat in London. I __2__ (live) there for six months. My boyfriend's name is Bruno. We __3__ (know) each other for two years. Bruno is Italian, but he __4__ (live) in England for over five years. He works for BBC Radio. He __5__ (have) this job for a year.

Lynne Carter

EXERCISE 6B

Lynne is meeting two clients, Ben and Patty Crawford. Ben and Patty are on holiday in London. Complete the conversation using the present perfect simple.

Lynne: How is your hotel?

Ben: Great! It's the best hotel I *'ve ever stayed* (ever | stay) in.

Patty: Yes, Ben is really pleased. He __1__ (never | slept) in such a big bed before. But he won't be so pleased when we get the bill. It's also the most expensive hotel we __2__ (ever | stay) in!

Lynne: __3__ (you | be) to London before, Ben?

Ben: No, I __4__ (not | be) here before, but Patty __5__ (be) a number of times. Haven't you, Patty?

Patty: That's right. But the last time was ten years ago and London __6__ (change) a lot since then.

Lynne: And what are you going to do this afternoon?

Patty: Well, I __7__ (never | see) Madame Tussaud's. We __8__ (hear) a lot about it from friends, so we thought we'd go there.

Lynne: I see. And what about dinner tonight? I know a very good Japanese restaurant. __9__ (you | ever | eat) Japanese food, Patty?

Patty: No, I haven't. Is it good?

Lynne: It's delicious.

Ben: I __10__ (not | try) Japanese food before either, so let's go there.

Patty: Yes, why not?

EXERCISE 6C

Every Saturday morning Simon and Sally clean the kitchen. Here are the jobs that they do:

SIMON AND SALLY	SALLY	SIMON
1 do the washing up	2 clean the cooker	3 empty the rubbish bin
4 clean the windows	5 de-frost the fridge	6 clean the floor

Look at the picture. It is ten to eleven on Saturday morning. What jobs have Simon and Sally done? What haven't they done yet?

Examples:

1 *They've done the washing up.*
2 *Sally hasn't cleaned the cooker yet.*

7 *Gone* and *been*

Compare *gone* and *been*:

*Mr Jones isn't here at the moment. He has **gone** to the hairdresser's.* (= He is there, or on his way there.)

*Mr Jones is back now. He has **been** to the hairdresser's.* (= He was there, but he has returned.)

EXERCISE 7A

Complete the sentences with *gone* or *been*.

'Where's Kate?'   'She's *gone* to the cinema.'

1 I'm sorry I'm late, everyone. I've ____ to the dentist's.
2 There's nobody at home. I think they've ____ away for the weekend.
3 You look very brown. Have you ____ on holiday?
4 Simon isn't here at the moment. He's ____ to a football match.
5 'Have you ever ____ to Scotland?'   'Yes, I've ____ there quite a few times.'

8 Present perfect with *just*, *yet* and *already*

We often use the present perfect with the adverbs *just*, *yet* and *already*:

1 We use *just* for very recent events; *just* goes after the auxiliary verb *have*.

*The taxi **has just** arrived.*
*They**'ve just** finished.*

2 We use *yet* when we are expecting something to happen; *yet* normally goes at the end of a clause.

*It's nearly 10 o'clock. Has Andrew woken up **yet**?*
*They haven't finished dinner **yet**.*

We use *yet* in this way only in questions and negatives.

20

3

We use *already* when something has happened sooner than expected; *already* normally goes after the auxiliary verb *have*.

*'Where's Kate?'   'She's **already** left.'*
*'Could you do the washing up?'   'I've **already** done it.'*

Already can also go at the end of a clause for emphasis.

*She's left **already**.*
*I've done it **already**.*

EXERCISE 8A

Put the words in brackets in the correct place in the sentences. Sometimes two answers are possible.

Example:

Has Ken come home from work? (just)   *Has Ken just come home from work?*

1 Have you done your homework? (yet)
2 I haven't worn my new coat. (yet)
3 'Is Sally here?'   'No, she's gone out.' (just)
4 Have you spoken to your parents? (just)
5 It's quite early. Has Jack gone to bed? (already)
6 I've cleaned the windows. (already)

9   Present perfect continuous

1

Form

We form the present perfect continuous with *have/has been* + . . .-*ing*.

AFFIRMATIVE			NEGATIVE			QUESTION		
I *you*	*have*		*I* *you*	*have not*		*have*	*I* *you*	
he *she* *it*	*has*	*been working*	*he* *she* *it*	*has not*	*been working*	*has*	*he* *she* *it*	*been working?*
we *you* *they*	*have*		*we* *you* *they*	*have not*		*have*	*we* *you* *they*	

This form is sometimes called the 'present perfect progressive'.

CONTRACTIONS

've = have   haven't = have not
's = has   hasn't = has not

When we add *-ing* to verbs, there are sometimes changes in spelling
eg *have* → *having*. See 188.3–6.

2   **Use**

Sentences with the present perfect always connect the present and the past:

a   We use the present perfect continuous to talk about something which started in the past and has been in progress up to the present.

More examples:
I've been working all day.
How long have you been sitting there?
They've been watching TV since 6 o'clock.

b   We also use the present perfect continuous when an action has been in progress up to the recent past, especially when the action has results in the present.

It's been snowing.

It's been snowing. (It isn't snowing now, but there is snow on the ground.)
Have you been running? (You aren't running now, but you look hot.)

c   We can use the present perfect continuous to talk about repeated actions or situations in a period up to the present (or the recent past).

I've been having driving lessons for six months.
How long have you been living in Manchester?

EXERCISE 9A

Complete the sentences using the present perfect continuous of the verbs in brackets.

Example:

I'm sorry I'm late. *Have you been waiting* (you | wait) long?

1 She ____ (not | live) in London for very long.
2 How long ____ (you | study) English?
3 Those two men ____ (stand) outside the house for over two hours. Do you think we should call the police?

4 You look tired. I think you ____ (work) too hard lately and you ____ (not | get) enough fresh air and exercise.
5 'Annie's clothes are very dirty. What ____ (she | do)?'   'She ____ (play) in the garden.'

EXERCISE 9B

Look at the people in the pictures.
What have they been doing?.

Example:

1 *She's been repairing the car.*

paint	onions
chop	on the beach
repair	some shelves
lie	in the garden
put up	the car
play	the kitchen

Note

—Some verbs eg *know, want* are not normally used in the continuous forms. See 27.

10   Present perfect continuous and present perfect simple

1 **Compare:**

PRESENT PERFECT CONTINUOUS

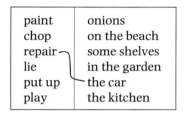

I've been cleaning my car.

When we use the present perfect continuous, the action may be finished or not finished.

More examples:

She's been doing her homework.
(= Perhaps she has finished it, perhaps she has not.)

PRESENT PERFECT SIMPLE

I've cleaned my car.

We use the present perfect simple when the action is finished.

She's done her homework. (= She has finished it.)

2 We use the present perfect continuous to talk about how long something has been in progress.

I've been typing letters all morning.
How long have you been having driving lessons?

We use the present perfect simple to talk about what has been achieved in a period of time.

I've typed four letters so far this morning.
How many driving lessons have you had?

3   We use the present perfect continuous for situations which are more temporary (continuing for a short time).

He's been living there for just a few weeks.
I've been working very hard recently.

We use the present perfect simple for situations which are more permanent (continuing for a longer time).

He's always lived there.

You've worked hard all your life.

4   Sometimes there is only a small difference in meaning between the two forms.

I've been living/I've lived in this flat for ten years.
How long has she been working/has she worked for the company?

EXERCISE 10A

Choose the correct form.

Example:

'Can I have a look at your newspaper?'   'Certainly. You can keep it if you like.
~~I've been reading~~/I've read it.'

1 *They've been repairing/They've repaired* the road all this week, but they haven't finished it yet.
2 I'm very sorry, but *I've been breaking/I've broken* this chair.
3 Sally *has been saving/has saved* nearly two thousand pounds so far this year.
4 What's the matter? *Have you been losing/Have you lost* something?
5 *I've always been working/I've always worked* in the music industry.
6 Someone *has been eating/has eaten* my chocolates. There aren't many left.

Note

–Some verbs eg *know, own* are not normally used in the continuous forms. For example, we cannot say, ~~I've been knowing him for years~~. See 27.

11   Present perfect with *for* and *since*

We often use *for* and *since* with the present perfect to talk about things that have continued over a period of time up to the present (or the recent past). Compare:

It's been raining for four days.

MONDAY   TUESDAY   WEDNESDAY   THURSDAY

It's been raining since Monday.

We use *for* when we mention the length of the period (eg *four days*); we use *since* when we mention the starting point of the period (eg *Monday*).

for + length of time		*since* + starting point	
	two hours		2 o'clock
	a week		10 April
for	six months	*since*	July
	twelve years		1977
	a long time		I was a child

I've been here for two hours.
He's been living in Paris for six months.

I've been here since 2 o'clock.
He's been living in Paris since July.

EXERCISE 11A

Complete the sentences using *for* or *since*.

Example:

I've been interested in jazz *since* I left school.

1 Lynne has been the manager of Timeways Travel in London ____ three years.
2 I've lived in Rome ____ I was two.

3 Mr Woods hasn't been feeling well ____ over a month.
4 Sally and her boyfriend Peter have been going out together ____ last winter.
5 I've only been waiting ____ a few minutes.
6 He's been in Japan ____ 1986.

12   Present perfect and past simple

1

The present perfect always connects the past and the present; the past simple tells us only about the past:

a

We use the present perfect to talk about something which started in the past and continues up to the present.

```
        ┌──10 years──┐
Past ───────────────┴─── Present
```

I've lived in London for ten years. (= I still live in London now.)

More examples:

He has worked in a shop for five years. (= He still works in the shop now.)

How long have you been here? (= You are still here now.)

We use the past simple to talk about something which started and finished in the past.

```
        ┌──10 years──┐
Past ───────────────┴─── Present
```

I lived in Manchester for ten years. (= I do not live in Manchester now.)

He worked in a factory for ten years. (= He does not work in the factory now.)

How long were you there? (= You are not there now.)

25

b

We also use the present perfect when the result of a past action is connected to the present.	We use the past simple when the result of a past action is not connected to the present.

I've lost my wallet. (= I have not got the wallet now.)	*I lost my wallet, but I've got it back again now.*
We often use the present perfect to announce 'news'.	We use the past to give details of the news.
Someone has stolen my motorbike.	*I left the bike outside for a few minutes and when I came back, it wasn't there.*

2

When we say a definite past time eg *yesterday, last week, six weeks ago*, we always use the past simple, never the present perfect.

I lost my wallet yesterday. (Not: ~~I've lost my wallet yesterday~~.)
Someone stole my bicycle last week. (Not: ~~Someone has stolen my bicycle last week~~.)

We use the present perfect to talk about an indefinite time up to the present eg *ever, never, recently*. Compare:

PRESENT PERFECT	PAST SIMPLE
Have you ever seen a ghost?	*Did you see your friend yesterday?*
I've never been to New York.	*I went to London last week.*
I've started taking driving lessons recently.	*I started taking driving lessons six weeks ago.*

In conversations, we often begin indefinitely, with the present perfect, then we use the past simple when we think about the definite time that something happened.

'Have you ever been to the United States?'   'Yes, I went there in 1985.'   'Did you go to New York (= when you were there in 1985)?'
I've seen that film. I enjoyed it (= when I saw it) very much.

3

We can use *today, this morning, this afternoon*, etc:

with the present perfect when these periods of time are not finished.	with the past when these periods of time are finished.
I've seen Peter this morning. (It is still morning.)	*I saw Peter this morning.* (It is now afternoon, evening, or night time.)

4

We normally use a past tense, not the present perfect, to ask when something happened.

When did you arrive home last night? (Not: ~~When have you arrived home last night?~~)

EXERCISE 12A

Lynne Carter, the manager of the Timeways Travel company, is interviewing a young man called Paul Morris for a job.

Choose the correct form.

Lynne: Your present company is Sun Travel, isn't it? How long *have you worked/ did you work* there?
Paul: (1) *I've worked/I worked* for them for two years.
Lynne: I see. And what were you doing before that?
Paul: (2) *I've worked/I worked* for a student travel company in Spain.
Lynne: Oh, really? How long (3) *have you been/were you* in Spain?
Paul: For nearly a year. (4) *I've moved/ I moved* back to London from Spain two years ago to join Sun Travel.
Lynne: I see. And do you drive, Paul?
Paul: Yes, I do. (5) *I've had/I had* a driving licence for five years.
Lynne: And have you got your own car?
Paul: No, not at the moment. (6) *I've had/I had* a car in Spain, but (7) *I've sold/I sold* it before (8) *I've come/I came* back to Britain.

EXERCISE 12B

Complete the conversations using the present perfect simple or the past simple of the verb in brackets.

1 'I know Sally Robinson.'   'Really? How long *have you known* (you | know) her?'   'Oh, for quite a long time now.'   'When ____ (you | first | meet) her?'
2 '____ (your husband | ever | have) pneumonia?'   'Yes, he ____ (have) it twice. He ____ (had) it ten years ago, and once when he ____ (be) a child.'
3 *(It's 10 o'clock in the morning.)* '____ (you | see) Mrs Carter this morning?'   'Yes, I ____ (saw) her when I ____ (arrive) in the office, but she ____ (go) out soon afterwards.'
4 *(It's the middle of the afternoon.)* I'm really hungry. I ____ (not | have) any breakfast this morning and I ____ (not | have) time to go out for anything to eat this afternoon.

13   Present perfect and present tense

To say how long something has continued, we can use the present perfect, but not the present continuous or present simple.
*She **has been waiting** for an hour.* (Not: *She is waiting for an hour*.)
I've lived here since last year. (Not: *I live here since last year*.)

EXERCISE 13A

Choose the correct form.

Example:

We've been working/We're working since 9 o'clock.

1 *I've been cleaning/I'm cleaning* my flat for the past two hours.
2 Look. Can you see Simon over there? *He's been sitting/He's sitting* in the corner.
3 'How long *have you been/are you* ill?'   'Since yesterday.'
4 *Have you known/Do you know* Sarah for very long?
5 *I've been learning/I'm learning* English since last year.
6 *They've lived/They live* in London now. *They've been/They're* there for the last six months.

14   Past perfect simple

1

Form

We form the past perfect simple with *had* + past participle.

AFFIRMATIVE			NEGATIVE			QUESTION		
I you he she it we you they	had	worked gone	I you he she it we you they	had not	worked gone	had	I you he she it we you they	worked? gone?

CONTRACTIONS

'd = had   *hadn't = had not*

Some verbs are 'regular', other verbs are 'irregular':

■ The past participle of regular verbs has an *-ed* ending eg *work* → *worked*. When we add *-ed* to verbs, there are sometimes changes in spelling eg *stop* → *stopped*. See 188.3,4,6. For the pronunciation of *-ed*, see 187.2.

■ Irregular verbs have different past participle forms eg *go* → *gone*; *see* → *seen*. See 190.

2 **Use**

a When we are talking about the past, we sometimes want to refer back to an earlier past.

Earlier Past —————————————— Past —————————————— Present

When I telephoned Sue,
she had gone out.

We use the past perfect (eg *she had gone out*) to talk about something which had happened before the past time we are thinking about (eg *when I telephoned*).

More examples:

*We arrived at the cinema at 8.00, but the film **had started** at 7.30.*
*When I spoke to the woman I realized I **had met** her somewhere before.*

b The past perfect is the past form of the present perfect. Compare:

PRESENT PERFECT	PAST PERFECT
I **haven't eaten** all day today, so I'm very hungry now.	I **hadn't eaten** all day yesterday, so I was very hungry when I got home.

c Compare the uses of the past perfect and past simple:

We got to the cinema at 8.00, but the film **had started** at 7.30.	We got to the cinema at 7.20 and the film **started** at 7.30.
When Sue arrived, we **had had** dinner. (We had dinner, then Sue arrived.)	When Sue arrived, we **had** dinner. (Sue arrived, then we had dinner.)

EXERCISE 14A

Complete the sentences using the past perfect simple of the verbs in brackets.

Example:

'Why were you so angry when I saw you yesterday?'   'Oh, I*'d just had* (just | have) a big argument with my parents.'

1 I tried contacting my pen pal when I was in the United States, but she _____ (change) her address and no one knew where she _____ (move) to.

2 He was very nervous when he first drove in Britain because he _____ (not | drive) on the left before.

3 When I heard his voice on the phone, I knew I _____ (speak) to him before. Then I remembered I _____ (already | meet) him. I also remembered that I _____ (not | like) him very much.

29

EXERCISE 14B

Choose the correct form.

Example:

Simon wasn't at home when I phoned. He *had gone*/~~went~~ out.

1 Sally was at home when we arrived, but she *had gone/went* out soon afterwards.
2 When I opened the safe, the money *had disappeared/disappeared*.
3 Andrew was late for school yesterday. When he got to the classroom, the lesson *had started/started*.
4 They waited until everyone was ready and then they *had started/started* the meeting.

EXERCISE 14C

Put one verb in each sentence into the past perfect simple and the other verb into the past simple.

Example:

'Did you catch your train yesterday?'   'No, it *had already left* (already | leave) when we *got* (get) to the station.'

1 Andrew ____ (do) the test before, so he ____ (find) it very easy.
2 I ____ (not | laugh) at the joke because I ____ (hear) it before.
3 We ____ (leave) the restaurant when we ____ (have) dinner.
4 When I found my wallet I ____ (discover) that somebody ____ (took) the credit cards out of it.

15   Past perfect continuous

1 | **Form**

We form the past perfect continuous with *had been + . . .-ing.*

AFFIRMATIVE		NEGATIVE		QUESTION		
I you he she it we you they	had been working	I you he she it we you they	had not been working	had	I you he she it we you they	been working?

This form is sometimes called the 'past perfect progressive'.

CONTRACTIONS

'd = had   hadn't = had not

When we add *-ing* to verbs, there are sometimes changes in spelling eg *stop → stopping.* See 188.3–6.

2 | **Use**

a When we are talking about the past, we sometimes want to refer back to an earlier past.

Earlier Past ————————————————— Past —————————————————— Present

*Sally **had been waiting** for an hour when the bus arrived.*

We use the past perfect continuous (eg *Sally had been waiting for an hour*) to talk about something which had been in progress up to the past time we are talking about (eg *when the bus arrived*).

More examples:

I'd been walking for about half an hour when it suddenly started to rain.
*Mr Woods **had been working** for 50 years when he finally retired in 1965.*

b The past perfect continuous is the past form of the present perfect continuous. Compare:

PRESENT PERFECT CONTINUOUS	PAST PERFECT CONTINUOUS
*I've **been working** hard all day, so I'm very tired now.*	*I'd **been working** hard all day, so I was very tired last night.*

EXERCISE 15A

Complete the sentences using the past perfect continuous of the verbs in brackets.

Example:

I'd been standing (stand) there for nearly a half an hour when I realized I was at the wrong bus-stop.

1 Maria's sister ____ (study) at university for eight years before she finally passed her exams.
2 'I'm really sorry I was so late last night.'   'That's OK. We ____ (not | wait) long.'
3 The strange thing was that we ____ (just | talk) about ghosts when we heard the noise upstairs.
4 'Robert moved from Manchester to London in 1988.'   'How long ____ (he | live) in Manchester?'

EXERCISE 15B

Join each idea in **A** with an idea from **B**. Make sentences using the past perfect continuous of the verbs in brackets.

Example:

1 *I felt very cold because I had been standing outside for over two hours.*

A

1 I felt very cold because
2 I (play) tennis so
3 The children's hair was wet because
4 I (not | feel) well for weeks before
5 They (travel) all day so
6 They (drive) for about half an hour when they realized

B

they were lost
they were very tired
I finally went to see the doctor
I (stand) outside for over two hours
they (swim) in the sea
I was feeling hot and sticky

Note

—Some verbs eg *know, want* are not normally used in the continuous forms. See 27.

16   Future: *will*

1

a

Form

will + infinitive without *to* (but see **b** below)

AFFIRMATIVE		NEGATIVE		QUESTION		
I you he she it we you they	will work	I you he she it we you they	will not work	will	I you he she it we you they	work?

CONTRACTIONS

'll = *will*   *won't* = *will not*

b

We use *will* with all persons (*I, you, he, they*, etc). We can also use *shall* instead of *will* with *I* and *we* eg *I/we shall work* (but, in everyday speech, we normally use the contractions *I'll* and *we'll*). The negative of *shall* is *shall not* (contraction: *shan't*).

2   **Use**

a   We can use *will* to predict the future.

Tomorrow **will be** *another cold day in all parts of the country.*

More examples:

In the future, machines **will do** *many of the jobs that people do today.*
Who do you think **will win** *the football match on Sunday?*
We **won't arrive** *home before midnight tonight.*

When we predict the future, we often use *will* with the following verbs and expressions:

think   expect   believe   be sure   be afraid

I **expect** *they***'ll be** *here at around 10 o'clock tomorrow morning.*
*I***'m sure** *you***'ll enjoy** *the film if you go and see it.*

We also use *will* in this way with adverbs of probability eg *probably, perhaps, certainly.*

Martin **will probably phone** *us this evening.*
Perhaps** I'll see** *you tomorrow.*

b   We also use *will* when we decide to do something at the moment of speaking.

'Would you like something to drink?'   *'Oh, thank you. I***'ll have** *some orange juice.'*
'There's someone at the door.'   *'Is there? Oh, I***'ll see** *who it is.'*
'I'm going out shopping.'   *'Oh, are you? I***'ll come** *with you, then. I need to get some things myself.'*

EXERCISE 16A

What will life be like in 50 years from now? Complete the predictions using *will/won't*.

Example:

people | eat | more artificial food
People will eat more artificial food.

1 the population of the world | be | much bigger
2 scientists | control | the weather
3 people | take | holidays in space

4 many people | not work | at all during their lives
5 people | live | longer
6 life | not be | better than it is now

Do you agree with these predictions?

EXERCISE 16B

Complete the sentences using *I'll* or *I won't* and the verbs in the box.

> ~~go~~   answer   not go   put on   not have
> lend   wait

Example:

I'm tired, I think *I'll go* to bed early tonight.

1 'I haven't got any money.'   'Haven't you? Oh, ____ you some if you like.'
2 'The telephone is ringing.'   'Oh, ____ it.'
3 I'm a bit cold. I think ____ on a sweater.
4 'Would you like something to eat?'   '____ anything at the moment, thank you. I'm not very hungry.'
5 'I'm going out for a walk.'   'It's raining.'
   'Oh, is it? Well, ____ out now, then, ____ until it's stopped.'

EXERCISE 16C

Complete the sentences using *will/won't* and the verbs in brackets.

Example:

You drive very well. I'm sure you*'ll pass* (pass) your driving test tomorrow.

1 Robert has got such a bad memory. Do you think he ____ (remember) the appointment?
2 'How long ____ (the meeting | last)?'   'I don't know exactly, but I'm sure it ____ (not | finish) before lunchtime.'
3 '____ (you | be) at home this evening?'   'No, I'm working tonight and ____ (not | get) home until very late.'   'Right. I ____ (phone) you tomorrow then.'

Note

–See also 18 Future: *will* and *going to*
–We also use *will* in these ways: offers eg *I'll help you.* (see 49.1); requests eg **Will** *you help me?* (see 48.2); refusals eg *The car* **won't** *start.* (see 52); promises eg *I* **will** *be careful, I promise.* (see 53); and threats eg *Stop making that noise or I'll scream!* (see 53).
–We also use *shall?* to ask for advice eg *What* **shall** *I do?* (see 42.4), and to make offers eg **Shall** *I help you?* (see 49.2) and suggestions eg **Shall** *we go out this evening?* (see 50.1).

17 Future: *going to*

1 Form

be + *going to* + infinitive

AFFIRMATIVE		
I am		
you are		
he		
she is	*going to work*	
it		
we		
you are		
they		

NEGATIVE		
I am not		
you are not		
he		
she is not	*going to work*	
it		
we		
you are not		
they		

QUESTION		
am I		
are you		
he		
is she	*going to work?*	
it		
we		
are you		
they		

CONTRACTIONS

'm = am
're = are   aren't = are not
's = is   isn't = is not

2 Use

Sentences with *going to* connect the future and the present:

a We use *going to* to talk about something in the future which we can see as a result of something in the present.

*Look at those black clouds in the sky. It's **going to rain**.*
*Those people **are going to get** wet.*

More examples:

*Hurry up! It's getting late. You're **going to miss** your train.*
*Look out! That ladder **is going to fall**!*

For this reason, sentences with *going to* are often about the near future.

b We also use *going to* to talk about what we intend to do in the future. We use *going to* when we have already decided to do something.

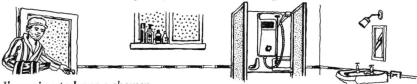

*I'm **going to have** a shower.*

More examples:
'Why have you moved all the furniture out of this room?'   'I'm going to clean the carpet.'
'Lynne has just sold her car.'   'Is she going to buy a new one?'

EXERCISE 17A

What is going to happen in the pictures?

Example:

She's going to answer the phone.

EXERCISE 17B

Complete the sentences using *going to* and the verbs in brackets.

Example:

'I've made up my mind I'*m going to change* (change) my job.'   'What *are you going to do* (you | do)?'   'I'm not sure yet.'

1 'What ____ (you | wear) at the party on Saturday?'   'I haven't decided yet.
  What about you? ____ (you | wear) your new black dress?'
2 'Why have you bought all that wallpaper? What ____ (you | do)?'   'I ____
  (decorate) the living room.'
3 He's decided that he ____ (not | leave) school this summer. He ____ (stay) on for
  another year.
4 'I ____ (buy) a new motorbike.'   'How ____ (you | pay) for it? You haven't got
  enough money.'   'I ____ (ask) my bank to lend me the money.'

Note

–See also 18 Future: *will* and *going to*.
–We use the past form *was/were* + *going to* to talk about the 'future in the past'
  eg I *was going to stay* at home last night, but I decided to go out instead. See 25.

18 Future: *will* and *going to*

1 We use both *will* and *going to* in predictions about the future, but there is a difference:

We use *will* to talk about what we think or believe will happen in the future.

We use *going to* to talk about something in the future which we can see as a result of something in the present.

That boat doesn't look very safe. It'll sink in that heavy sea.

Look at that boat! It's going to sink.

Don't climb up that tree. You'll fall and hurt yourself.

Look out! You're going to fall!

2 We also use both *will* and *going to* to talk about what we intend to do, but there is a difference here also:

We use *will* when we decide to do something at the moment of speaking.

'Oh dear! I've spilt some wine on my jacket.'   'Don't worry. I'll clean it for you.'
What shall I do tomorrow? I know! I'll paint the kitchen.

We use *going to* when we have already decided to do something.

'Why have you moved all the furniture out of this room?'   'I'm going to clean the carpet.'
'Why are you putting on those old clothes?'   'I'm going to paint the kitchen.'

EXERCISE 18A

Complete the sentences using *will* or *going to* and the verbs in brackets.

Example:

'Would you like tea or coffee?'   'Oh, thank you, I*'ll have* (have) tea, please.'

1 'Someone told me that you're moving from London.'   'That's right. I ____ (live) in Manchester.'
2 'Would you like to come to my house this evening?'   'Yes, all right. I ____ (come) at 9 o'clock.'
3 I don't feel very well. I think I ____ (faint).
4 'It's Simon's birthday soon. I've decided to buy him the new Blues Brothers record.'   'Oh, he doesn't like the Blues Brothers any more.'   'Oh, really? Well, I ____ (get) him something to wear.'
5 Oh, no! Look at those cars! They ____ (crash)!
6 'I could lend you some money if you like.'   'Could you? I ____ (pay) you back on Friday.'

19   Present continuous for the future

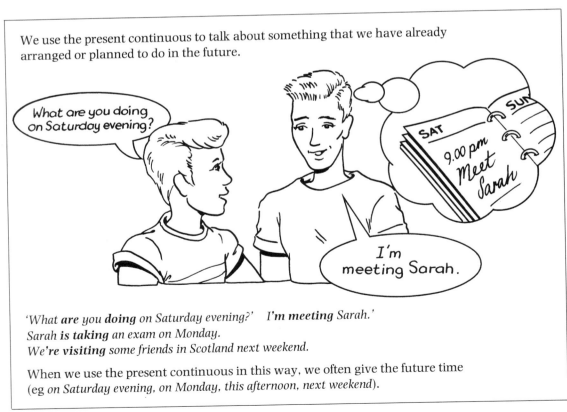

We use the present continuous to talk about something that we have already arranged or planned to do in the future.

'What **are** you **doing** on Saturday evening?'   I'm meeting Sarah.'
Sarah **is taking** an exam on Monday.
We're **visiting** some friends in Scotland next weekend.

When we use the present continuous in this way, we often give the future time (eg *on Saturday evening, on Monday, this afternoon, next weekend*).

EXERCISE 19A

Today is Friday, April 15th, Sally and Peter are trying to arrange to meet soon.
Look at Sally's arrangements for the weekend.

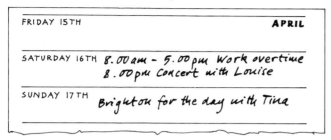

FRIDAY 15TH   **APRIL**

SATURDAY 16TH   *8.00 am - 5.00 pm Work overtime*
                8.00 pm Concert with Louise

SUNDAY 17TH   *Brighton for the day with Tina*

Complete the conversation using the present continuous of the verbs in the box.
Use some verbs more than once.

> do   spend   go   meet   work

Peter: Why don't we meet tomorrow afternoon?
Sally: I can't, Peter. I*'m working* overtime tomorrow.
Peter: What about tomorrow evening? __1__ (you) anything then?
Sally: Yes, I __2__ my friend Louise. We __3__ to a concert. And I __4__ to
            Brighton on Sunday with Tina. We __5__ the day there. Listen, Peter. What
            __6__ (you) on Sunday evening?
Peter: I __7__ (not) anything special, I don't think.
Sally: Let's meet on Sunday evening, then.
Peter: All right.

Note

–For the form of the present continuous, see 1.1.
–Some verbs eg *be, like* are not normally used in the continuous forms. For
  example, we cannot say ~~I'm being at home tonight~~. See 27.

20   Future: present continuous and *going to*

1 | When we talk about things which we have already arranged to do or planned to
do in the future, we can use the present continuous (see 19) or *going to* (see 17).

I'm having lunch with Lynne tomorrow.
I'm going to have lunch with Lynne tomorrow.

2 | When we make predictions about the future, we can use *going to* (or *will*), but not
the present continuous.

It's going to rain tomorrow. (*It's raining* tomorrow is not possible.)

EXERCISE 20A

Complete the sentences using the present continuous or *going to*. Sometimes either structure is possible.

Examples:

I (see) Sarah this afternoon.   *I'm seeing Sarah this afternoon./I'm going to see Sarah this afternoon.*
Hurry up! We (miss) our bus.   *Hurry up! We're going to miss our bus.*

1 It (snow) later tonight.
2 She (meet) them tomorrow morning.
3 What (you | do) this afternoon?
4 Be careful! You (break) that glass.
5 He (not | come) next Saturday.
6 Look out! You (hurt) yourself with that knife.

Note

–Some verbs eg *be, like* are not normally used in the continuous forms. For example, we can say *I'm going to be in London next Saturday*, but not ~~I'm being in London next Saturday~~. See 27.

21   Present simple for the future

We use the present simple to talk about future events which are part of a fixed timetable or fixed programme.

Here are some of the programmes on TV tomorrow evening.

```
TOMORROW'S TV
6.15  TENNIS from WIMBLEDON
7.30  FILM Annie Hall
      with Woody Allen
9.00  THE NEWS and WEATHER
```

*'What time **does** the tennis **start** tomorrow evening?'*   *'At 6.15.'*
*The film **starts** at 7.30 and **finishes** at 9.00.*

More examples:

*What time **does** your plane **leave** tomorrow?*
*Next summer the school holidays **begin** on July 25th and **end** on September 10th.*

We use the present simple in this way when we think of something in the future as a fact, or as an arrangement or plan which cannot change.

EXERCISE 21A

Complete the sentences using the present simple of the verbs in brackets.

Example:

Our boat *leaves* (leave) Dover at 2.00 on Friday and *arrives* (arrive) in Calais at 6.00.

1 The conference ____ (start) on June 3rd, and ____ (finish) on June 10th.
2 We've got plenty of time. Our plane ____ (not | take off) until 9 o'clock.
3 Tonight's concert ____ (begin) at 8.00 and it ____ (not | end) until 11.00.
4 When ____ (the next train | leave) for Bristol?

22   Present simple for the future after *when, if,* etc

We use the present simple to refer to the future in clauses of time and condition after *when, while, as soon as, after, before, until, if, unless, as/so long as* and *provided/ providing (that).*

will/won't	present simple
I'll phone you	***when** I **get** home.*
We won't go out	***until** it **stops** raining.*
We'll go to the beach	***if** the weather **is** nice.*
I'll go to the party	***provided** you **go** too.*

EXERCISE 22A

Put one verb in each sentence into the present simple and the other verb into the *will/won't* form.

Examples:

If I *fail* (fail) the exam, I*'ll take* (take) it again.

1 When I ____ (see) him I ____ (give) him your message.
2 She ____ (phone) us as soon as she ____ (arrive) in Paris.
3 If the weather ____ (be) nice tomorrow, we ____ (go) sailing.
4 I ____ (look after) your cat while you ____ (be) on holiday.
5 He ____ (not | do) anything until he ____ (hear) from us.
6 Unless we ____ (hurry), we ____ (be) late.
7 We ____ (play) tennis this evening as long as it ____ (not | rain).
8 I ____ (lend) you the money provided you ____ (pay) me back tomorrow.

Note

–We can also use the present perfect after *when, if,* etc to show that the first action will be finished before the second eg *I'll lend you the book **when I've finished** it.*

41

23 Future continuous: *will be + ...-ing*

1 | **Form**

a | *will be + ...-ing* (but see **b** below)

AFFIRMATIVE		NEGATIVE		QUESTION		
I you he she it we you they	will be working	I you he she it we you they	will not be working	will	I you he she it we you they	be working?

This form is sometimes called the 'future progressive'.

CONTRACTIONS

'll = will   *won't = will not*

When we add *-ing* to verbs, there are sometimes changes in spelling
eg *live* —> *living*. See 188.3–6.

b | We can use *shall* instead of *will* with *I* and *we* eg *I/we shall be working* (but, in everyday speech, we normally use the contractions *I'll* and *we'll*). The negative of *shall* is *shall not* (contraction: *shan't*).

2 | **Use**

a | We use *will be + ...-ing* to talk about something which will be in progress at a time in the future.

*I'll **be having** dinner at 7.00.*
*Don't phone me at 8.00. I'll **be doing** my homework then.*
*This time tomorrow we'll **be flying** to Greece on our holidays.*

b We also use *will be* + . . .*-ing* to talk about things in the future which are already planned, or which are part of a regular routine.

*I'll **be going** into town later on. Do you want me to get you anything from the shops?*

*'Would you like me to give Peter a message for you?'   'Oh, I don't want to trouble you.'   'It's no trouble, really. I'll **be seeing** Peter tomorrow anyway.'*

We often use *will be* + . . .*-ing* as a polite way of asking about someone's plans, especially when we want someone to do something for us.

***'Will** you **be going** out this morning?'   'Yes, why?'   'Oh, could you get me a newspaper?'*
***Will** you **be using** your camera at the weekend? I wondered if I could borrow it.*

When we use *will be* + *-ing* form in this way, it often suggests that we do not want to change the other person's plans.

EXERCISE 23A

Lynne Carter is going from London to Manchester on business tomorrow. Look at Lynne's plans.

What will Lynne be doing at these times tomorrow?

Example:
8.30
At 8.30 tomorrow she'll be flying to Manchester.

8.00 – 8.55	Fly to Manchester.
10.00 – 12.00	Visit the ABC travel company.
13.00 – 14.30	Have lunch with Mary and Ron King.
15.00 – 16.00	Visit Derek Hall.
16.15 – 16.45	Take a taxi to the airport.
17.15 – 18.05	Fly back to London.

1 11.00   **2** 13.30   **3** 15.30   **4** 16.30
5 17.30

EXERCISE 23B

Complete the sentences using the *will be* + *-ing* form of the verbs in brackets.

Example:

I*'ll be going* (go) shopping later. Do you want me to get you anything?

1 ____ (you | speak) to Robert in the next few days? I've got a message for him.
2 I ____ (not | use) my car this evening. Do you want to borrow it?
3 We ____ (get) some concert tickets for ourselves. Would you like us to get you one?
4 When ____ (you | visit) your grandparents again?

Note

–Some verbs eg *be, know* are not normally used in the continuous forms. For example, we cannot say ~~I'll be being at home this evening~~. See 27.

24 Future perfect: *will have* + past participle

1

a

Form

will have + past participle (but see **b** below)

AFFIRMATIVE			NEGATIVE			QUESTION			
I you he she it we you they	will have	finished gone	I you he she it we you they	will not have	finished gone	will	I you he she it we you they	have	finished? gone?

CONTRACTIONS

'll = will   *won't = will not*

Some verbs are 'regular', other verbs are 'irregular':

■ The past participle of regular verbs ends in *-ed* eg *finish* ⟶ *finished*. When we add *-ed* to verbs, there are sometimes changes in spelling eg *stop* ⟶ *stopped*. See 188.3,4,6. For the pronunciation of *-ed*, see 187.2.

■ Irregular verbs have different past participle forms eg *go* ⟶ **gone**; *be* ⟶ **been**. See 190.

b We can use *shall* instead of *will* with *I* and *we* eg *I/we shall have finished* (but, in everyday speech, we normally use the contractions *I'll* and *we'll*). The negative of *shall* is *shall not* (contraction: *shan't*).

2

Use

We can use *will have* + past participle to talk about something that will be completed by (not later than) a certain time in the future.

Past ——— Present ——————————————————— Future

When we use this structure, we think of a future time and look back from that future time to say that something will be complete.

I'll have finished dinner by 8.00.

'I'll phone you at 11.00.'   'No, I'll have gone to bed by then. Can you phone earlier?'
I'll have worked here for a year next September.

EXERCISE 24A

Complete the sentences using the *will have* + past participle form of the verbs in brackets.

Example:

I need my car first thing tomorrow morning. Do you think *you will have repaired* (you | repair) it by then?

1 Let's hurry. The film ____ (start) by the time we get to the cinema.
2 I'll meet you outside your office this evening. ____ (you | finish) work by 6.00?
3 'I'll come round to your house at 7.00.'   'No, that's too late. I ____ (go) out by then.'
4 I'm sure they'll be hungry. When they arrive here, they ____ (not | eat) anything since this morning.

Note

–A continuous form is also possible: *will have been* + . . .*-ing* eg *They'll be tired when they arrive. They'll have been travelling all day.*

25   Future in the past: *was/were going to*

We can use *was/were going to* + infinitive to say that something was planned for the future at a past time.

Future————————→
Past————————————————Present————————Future

They were going to get married, but in the end they changed their minds.

Note that when we use this structure, it often means that the planned future action did not happen.

I was going to stay at home last night, but I decided to go out instead.
We were going to eat at the Italian restaurant, but it was full, so we ate somewhere else.
I thought you were going to visit me yesterday. Why didn't you?

EXERCISE 25A

Join each idea in **A** with an idea from **B**. Make sentences using *was/were going to* and the verbs in brackets.

Example:

1 *I was going to take a taxi home last night, but I didn't have enough money, so I had to walk.*

A

1 I (take) a taxi home last night,
2 We (write) to them when we were on holiday,
3 She (drive) to Scotland last weekend,
4 We (play) tennis yesterday afternoon,
5 She (watch) the film on TV last night,
6 I (change) my job last year.

B

but it rained all afternoon, so we stayed at home.
but my boss offered me more money, so I decided to stay.
but I didn't have enough money, so I had to walk.
but she had seen it before, so she went to bed early.
but her car broke down, so she went by train.
but we changed our minds and phoned them instead.

Note

–Sometimes we can also express the future in the past with *would* eg *I was very surprised you failed the exam. I thought you **would** pass easily.*

26   Continuous forms with *always*

1   We can use *always* with the present continuous or past continuous to mean 'too often'.

*He's **always saying** stupid things.*
*Our neighbours **are always having** arguments.*
*She **was always crying** when she was a baby.*

This use of *always* often expresses anger or irritation (that something happens too often).

2   *Always* normally means 'on all occasions'. In this meaning, we use *always* with simple forms, not continuous forms. Compare:

always with simple forms	*always* with continuous forms
*She **always comes** to work at 8.30.*	*She's **always coming** to work late.*
*I **always pay** my rent by cheque.*	*I'm **always paying** for you when we go out. Why don't you pay sometimes?*
*They **always had** dinner at 8 o'clock.*	*They **were always having** arguments.*

Note that *always* goes before a full verb (eg *she **always comes***), but after the auxiliary verb *be* (eg *she's **always coming***).

3 | When we use a continuous form to talk about something that happens too often, we can use words like *forever* and *continually* instead of *always*.

You're forever losing things.
He's continually saying stupid things.

4 | We do not only use *always* with a continuous form in a negative sense (to say that something happens too often). We also use this structure when something happens more often than expected.

She's always helping other people.
I'm always meeting Maria in the park. (by accident)

EXERCISE 26A

Complete the sentences using *always* and the present continuous or past continuous of the verbs in brackets.

Examples:

He's a really miserable man. He's *always complaining* (complain) about something.
When I was a child, my sister *was always teasing* (tease) me.

1 Simon is very untidy. He ____ (leave) his clothes lying on the bathroom floor.
2 When we were children, my brother was bigger than me and he ____ (hit) me.
3 My sister really makes me angry. She ____ (borrow) my things without asking me.
4 My memory is getting very bad these days. I ____ (forget) things.
5 Our old car was very unreliable. It ____ (break down).
6 My parents are very lucky. They ____ (win) prizes in competitions.

27   Verbs not used in the continuous

1 | Some verbs (eg *like*, *understand*) are normally used only in the simple forms, not the continuous forms. We can say *I like* or *she didn't understand*, but we cannot say *I'm liking* or *she wasn't understanding*.

Here are some of the most important verbs which are not normally used in the continuous forms:

a | **Verbs of thinking**

think (= believe)	*believe*	*understand*	*know*
see (= understand)	*recognize*	*suppose*	*remember*
imagine	*forget*	*mean*	*realize*

I think you're right. (Not: ~~I'm thinking . . .~~)
Do you know Billy Palmer? (Not: ~~Are you knowing . . . ?~~)
She didn't understand what you said. (Not: ~~She wasn't understanding . . .~~)

47

b | **Verbs of feeling**

> like   dislike   hate   love   prefer   want   wish

I **like** this music. (Not: ~~I'm liking ...~~)
Do you **want** to go now? (Not: ~~Are you wanting ...?~~)

c | **Verbs of perception**

> see   hear   smell   taste   feel

We **heard** someone outside. (Not: ~~We were hearing ...~~)
This spaghetti **tastes** delicious. (Not: ~~This spaghetti is tasting ...~~)

d | **Other verbs**

> have (= possess)   own   belong to   owe   need
> include   cost contain   weigh
> sound   be   seem   deserve

How long **has** Sally **had** her motorbike? (Not: ~~How long has Sally been having ...?~~)
I **weigh** 70 kilos. (Not: ~~I'm weighing ...~~)
We **were** at home last night. (Not: ~~We were being ...~~)

2 | But note that some of the above verbs have more than one meaning; we can use these verbs in the continuous when they describe actions. Compare:

SIMPLE USES	CONTINUOUS USES
I **think** you're right. (*think* = believe)	Ssh! I'**m thinking**. (*think* = use the mind)
I'**ve had** my car for six months. (*have* = possess)	I'**ve been having** lunch. (*have* = eat)
Do you **see** what I mean? (*see* = understand)	Are you **seeing** the doctor tomorrow? (*see* = visit)

Compare also these simple and continuous uses of *be*:

He'**s** stupid. (generally)	He'**s being** stupid. (He is behaving in a stupid way at the moment.)

3 | We often use *can* and *could* with the verbs of perception *see, hear, smell, taste, feel* and some verbs of thinking eg *understand, remember.*

I **can see** you.
We **could hear** someone outside.

4 | Compare *hear*, *see* and *listen*, *look*, *watch*.

When we *hear* or *see*, it is not always a deliberate action, and we do not normally use the continuous.

*When I was in the garden I **heard** the telephone ring.*

When we *listen*, *look* or *watch*, it is a deliberate action, and we can use the continuous.

*Ssh! I**'m listening** to the radio.*
*They **were watching** TV last night.*

5 | Verbs of physical feeling, for example, *feel*, *ache* and *hurt*, can be used in either the continuous or simple forms.

*I **am feeling**/I **feel** ill.*
*My head **is aching**/My head **aches**.*

EXERCISE 27A

Choose the correct form.

Example:

She says she didn't take the money, but *I don't believe*/~~I'm not believing~~ her.

 1 You're very quiet. What *do you think/are you thinking* about?
 2 What *do you think/are you thinking* about my idea?
 3 How long *has Simon known/has Simon been knowing* Maria?
 4 What *does this word mean?/is this word meaning?*
 5 *Did you hear/Were you hearing* the news?
 6 *You don't watch/You aren't watching* the TV at the moment. Why don't you switch it off?
 7 I'm sorry, but *I didn't remember/I wasn't remembering* to get your newspaper when I went shopping.
 8 *Do you like/Are you liking* this painting?
 9 *She has always wanted/She has always been wanting* to be a doctor.
10 The man was a stranger to me. *I had never seen/I had never been seeing* him before.

Note

—Verbs which are not used in the continuous do have *-ing* forms, which are used, for example, as subjects eg ***Knowing** how to drive is very useful*, and after prepositions eg *I'm looking forward to **having** a car of my own.*

28 Review of the present and the past

EXERCISE 28A

Complete the sentences using a suitable present or past form of the verbs in brackets.

(i) Maria Fernandez is Spanish. She *lives* (live) in Madrid, where she __1__ (work) for an export company. She __2__ (be) with this company for two years now. At the moment she __3__ (study) English on a one-month intensive course in London. She __4__ (be) in London for one week now. She __5__ (arrive) there last Saturday. This is not Maria's first time in Britain. She __6__ (be) there twice before.

(ii) I woke up when I __1__ (hear) a noise downstairs. I __2__ (get) out of bed quietly because my wife __3__ (still | sleep) and __4__ (go) to the top of the stairs. It was dark, but I could see two men downstairs in the living room. They __5__ (try) to open the safe. When I __6__ (switch on) the light, the two men __7__ (run) into the kitchen and __8__ (escape) out of the back door. Then, before I __9__ (have) a chance to do anything, I __10__ (hear) a police car pull up outside the house. A neighbour of mine __11__ (see) the men breaking into my house and __12__ (phone) for the police.

EXERCISE 28B

Choose the correct form.

(i) It's 6.30 in the evening and Sally has just come home. Simon is in the kitchen.

Sally: Hi, Simon. Something *smells/is smelling* nice. What (1) *do you cook/are you cooking?*
Simon: (2) *I make/I'm making* some onion soup. Would you like some?
Sally: No, thanks. I'm not hungry at the moment. (3) *I've just had/I just have* something to eat in town.
Simon: Oh? What (4) *did you have/do you have?*
Sally: I (5) *I've met/I met* Peter at 5.00 and (6) *we were going/we went* to Alfredo's for a pizza. Can I just taste the soup? (7) *It's looking/It looks* delicious. Umm! Very good. I think it's the best onion soup (8) *I've ever tasted/I've ever been tasting*!

50

(ii) Andrew's friend, Les, has bought a new bicycle.

Les: Hi, Andrew. (1) *Do you like/Are you liking* my new bike?

Andrew: Yes, very much! I didn't know you'd bought a bike. How long (2) *have you had/did you have* it?

Les: Oh, (3) *I've only had/I've only been having* it for a few days. (4) *I bought/I've bought* it last weekend.

Andrew: How much (5) *did it cost/has it cost*?

Les: £120. (6) *I'd been saving/I'm saving* for over a year to buy it.

(iii) Mrs Wood has hurt her arm. She is at the doctor's.

Doctor: Does your arm hurt when you move it, Mrs Woods?

Mrs Woods: Yes, a little. (1) *It's hurting/It's been hurting* me for about a week now. (2) *I fell/I was falling* off a ladder when (3) *I cleaned/I was cleaning* the windows at home last Tuesday. (4) *Are you thinking/Do you think* that (5) *I've broken/I've been breaking* my arm, doctor?

Doctor: No, (6) *you aren't breaking/haven't broken* it, Mrs Woods. But I think you should go to hospital for an X-ray.

29   Review of the future

EXERCISE 29A

Choose the correct form.

Example:

I can't go to the beach this afternoon. ~~*I'll play*~~/*I'm playing* tennis.

1 *It's raining/It's going to rain* tomorrow.
2 *Do you do/Are you doing* anything this evening?
3 I'll write to you when *I arrive/I'll arrive* in Brazil.
4 I feel terrible. I think *I'll be/I'm going to be* sick.
5 'I've got wine or beer. Which would you like?'   'Oh, thank you. *I'll have/I'm going to have* beer, please.'
6 If the weather *is/will be* nice this afternoon, we'll have a picnic.
7 'What are you doing with that ladder?'   '*I'll repair/I'm going to repair* the roof.'
8 'It's raining outside. Would you like to borrow an umbrella?'   'Oh, thank you. *I'll bring/I'm going to bring* it back tomorrow.'
9 We're going on holiday next Monday. This time next week *we'll be lying/we'll lie* on a beach in Turkey.
10 Ben and Patty Crawford are on holiday in Europe. *They'll have visited/They'll be visiting* seven countries by the time they get home to Canada at the end of the month.

30 Imperative and *let's*

1 **Imperative**

a We use the imperative in many different ways, for example, to give orders, to make offers, suggestions and requests, and to give warnings.

Stop!
Have some more coffee.
Tell your boss you can't work late tonight.
Help me with these bags, please.
Look out! Be careful.

b The imperative has the same form as the infinitive without *to*.

Sit down.
Open the window.

c We make the negative imperative with *don't/do not*.

Don't sit down.
Don't open the window.
Do not feed the animals. (eg on a notice in a zoo)

d We can make an imperative more emphatic by putting *do* in front of it. We do this, for example, when we want to be polite, or when we want to express impatience.

Do sit down.
Do stop making that noise!

e The imperative does not normally have a subject, but we can use a noun or pronoun to make it clear who we are speaking to.

Andrew shut the door, please.
Have some more coffee, Kate.
Sit down, everybody.

f After the imperative, we can use the question tags *will/won't/would you?* and *can/can't/could you?*

Shut the door, will you?
Sit down, won't you?
Help me with these bags, could you?

2 *Let's*

a We use *let's* (= *let us*) + infinitive without *to*, as a kind of first person plural imperative, to make suggestions.

We're late. Let's hurry.
'What shall we do this evening?'   'Let's stay at home.'

b We can make negatives with *let's not* or *don't let's*.

Let's not wait./Don't let's wait.

Some people think that *let's not* is more 'correct'.

c | We can use *do* before *let's* for emphasis.
***Do let's* hurry.**

d | After *let's* we can use the question tag *shall we?*
Let's* go to the cinema, *shall we?

EXERCISE 30A

What are these people saying? Find the words in the box.

Example:

Put	that! It's hot.
Take off ⟍	me the spanner.
Do turn ⟍	your shirt, please.
Please take	that music down, Andrew!
Don't touch	a seat, Mr Woods.
Pass	this in the fridge, could you?

Take off your shirt, please.

EXERCISE 30B

You are with a friend. Reply to your friend by making suggestions. Use *Let's* and the words in the box.

Example:

Friend: 'I'm hungry.'   You: *'Let's have something to eat.'*

1 'I'd like to see a film.'
2 'I don't feel like waiting for the bus.'
3 'I'm cold.'
4 'It's Sue's birthday soon.'
5 'It's raining hard outside.'

have ⟍	a taxi
buy	in this evening
take ⟍	something to eat
light	her a present
go	a fire
stay	to the cinema

31 Be

1 Form

a Present form of *be*

AFFIRMATIVE		NEGATIVE		QUESTION	
I	am	I	am not	am	I?
you	are	you	are not	are	you?
he she it	is	he she it	is not	is	he? she? it?
we you they	are	we you they	are not	are	we? you? they?

CONTRACTIONS

'm = am
're = are   aren't = are not
's = is   isn't = is not

b Past form of *be*

AFFIRMATIVE		NEGATIVE		QUESTION	
I	was	I	was not	was	I?
you	were	you	were not	were	you?
he she it	was	he she it	was not	was	he? she? it?
we you they	were	we you they	were not	were	we? you? they?

CONTRACTIONS

wasn't = was not
weren't = were not

2 Use

We use *be* to ask for and give information about people and things.

*My name **is** Maria. **I'm** from Spain.*
***Is** Ken ready No, he **isn't**.*
*'**Were** you at home last night?'   'No, I **wasn't**. I **was** at the cinema.'*
*Anna Pavlova **was** a famous Russian dancer.*

EXERCISE 31A

Complete the conversations using the words in the box.

am ('m)	am not ('m not)
are ('re)	are not (aren't)
is ('s)	is not (isn't)

(i) James is at a party. He has just seen his friend Rosie.

James: Hello, Rosie. How *are* you?
Rosie: Oh, hello, James. I __1__ fine, thanks. How __2__ you?
James: I __3__ too bad, thank you.

(*a few moments later*)

James: Who __4__ that girl over there? Do you know her?
Rosie: Yes, her name __5__ Carla. She __6__ Italian.
James: __7__ she a student at the college?
Rosie: No, she __8__.

(ii) Sally is waiting outside the bus station. Her friend Peter is late.

Peter: Hello, Sally. Sorry. __1__ I very late?
Sally: Yes, you __2__.
Peter: What __3__ the time?
Sally: It __4__ almost half past seven.
Peter: Really? Oh, I __5__ sorry, Sally. __6__ you angry?
Sally: No, I __7__ angry, but I __8__ very hungry. Let's go for something to eat.

(iii) Mr and Mrs Ash are from Canada. They have just arrived in England. They are speaking to a customs officer at Heathrow Airport in London.

Officer: Where __1__ you from?
Mrs Ash: We __2__ from Canada.
Officer: __3__ you here on holiday?
Mrs Ash: Yes, we __4__.
Officer: __5__ this your first visit to England?
Mrs Ash: Well, it __6__ my husband's first visit, but I've been here before.
Officer: I see. __7__ these your suitcases?
Mrs Ash: Yes, they __8__.
Officer: And what about this bag? __9__ this yours, too?
Mrs Ash: No, it __10__.

EXERCISE 31B

There **was** a robbery in London at 10 o'clock last night. A police inspector is interviewing Eddie Cooper about the robbery.

Complete the conversation. Use *was* and *were*.

Inspector: *Were* you in London last night, Cooper?
Cooper: Yes, I __1__.
Inspector: Where __2__ you at 10 o'clock last night?
Cooper: At 10 o'clock? I __3__ in a pub called The Bell.
Inspector: And what about your friends Jack Callaghan and Frankie Dobbs? __4__ they in the pub with you?
Cooper: No, they __5__ n't, Inspector.
Inspector: Where __6__ they, then?
Cooper: I don't know where they __7__, but they __8__ n't with me.
Inspector: __9__ you on your own in The Bell?
Cooper: No, I __10__ n't. My girlfriend Diana __11__ with me.
Inspector: And __12__ she with you all evening?
Cooper: Yes, she __13__.

Note

–For *there + be* eg **There's** *a bank in West Street*, see 32.
–We also use *be* as an auxiliary verb (a helping verb) in the continuous forms eg *He's working* (present continuous), *He* **was** *working* (past continuous); and with *going to* eg *He's going to work*. For the continuous forms, see 1,5,9,15,23; for *going to*, see 17,20. We also use *be* as an auxiliary verb in the passive eg *It* **was** *made in Japan*. See 59–60.

32   *There is, there are*

| 1 | When we say that something exists, we normally begin the sentence with *there + be* and put the subject after *be*. |

There is *a bank in West Street*. (We do not normally say: *A bank is in West Street*.)

We use this structure with 'indefinite' subjects (eg *a man, some letters, anybody*).

There's *a man at the door.*
There are *some letters for you.*
'Is there anybody at home?'   *'No, there isn't.'*

2   We can use this structure with different forms of *be*. For example:

There is *a bank in West Street.* (present tense)
There was *a telephone call for you last night.* (past tense)
There has been *an accident.* (present perfect)
There will be *a lot of people at the party.* (*will* form) etc

Note that if the subject is plural, *be* takes a plural form also. Compare:

There's *a man at the door.*	***There are*** *some men at the door.*
There was *a telephone call for you last night.*	***There were*** *two telephone calls for you last night.*
There has been *an accident.*	***There have been*** *a lot of accidents recently.*

3   Compare *there is/are* and *it is/they are*:

We use *there + be* to say that something exists; we use a personal pronoun eg *it*, *they + be* (or another verb) to give more details.

There's *a letter for you.* ***It's*** *from Australia.*
'***There's*** *a man at the door.'*   '***It's*** *Mr Davis.'*
There are *some biscuits in the kitchen.* ***They're*** *in the cupboard.*

EXERCISE 32A

Complete the sentences using *there* and the verb forms in the box.

is   are   was   were   has been   will be

Example:

There was a terrible accident in Western Road yesterday.

1 Look. ____ a policeman over there. Can you see him?
2 How many people ____ at the party last night?
3 I think ____ some snow later this evening.
4 Excuse me. ____ a post office near here?
5 ____ six hotels in this street ten years ago, now ____ only two.
6 ____ a lot of cold weather recently.

EXERCISE 32B

Complete the sentences using the words in the box.

there   it   they   is   are

Example:

'*Is there* a police station near here?'   'Yes, *there is. It's* in East Street.'

1 ____ a good programme on TV this evening. ____ about the history of pop music.
2 ____ some envelopes in my bedroom. ____ on my desk.
3 '____ any beer in the kitchen?'   'Yes, ____ in the fridge.'
4 '____ a man waiting outside. Who ____?'   '____ Jim Brown.'
5 'Look! ____ a light on in my bedroom!'   '____ somebody in there.'

33 *Have* and *have got*

1 In British English we often use *have got* instead of *have* when the meaning is 'possess'.

I've got a new camera. | *I have a new camera.*
I haven't got any money. | *I don't have any money.*
Have you got a pen? | *Do you have a pen?*
He's got brown eyes and black hair. | *He has brown eyes and black hair.*

Have got means exactly the same as *have* in these uses; *got* is an 'empty' word here. *Have got* is more informal; we use it very often in conversations and, for example, when we write to friends.

2 **Form**

a Present form of *have got*

AFFIRMATIVE		NEGATIVE		QUESTION		
I you	have got	I you	have not got	have	I you	
he she it	has got	he she it	has not got	has	he she it	got?
we you they	have got	we you they	have not got	have	we you they	

CONTRACTIONS

've got = have got   *haven't got = have not got*
's got = has got   *hasn't got = has not got*

b Present form of *have* (1)

AFFIRMATIVE		NEGATIVE		QUESTION		
I you	have	I you	do not have	do	I you	
he she it	has	he she it	does not have	does	he she it	have?
we you they	have	we you they	do not have	do	we you they	

CONTRACTIONS

don't = do not
doesn't = does not

c   Present form of *have* (2)

We can also form *have* without *got* and without *do/does* in negatives and questions:

AFFIRMATIVE	NEGATIVE	QUESTION
I you have	I you have not	have I? you?
he she has it	he she has not it	he? has she? it?
we you have they	we you have not they	we? have you? they

CONTRACTIONS

'*ve = have*   *haven't = have not*
'*s = has*   *hasn't = has not*

But this is not very common in everyday speech.

3   When we talk about something that happens repeatedly, we normally use *have* (with *do/does* in negatives and questions), not *have got*. Compare:

*I often **have** headaches.*	*I**'ve got** a terrible headache at the moment.*
*I **don't** usually **have** much time for lunch.*	*I **haven't got** much time today.*

We do not use *have (got)* in the continuous forms when the meaning is 'possess'. For example, we do not say ~~I'm having got a new camera~~.

When we talk about the past, we normally use *had*, not *had got*.

*I **had** a headache last night.* (Not: ~~I had got a headache . . .~~)

We use *did* in past negatives and questions.

*I **didn't have** a pen.*
***Did** you **have** a key?*

We do not use *got* in short answers.

'Have you got a pen?'   *'Yes, I **have**.'* (Not: ~~Yes, I have got.~~)

EXERCISE 33A

Complete the sentences using *have got* where possible. If a form of *have got* is not possible, use the correct form of *have*.

Example:

'Excuse me, *have you got* (you) the time?'   'Yes, it's twenty-five past six.'

1 'I want to make a telephone call, but I ___ (not) any change. ___ (you) any?'
  'Let's see. Yes, I ___ two 20p coins.'
2 My brother ___ dark hair now, but when he was a child he ___ fair hair.
3 'I'll phone you tomorrow.'   '___ (you) my telephone number?'
4 '___ (we) any aspirins?'   'Yes, there are some in the bathroom cupboard.
  Why? ___ (you) a headache?'   'No, I'm fine, but Andrew ___ a terrible toothache.'
5 '___ (your sister) a car at the moment?'   'Yes, she ___.'
6 I couldn't get the concert tickets yesterday because I ___ (not) enough money.

Note

–We use *have to* and *have got to* to talk about necessity or obligation eg *I **have to** go/
 have got to go* now. See 38–39.
–We also use *have* (not *have got*) as an auxiliary verb (a helping verb) in the perfect
 forms eg *I **have** worked* (present perfect). For the perfect forms, see 6,9,14,15,24.

34   *Have* for actions

1 | We can use *have* to talk about actions in a number of expressions. For example:

> *have breakfast/lunch/dinner/a meal/a drink/a cup of tea/
>   some coffee/a beer/a cigarette*
> *have a bath/a shower/a wash/a shave/a sleep/a rest/a dream*
> *have a swim/a walk/a game of tennis, a game of football, etc*
> *have a holiday/a day off work/a party/a good time, a bad time, etc*
> *have a conversation/a talk/a chat/a quarrel/a row/a fight/
>   a disagreement/an argument*
> *have a baby* (= give birth to a baby)
> *have a look* (= look)
> *have a try/a go* (= try)

2 | *Have got* is not possible in these expressions.

*I usually **have** lunch at around 1 o'clock.* (Not: ~~I usually **have got** lunch . . .~~).

3 | We can use continuous forms of *have* with these expressions (because they describe actions).

*Sally **is having** a shower at the moment.*
*Are you **having** a good time?*
*We **were having** dinner when Peter arrived.*

4 | We form negatives and questions with *do/does* in the present simple and *did* in the past simple.

I **don't** usually **have** a big breakfast.
What time **does** Lynne usually **have** lunch?
Did you **have** a nice holiday?

5 | Contractions of *have* (*'ve, 's*) and *had* (*'d*) are not normally used.

I **have** a swim every day. (Not: ~~I've a swim . . .~~)
They **had** an argument about money. (Not: ~~They'd an argument . . .~~)

EXERCISE 34A

Complete each sentence using the correct form of the most suitable expression in the box. Use each expression only once.

> have a look   have a rest   have a shave
> ~~have breakfast~~   have a game of tennis   have a cigarette
> have a swim   have a baby   have a good time

Example:

'Are you hungry?'   'No, I *'ve just had breakfast* (just), thank you.'

1 'Have you stopped smoking?'   'Yes, I ____ (not) since the beginning of the New Year.'
2 Can I ____ at that photo?
3 'Simon and I ____ yesterday.'   'Who won?'
4 She usually ____ in the sea every morning before breakfast.
5 What was the party like last night? ____ (you)?
6 'My sister ____ (just).'   'Is it a girl or a boy?'
7 'I'm tired.'   'Let's ____ for a few minutes, then.'
8 Are you going to ____ today, or are you growing a beard?

35   Modal verbs: general

The 'modal auxiliary verbs' or 'modal verbs' are *can, could, may, might, will, would shall, should, ought to, must, need* and *dare.*

1 | **Use**

We use modal verbs to talk about, for example, possibility, willingness, ability, obligation, certainty and permission.

It **might** rain. (possibility)   You **must** be home by 11 o'clock. (obligation)
Will you help me? (willingness)   You haven't eaten all day. You **must** be hungry. (certainty)
Can she swim? (ability)   **May** I borrow your car? (permission)

2 **Form**

a We form the affirmative by putting the modal verb between the subject and the full verb.

I can swim.
We should go now.

Modal verbs take the same form in all persons. There is no *-s* ending in the third person singular.

She can swim (Not: ~~She cans . . .~~)
He should go now. (Not: ~~He shoulds . . .~~)

After all modal verbs (except *ought*) we use the infinitive without *to* eg *swim, go.*
After *ought* we use *to +* infinitive eg *to swim, to go.*

We ought to go now.

b We form the negative by putting *n't/not* after the modal verb.

She can't swim.
We shouldn't go.
It might not rain.

We form questions by inverting the subject and the modal verb. Compare:

She can swim. ⟶ *Can she swim?*

We should go. ⟶ *Should we go?*

Note that we do not use *do* in questions and negatives. For example, we do not say ~~Does she can swim? She doesn't can swim~~, etc.

c We can use the structure modal verb + *be* + . . .*-ing.*

It's getting late. We really must be going now.
I may be working late tomorrow.

d We sometimes use expressions such as *be able to, be allowed to* and *have to* instead of modal verbs. These expressions give us certain meanings and forms which are not possible with modal verbs.

I'd like to be able to play the piano. (*Can* has no infinitive; we cannot say ~~I'd like to can play . . .~~)
She had to go to the doctor's yesterday. (*Must* is not used to talk about the past; we cannot say ~~She must go . . . yesterday~~.)

e When we talk about the past, we can use modal verb + *have* + past participle. We use this structure, for example, to talk about things that possibly happened or things that did not happen.

'Peter is late.' 'He may have missed his train.' (= Perhaps he missed/has missed his train.)
I feel really tired today. I shouldn't have stayed up so late last night. (But I stayed up late last night.)

–For details of modal verbs, see 36–55.

36 Ability: *can, could, be able to*

1 | ***Can***

We use *can* to talk about ability. The negative of *can* is *cannot* (contraction: *can't*).

***Can** you swim?*
*He **can** play the guitar.*
*I **can't** open this bottle.*
***Can** you come to a party tomorrow evening?*

We can use *be able to* instead of *can* eg ***Are** you **able to swim**?* but *can* is more common.

2 | ***Could** and **was/were able to***

a | We can use *could* to say that someone had the general ability to do something in the past.

*I **could** swim when I was 4 years old.*
*My grandmother **could** speak Italian and Spanish.*

We also use *was/were able to* with this meaning.

*I **was able to** swim when I was 4 years old.*

b | But when we want to say that someone had the ability to do something, and that they did it in a particular situation, we must use *was/were able to* (*could* is not possible).

*Even though I'd hurt my leg, I **was able to** swim back to the boat.* (Not: . . . ~~I could swim back . . . .~~)
*The manager wasn't in the office for very long, but we **were able to** speak to him for a few minutes.* (Not: . . . ~~we could speak to him . . . .~~)

We can use *managed to* (+ infinitive) or *succeeded in* (+ *-ing* form) instead of *was/were able to* in this meaning.

*Even though I'd hurt my leg, I **managed to swim** back to the boat/I **succeeded in swimming** back to the boat.*

We normally use *managed to* or *succeeded in* when the action was difficult to do.

c | There is an exception with the verbs of perception *see, hear, smell, taste, feel,* and some verbs of thinking eg *understand, remember*. We use *could* with these verbs when we actually did these things in particular situations.

*We **could see** a man in the garden.*
*She didn't speak very clearly, but I **could understand** what she said.*

d | We use *could not* (contraction: *couldn't*) for both general ability and particular situations.

*My grandmother **couldn't speak** German.*
*He tried very hard, but he **couldn't swim** back to the boat.*

3 | *Could have ...*

We use *could have* + past participle to say that someone had the ability or the opportunity to do something in the past but did not do it.

You **could have helped** me. *Why didn't you?*
I **could have gone** *to university when I was younger, but I decided not to.*

4 | Expressing ability in other forms: *be able to*

Can has no infinitive, *-ing* form or participles. So, when necessary, we make these forms with *be able to*.

I'd like **to be able to** *play the piano.* (We cannot say ~~I'd like to can play ...~~)
In the future, people **will be able to** *live on other planets.* (We cannot say ~~... people will can live ...~~)
She enjoys **being able to** *speak foreign languages.* (We cannot say ~~She enjoys canning ...~~)
I've **been able to** *drive since I was 18.* (We cannot say ~~I've could ...~~)

EXERCISE 36A

Complete the sentences using *can* or *could* where possible. If *can* or *could* is not possible, use a form of *be able to*.

Examples:
He has been living in France for 6 months. He *can* speak French very well now.
I'll *be able to* go shopping later today.

1 When Robert was younger he ＿＿ run quite fast.
2 Look! You ＿＿ see the mountains from this window.
3 Kate ＿＿ sing beautifully when she was a child.
4 How long have you ＿＿ play the guitar?
5 Look! I ＿＿ lift this chair with one hand!
6 I'm sorry, but I won't ＿＿ come to the party on Saturday.

EXERCISE 36B

Complete the sentences using *could* or *was/were able to*.
Sometimes either form is possible.

Example:
Simon *could/was able to* read music when he was 7.

1 We ＿＿ put out the fire before much damage was done.
2 My daughter ＿＿ walk when she was only 11 months old.
3 I ＿＿ finish all the work you wanted me to do yesterday.
4 '＿＿ (you) speak French before you went to live in Paris?'   'I ＿＿ (not) speak it very well.'
5 They were talking quite loudly. I ＿＿ hear everything they said.

EXERCISE 36C

Robert Wells is 52 years old. Sometimes he feels that he has wasted his life.

Read about Robert. Replace the words in italics with *could have . . .*, as in the example.

Example:

When Robert was 26 *he had the chance to get* married, but he decided not to.
When Robert was 26 *he could have got* married, but he decided not to.

1 *Robert had the ability to go* to university, but he didn't want to go.
2 *He had the intelligence to pass* his final exams at school, but he didn't take them.
3 A lot of people thought *he had the ability to be* a professional footballer when he was younger, but he didn't try.
4 *He had the opportunity to start* his own business once, but he didn't want to.
5 *He had the chance to emigrate* to Australia a few years ago, but he decided not to.

Note

–For the form of modal verbs like *can* and *could*, see 35.2.
–We use *can/could* (= 'ability') in requests eg **Can** *you help me?* (see 48), and offers eg *I* **could** *lend you some money* (see 49.3).
–*Could* also has the conditional meaning 'would be able to' eg *I* **could** *repair the car if I had the right tools.* (= I would be able to repair the car . . .) See 69.3,71.3.

37   Permission: *can, could, may, might, be allowed to*

1   **Asking for permission**

Can I borrow your dictionary?

We can use *can*, *could* and *may* to ask for permission.

Can I use your phone?
Could I ask you a personal question?
May I make a suggestion?

Could is less direct and more polite than *can* here, *May* is more formal (and some people think it is more 'correct') than *can* or *could*, but *can* and *could* are more common.

We can also use *might* to ask for permission in a less direct, more formal style.

Might I make a suggestion?

2 | **Giving permission**

When we give permission, we use *can* or *may* (but not *could* or *might*).

'*Can I use your phone?*'   '*Yes, of course you **can**.*'
You **can** borrow my camera if you want to.
'*Could I make a suggestion?*'   '*Of course you **may**.*'

3 | **Talking about permission**

When we talk about things that are already permitted or not permitted (eg when there is a law or a rule), we use *can('t)* or *be (not) allowed to*.

You **can't** smoke/**aren't allowed to** smoke in this room.

More examples:

You **can** drive/**are allowed to** drive a car in Britain when you are 17. (That's the law.)
The children normally go to bed at 9 o'clock, but they **can** stay up/**are allowed to** stay up later on Saturdays. (Their parents have decided this.)

4 | ***Could* and *was/were allowed to***

a | We use *could* to say that we had general permission to do something in the past.

When we were children, we **could** stay up late on Saturday nights.
When I lived at home, I **could** borrow my parents' car whenever I wanted to.

Was/were allowed to is also possible in this meaning.

When we were children, we **were allowed to** stay up late on Saturday nights.

b | But when we want to say that someone had permission to do something and they did it in a particular past situation, we must use *was/were allowed to* (*could* is not possible).

The children **were allowed to** stay up until midnight last night. (Not: ~~The children could stay up . . .~~)

This is like the difference between *could* and *was/were able to* (see 36).

EXERCISE 37A

What are these people asking? Find their questions in the box.

Example:

Could I have a look at your magazine?

May I sit	in?
Do you think I could close	a look at your magazine?
Could I have	this on?
Can I try	here?
May I come	your bike for half an hour?
Can I borrow	the window?

EXERCISE 37B

What do these notices mean? Make sentences using the words in the box. Make two sentences for each notice, as in the example.

Example:

You can't take photographs.
You aren't allowed to take photographs.

You	can('t)	take in this street.
	are(n't) allowed to	park in this room.
		feed on the grass.
		smoke photographs.
		turn the animals.
		walk left.

67

EXERCISE 37C

Complete the sentences using *could* or *was/were allowed to*.
Sometimes either form is possible.

Example:

I *was allowed to* see him for a few moments yesterday.

1 Andrew ＿＿ leave school early yesterday because he wasn't feeling well.
2 Until the 19th century, people ＿＿ travel freely between most countries without a passport.
3 Sue's children ＿＿ watch the film on TV last night.
4 Her son has to wear a uniform in his new school, but in his old school he ＿＿ wear whatever he liked.

Note

–For the form of modal verbs like *can, could, may* and *might*, see 35.2.

38   Obligation and necessity (1): *must, have to, have got to*

1

a

Must and **have to**

We use both *must* and *have to* to express obligation or necessity, but there is sometimes a difference between them:

We normally use *must* when the authority comes from the speaker.

*You **must** be home by 10 o'clock.* (I insist.)
*I've got a terrible pain in my back. I **must** go and see the doctor.* (I think it is necessary.)
*You **must** drive carefully.* (I insist.)

We normally use *have to* when the authority comes from outside the speaker.

*I **have to** be home by 10 o'clock.* (My parents insist.)
*I **have to** go and see the doctor at 9.00 tomorrow morning.* (I have got an appointment.)
*You **have to** drive on the left in Britain.* (That is the law.)

68

b   We only use *must* (+ infinitive) to talk about the present and the future. When we talk about past obligation or necessity, we use *had to*.

I **had to** work late yesterday. (Not: ~~I must work late yesterday.~~)

c   *Must* has no infinitive, -*ing* form or participles. So, when necessary, we make these forms with *have to*.

I'll **have to** work late tomorrow. (We cannot say ~~I'll must . . .~~)
He hates **having to** get up early. (We cannot say ~~He hates musting . . .~~)
She's **had to** work hard all her life. (We cannot say ~~She's musted . . .~~)

Note that in questions and negatives with *have to* we use *do/does* in the present simple and *did* in the past simple.

What time **do** you **have to** start work?
We **don't have to** hurry. We've got plenty of time.
Did you **have to** walk home last night?

2   **Have got to**

We often use *have got to* instead of *have to* to talk about obligation and necessity. *Have got to* is more informal.

I **have to** go now.	I**'ve got to** go now.
Do you **have to** leave tomorrow?	**Have** you **got to** leave tomorrow?

We normally use *have to*, not *have got to*, for things that happen repeatedly, especially when we use one-word adverbs of frequency eg *always, often*. Compare:

I **always have to** work late on Wednesday evenings.	I**'ve got to** work late this evening.
Do you **often have to** get up early?	**Have** you **got to** get up early tomorrow?

We use *got* mostly in the present. To talk about the past, we normally use *had to*, not *had got to*.

I **had to** work late last night. (Not: ~~I had got to work late last night.~~)

These differences are like the differences between *have* and *have got* used to talk about 'possession' (see 33).

EXERCISE 38A

(i) Mrs Woods isn't very well. The doctor is speaking to her. Complete what the doctor says using *must* and the verbs *drink, take, stay* and *continue*. Use each verb only once.

Doctor: Well, Mrs Woods, your temperature is a little high, so you __1__ in bed for the next few days. You can eat whatever you like, but you __2__ plenty of liquids. And I'll give you some medicine. You __3__ it three times a day after meals. And you __4__ to take it for the next ten days.

(ii) Now Mrs Woods is explaining the doctor's instructions to Mr Woods. Complete what Mrs Woods says using *have to* and the verbs *drink, take, stay* and *continue*. Use each verb only once.

Mrs Woods: The doctor gave me some medicine. I __1__ it three times a day after meals. And I __2__ to take it for the next ten days. I'm not allowed to get up at the moment. I __3__ in bed for the next few days. Oh, and I'm allowed to eat whatever I like, but I __4__ plenty of liquids.

EXERCISE 38B

Complete the sentences using *must* or a form of *have to*. Sometimes two answers are possible.

Examples:

I couldn't go to the party last night because I *had to* babysit for my sister.
I *have to/must* get up early tomorrow morning.

1 You ___ get a visa to visit the United States.
2 Annie will ___ do her homework tomorrow.
3 It's getting very late. We ___ go now.
4 I ___ stay in bed yesterday because I wasn't very well.
5 Mr Mason ___ wear glasses since he was a child.
6 I don't like ___ work at weekends.

Note

–For the form of modal verbs like *must*, see 35.2.
–For the negatives *mustn't, don't have to, haven't got to, needn't* and *don't need to*, see 39.

39   Obligation and necessity (2): *mustn't, don't have to, don't need to, haven't got to, needn't*

We use *mustn't* when there is an obligation not to do something.	We use *don't have to* when it is not necessary to do something.
*You **mustn't** get up today.* (= Do not get up.)	*I **don't have to** get up today.* (= It is not necessary to get up.)
*You **mustn't** wash that sweater. It has to be dry-cleaned.* (= Do not wash it.)	*You **don't have to** wash that shirt. It isn't dirty.* (= It is not necessary to wash it.)

2   We can also use *don't need to, haven't got to* or *needn't* to say that it is not necessary to do something.

*I **don't need to** get up today.*
*I **haven't got to** get up today.*
*I **needn't** get up today.*

Note that we often use *needn't* when the speaker gives someone permission not to do something.

*You **needn't** pay me back the money you owe me until next week.* (= I give you permission not to pay me back the money until then.)

EXERCISE 39A

Choose the correct form.

Example:

You've been late for work twice this week. You *mustn't*/~~needn't~~ be late again tomorrow.'

1 You *mustn't/don't have to* open the door before the train stops. You could fall out.
2 We *mustn't/don't have to* hurry. We've got plenty of time.
3 We *mustn't/haven't got to* make any noise going into the house. It's very late and everybody is asleep.
4 You *mustn't/needn't* tell Nicki about the party. I've already told her.
5 You *mustn't/don't need to* phone the station about the time of the trains. I've got a timetable.
6 I *mustn't/haven't got to* go now. I can stay a bit longer if you want me to.

Note

–For the form of modal verbs like *must* and *needn't*, see 35.2.
–See also 41 *Needn't have* and *didn't need to*.

40 Review of permission and obligation: *can, can't, must, mustn't, needn't, be allowed to, have to, don't have to*

EXERCISE 40A

Complete these sentences using the modal verbs in the box. Sometimes two answers are possible.

must mustn't can can't needn't

Examples:

You needn't wait any longer, You *can* go now.
We mustn't make a noise. We *must* be quiet.
You must move your car. You *can't/mustn't* park here.

1 You mustn't leave the door unlocked. You ____ lock it.
2 You can only smoke in the canteen. You ____ smoke in this room.
3 We needn't do the washing up now. We ____ do it tomorrow.
4 We can stay a bit longer. We ____ go now.
5 You can't keep on using my tennis shoes. You ____ buy your own.
6 You can keep those magazines. You ____ give them back to me.

EXERCISE 40B

What do these signs and notices mean? Find the explanations in the box.

Example:

		swim here.
You	are allowed to aren't allowed to	~~stop~~. overtake. walk here.
	have to don't have to	be a member to get in. park here. be quiet.

You have to stop.

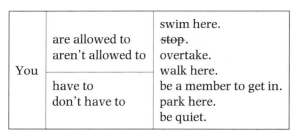

1 **SILENCE!**
2
3 Non Members Welcome

4 **P**
5 **NO SWIMMING**
6

41 *Needn't have* and *didn't need to*

1   *Needn't have* + past participle says that someone did something, but it was not necessary – it was a waste of time.

*I **needn't have made** so much food for the party. Nobody was very hungry.* (= It was not necessary to make so much food, but I did.)
*I **needn't have taken** my umbrella with me when I went out. It didn't rain.* (= It was not necessary to take my umbrella, but I did.)

2   *Didn't need to* + infinitive says that something was not necessary (but it does not say if someone did it or not).
Compare:

*She **needn't have gone** out.* (= It was not necessary to go out, but she did.)	*She **didn't need to go** out.* (= It was not necessary to go out; we don't know if she did or not.)
*They **needn't have hurried**.* (= It was not necessary to hurry, but they did.)	*They **didn't need to hurry**.* (= It was not necessary to hurry; we don't know if they did or not.)

3   When we use *didn't need to*, it often means that someone did not do something (because it was not necessary).

*She **didn't need to go** out, so she stayed at home.*
*I **didn't need to unlock** the door because it was already unlocked.*

But we can also use *didn't 'need to* (with stress on *need*) when something was not necessary, but someone did it.

*She **didn't 'need to go** out, but she went anyway.*

EXERCISE 41A

Complete the sentences using *needn't have* where possible. If *needn't have* is not possible, use *didn't need to*.

Examples:

'Did you water the garden?'   'Yes, but I *needn't have done* (do) it. Just after I'd finished it started to rain!'
I *didn't need to wake* (wake) her up because she was awake before me.

1   She ＿＿ (get up) early last Saturday, so she stayed in bed until 10 o'clock.
2   I didn't wear my coat when I went out. I ＿＿ (wear) it. It wasn't cold.
3   He was very anxious before the exam, but he ＿＿ (worry). It wasn't as difficult as he'd expected.
4   They ran all the way to the station, but they ＿＿ (hurry) because the train was late.
5   We ＿＿ (hurry), so we took our time.
6   Thank you very much for the flowers, but you really ＿＿ (buy) them for me.

42 Obligation and advice: *should, ought to, had better, be supposed to, shall*

1

a

Should and ought to

We can use both *should* and *ought to* to talk about obligation and duty, to ask for and give advice, and, in general, to say what is right or good.

*You **should** stop smoking./You **ought to** stop smoking.*
*You **shouldn't** tell lies./You **oughtn't to** tell lies.*
*What do you think I **should** do?/What do you think I **ought to** do?*

Should and *ought to* are very similar in meaning, but we often prefer *ought to* to talk about authority which comes from outside the speaker eg from laws or rules.

Note that after *should*, we use the infinitive without *to* eg *stop, tell*, but after *ought*, we use *to* + infinitive eg *to stop, to tell*.

b

We use *should have/ought to have* + past participle to say that someone did the wrong thing in the past.

*I **should have posted** this letter yesterday, but I forgot.* (I did not post it.)
*I'm really tired this morning. I **shouldn't have stayed up** so late last night.* (I stayed up late.)
*We had a really good time in London yesterday. You **ought to have** come with us.* (You did not come.)

2

Had better

Had better (+ infinitive without *to*) expresses a strong recommendation in a particular situation.

*It's very late. I**'d better go** now.*
*I think it's going to rain. You**'d better take** an umbrella with you when you go out.*

(*'d better = had better*)

We always use *had* (not *have*) with *better* in this structure, but the meaning is present or future, not past.

We form the negative with *had better not*.

*We**'d better not be** late.*

Had better often suggests a kind of threat or warning, and is stronger than *should* or *ought to*.

3

Be + supposed to

We can use *supposed to* to talk about what people are expected to do because of an arrangement, a rule, or a duty.

*You**'re supposed to start** work at 8.00 every morning.*
*I**'m supposed to see** Maria this afternoon.*

We use *not supposed to* to express prohibitions.

*You know you**'re not supposed to smoke** in here.*

There is often a difference between what is supposed to happen and what really happens.

*I**'m supposed to see** Maria this afternoon, but I'm not going to have enough time.*
*Put that cigarette out! You know you**'re not supposed to smoke** in here.*
*He **was supposed to phone** me yesterday, but he didn't.*

Note that we also use *supposed to* to mean 'said to' eg *I'd like to read that book. It**'s**
supposed to be very good.* See 64.2.

4   **Shall**

We can use *shall I?* when we want to know someone's opinion, or when we want
advice or instructions.

*I've missed my last bus. What **shall I** do?*
*I'm not sure what to do. **Shall I** apply for the job or not?*
*How long **shall I** cook this spaghetti?*

EXERCISE 42A

Complete the advice using *should* or *ought to*; find the advice for the problems.

Example: **1** 'I've lost my credit card.'
'You should report it to the credit card company immediately.'/
'You ought to report it to the credit card company immediately.'

PROBLEMS	ADVICE
1 'I've lost my credit card.'	'I think you | sell it.'
2 'I can't wake up in the mornings.'	'Perhaps you | look for another job.'
3 'I'm bored with my job.'	'Don't you think you | apologize to them?'
4 'I've got a terrible cough.'	'Perhaps you | buy a new alarm clock!'
5 'I was very rude to my parents.'	'You | report it to the credit card company immediately.'
6 'My car keeps on breaking down.'	'Don't you think you | give up smoking?'

EXERCISE 42B

Make sentences using *should(n't) . . ., ought(n't) to . . ., should(n't) have . . .* or
ought(n't) to have . . . and the words in brackets.

Example: My car is always dirty. (I | clean | it more often.)
I should clean it more often./I ought to clean it more often.

1 You think your friend works too hard. You tell him/her:
   (You | not work | so hard.) (You | relax | more.)
2 Your friend didn't go with you to a party on Saturday. The party was really
   good. You tell your friend: (You | come.)
3 Kate had a bad cold yesterday, but she went to work and now she feels terrible.
   (She | not go | to work yesterday.) (She | stay | in bed.)
4 Mr Woods walked straight out into the road without looking. He was nearly
   killed by a bus. (He | not walk | into the road without looking.) (He | look | first.)

EXERCISE 42C

Complete the sentences using *had better* and the verbs in the box.

Example: It's cold today. You*'d better wear* a coat when you go out.

park   stay   hurry   ~~wear~~   put out   be   not leave

1 This knife is very sharp. You ____ careful when you use it.
2 Oh no! Look! There's a 'No Parking' sign here. We ____ somewhere else.
3 You're not very well. I think you ____ in bed today.
4 We're late. We ____.
5 There's a lot of crime in this area. We ____ any doors or windows unlocked.
6 The plane is just going to take off. You ____ that cigarette.

EXERCISE 42D

Complete the sentences using the correct form of *be + supposed to* and the verbs in the box.

Example: I'm on a diet, so I*'m not supposed to eat* cream cakes.

arrive   ~~not eat~~   go   not open   not park   have

1 What are you doing with your birthday presents? You ____ them until your birthday!
2 I ____ to work yesterday, but I couldn't because I was ill in bed.
3 You ____ your car here at any time.
4 We ____ in Manchester at 6 o'clock this morning, but our plane was delayed.
5 Peter ____ a one-hour lunch break, but he sometimes takes a bit longer.

EXERCISE 42E

Complete each question using *shall I* and the most suitable verb in the box.

Example: How much money *shall I get* from the bank?

paint   invite   ~~get~~   tell   put

1 Who ____ to my party, do you think?
2 Where ____ all these dirty plates and glasses?
3 What do you think? ____ my parents what has happened?
4 What colour ____ my bedroom? Have you got any ideas?

Note
–For the form of modal verbs like *should, ought to* and *shall,* see 35.2.

43 Possibility: *may, might, could*

1　**Present and future possibility**

a　We use *may, might* and *could* to talk about present or future possibility.

'There's someone at the door.'　*'It **may** be Sarah.'* (= Perhaps it is Sarah.)
*We aren't sure what we are going to do tomorrow. We **might** go to the beach.*
(= Perhaps we will go to the beach.)
'Where's Simon?'　*'He **could** be in the living room.'* (= Perhaps he is in the living room.)

Might is normally a little less sure than *may*. *Could* is normally less sure than *may* or *might*.

$+++$*may*　　$++$*might*　　$+$*could*

b　We use the negatives *may not* and *might not* (contraction: *mightn't*) with this meaning, but not *could not*.

*Simon **may not** be in the living room* (= Perhaps he is not in the living room.)
*We **might not** go to the beach.* (= Perhaps we will not go to the beach.)

c　Note the form: *may/might/could + be + . . .-ing.*

*They **may be having** dinner at the moment.* (= Perhaps they are having dinner.)

2　**Possibility in the past**

a　We can use *may/might/could + have +* past participle to talk about possibility in the past.

'Where was Sally last night?'　*'I think she **may have been** at the cinema.'* (= I think perhaps she was at the cinema.)
'Peter is late.'　*'He **might have missed** his train.'* (= Perhaps he missed/has missed his train.)
'I can't find my wallet anywhere.'　*'You **could have left** it at home.'* (= Perhaps you left/have left it at home.)
'She walked straight past me without saying hello.'　*'She **might not have seen** you.'*
(= Perhaps she didn't see you.)

b We also use *could* and *might* (but not *may*) with *have* + past participle to say that something was possible in the past but did not happen.

'I forgot to lock my car last night.' *'You were very lucky. Someone **could have stolen** it.'*
*You were stupid to try to climb that tree. You **might have killed** yourself.*

EXERCISE 43A

Rephrase these sentences using the modal verbs in brackets.

Example:

Perhaps she is ill. (may) *She may be ill.*
Perhaps they went out. (might) *They might have gone out.*

1 Perhaps you're right. (could)
2 Perhaps it'll rain later. (might)
3 Perhaps she forgot about the meeting. (may)
4 Perhaps they were asleep. (might)
5 Perhaps he doesn't know the address. (may)
6 Perhaps they left early. (could)
7 Perhaps he isn't coming now. (might)
8 Perhaps I'll see you tomorrow. (may)
9 Perhaps they're going on holiday. (could)
10 Perhaps she didn't catch the bus. (may)

Note

–For the form of modal verbs like *may*, *might* and *could*, see 35.2.
–We also use *could* to suggest possible actions. eg *We **could** go out tonight.* See 50.3.
–*Might* also has the conditional meaning 'would perhaps' eg *If I won a lot of money,
  I **might** stop working.* (= . . . I would perhaps stop working). See 69.3, 71.3.

44 Possibility: *can*

1 We use *can* to talk about 'theoretical possibility'.

*Anyone **can** learn to swim.* (= It is possible for anyone to learn to swim.)

In this use, *can* often has a similar meaning to 'sometimes'.

*My brother **can** be very nice.* (= My brother is sometimes very nice.)

We use *may*, *might* or *could*, not *can*, to say that perhaps something will happen in the future or that perhaps something is true at the moment of speaking (see 43).

*It **may** rain later.* (Not: ~~It can rain later.~~)
'Where's Ken?' *'He **could** be outside.'* (Not: ~~'He can be outside.'~~)

Compare:

*It **can** be cold in England.* (= It is sometimes cold in England.)

*It **may** be cold tomorrow.* (= Perhaps it will be cold tomorrow.)

2 We use *could* to talk about theoretical possibility in the past.

*My brother **could** be really horrible when he was a child.*

EXERCISE 44A

Complete the sentences using *can* or *could* and the verbs in the box. Use each verb only once.

grow   ~~be~~   make   reach   live   survive   cross

Example:

Tigers *can be* dangerous.

1 Elephants ____ for up to 70 years.
2 Temperatures near the South Pole ____ minus 43 degrees centigrade.
3 A hundred years ago ships ____ the Atlantic in 10 days.
4 Camels ____ for up to 17 weeks in the desert without water.
5 Dinosaurs ____ up to 5 metres long.
6 Anyone ____ mistakes.

Note

–For the form of modal verbs like *can*, see 35.2.
–We also use *can* to suggest possible actions. eg *We **can** have dinner now if you like.* See 50.3.

45   Probability: *should, ought to*

1   We can use *should* or *ought to* to say that something is probable at the moment of speaking, or in the future.

*Sally **should** be at work by now. She's normally there at this time.* (= Sally is probably at work by now.)
*I **should** finish work early today. I haven't got much to do.* (= I will probably finish work early today.)
*He **ought to** pass his driving test easily. He's a very good driver.* (= He will probably pass his driving test easily.)

2 | **Should have . . .** and **ought to have . . .**

We use *should have/ought to have* + past participle when we expected something to happen and we do not know if it happened.

They **should have arrived** by now. (But I do not know if they have arrived.)
'I wonder if he passed his driving test this morning.'   'He **ought to have passed** it easily.' (But I do not know if he passed it.)

We also use this structure when we expected something to happen but it did not happen.

They **should have arrived** by now, but they aren't there yet.
He **ought to have passed** his driving test easily. I was surprised that he failed.

EXERCISE 45A

Complete the sentences using *should* or *ought to* and the correct form of the verbs in the box. Use each verb only once.

| pass ~~be~~ win   not take |
| sell   arrive   receive |

Example:
I've only got £15, but that *should be/ought to be* enough. We won't need to buy very much.

1 You ____ my letter first thing tomorrow morning. I posted it early today.
2 I was surprised Liverpool lost the football match. They ____ easily.
3 I ____ my car easily. I only want £950 for it and it's in very good condition.
4 Andrew ____ the exams last week. He worked very hard for them.
5 'How long will it take to drive to the park?'   'Well, it ____ long. It isn't very far.'
6 I'm still waiting for the 7 o'clock bus. It ____ half an hour ago.

Note

–For the form of modal verbs like *should* and *ought to*, see 35.2.

46 Deduction: *must, can't*

1 | ***Must, can't***

a | We use *must* in deductions to say that we are sure about something.

*There is a light on in the house, so someone **must** be at home.* (= I am sure that someone is at home.)
*Mrs Woods **must** know London very well. She has lived there all her life.* (= I am sure that she knows London very well.)

b | We use *can't* (not *mustn't*) as the negative of *must* in this meaning. We use *can't* in deductions to say that something is impossible.

*You've just had lunch. You **can't** be hungry already.* (= It is impossible that you are hungry already.)
*Annie **can't** be asleep. There's a light on in her bedroom.* (= It is impossible that she is asleep.)

c | Note the form: *must/can't + be + . . .-ing.*

*You've been working hard all day. You **must be feeling** tired.* (= I am sure that you are feeling tired.)
*Simon has bought two tickets for the concert, so he **can't be going** on his own.* (= It is impossible that he is going on his own.)

d | We also use *can* in questions about possibility.

*The telephone is ringing. Who **can** that be?*
*Sally is late. Where **can** she be?*

2 | ***Must have . . .*** and ***can't have . . .***

a | We use *must/can't + have + past participle for deductions about the past.*

*Those shoes you bought are very nice. They **must have been** expensive.* (= I am sure that they were expensive.)
*You **can't have been** at the swimming pool yesterday! The swimming pool was closed all day yesterday!* (= It is impossible that you were at the swimming pool!)

We can use *couldn't have . . .* instead of *can't have . . .* here.

*You **couldn't have been** at the swimming pool yesterday! The swimming pool was closed all day yesterday!*

b | We use *can have . . .* and *could have . . .* in questions about past possibility.

*Where **can** they **have gone**?*
*Sally is very late. What **could have happened** to her?*

EXERCISE 46A

Answer the questions in **A** using *must* or *can't*, give a reason from **B**.

Example:

1 They *must be* hungry. They haven't eaten all day.

A
1 Are they hungry?
2 Does he earn much money?
3 Is he at work today?
4 Are they asleep?
5 Is she happy?
6 Do they know each other?

B
They haven't met before.
He's on holiday this week.
He's always borrowing money from his friends.
They haven't eaten all day.
All the lights are off.
She's just passed her driving test.

EXERCISE 46B

There was a robbery at the Central Art Gallery in London yesterday. A detective is questioning Billy Palmer about the robbery. The detective knows that Palmer is lying to him. Look at what Palmer says on the left. Then look at the clues on the right.

1. I STAYED IN BED ALL MORNING YESTERDAY.
2. I HAD LUNCH AT LUIGI'S RESTAURANT.
3. I WENT FOR A DRIVE IN MY CAR YESTERDAY AFTERNOON.
4. I STAYED AT HOME LAST NIGHT.
5. I'VE NEVER BEEN INSIDE THE CENTRAL ART GALLERY.

* Someone phoned Palmer's flat at 9.00 last night and there was no reply.
* Palmer's car was outside his flat all yesterday afternoon.
* Palmer's fingerprints were found in the gallery.
* Someone saw Palmer in town at 10.00 yesterday morning.
* Luigi's restaurant was closed all day yesterday.

Make deductions using *must have . . .* or *can't/couldn't have . . . .* Give the reason for each deduction.

Example:

1 *Palmer can't/couldn't have stayed in bed all morning yesterday. Someone saw him in town at 10.00 yesterday morning.*

Note

—For the form of modal verbs like *must, can('t)* and *could(n't)*, see 35.2.

47 Review of possibility, probability and deduction: *may, might, could, should, ought to, must, can't*

EXERCISE 47A

Look at the examples:

Find the correct place in the table for the words in the box.

might ~~*should*~~ *must* ~~*may*~~	
ought to *can't* *could*	

Saying how sure we are:

YES definitely   ____
     probably   *should*; ____
     possibly   *may*;   ____; ____
NO definitely not ____

EXERCISE 47B

Rephrase the sentences using the correct form of the words in brackets.

Examples:

I'm sure she is in bed. (must) *She must be in bed.*
We'll probably arrive before 11 o'clock. (should) *We should arrive before 11 o'clock.*
Perhaps he was ill. (may) *He may have been ill.*
It's impossible that they missed the plane. (can't) *They can't have missed the plane.*

1 Perhaps she'll phone later. (might)
2 I'll probably be at home by 6 o'clock. (should)
3 Perhaps they went home. (could)
4 It's impossible that he's telling the truth. (can't)
5 I'm sure you've heard the news. (must)
6 Perhaps I won't go out this evening. (may)
7 It's impossible that she saw us. (can't)
8 I'm sure the bus has left. (must)
9 Perhaps he didn't apply for the job. (might)
10 She'll probably be here soon. (ought to)

48 Requests: *can, could, may, will, would*

1 | **Asking for something**

We can ask for things with *can, could* and *may*.

Can I have a glass of water, please?
Could I have the bill, please? (eg in a restaurant)
May I have some more coffee?

Could is less direct and more polite than *can* here; *may* is more formal than *can/could*.

2 | **Asking for permission**

We also use *can, could* and *may* to ask for permission (see 37.1).

Can I borrow your dictionary?
Could I ask you a personal question?
*Excuse me. **May** I have a look at your newspaper?*

3 | **Asking someone to do something**

a | We often use *can you?* (= are you able to?) to ask someone to do something for us.

Can you help me?
Can you switch on the light, please?

We use *could* as a less definite, more polite form of *can* in this meaning.

Could you lend me some money?
Could you do me a favour?

b | We also use *will you?* (= are you willing to?) to ask someone to do something.

Will you switch on the light, please?

We use *would* as a less definite, more polite form of *will* in this meaning.

Would you post this letter for me?
'The phone is ringing.'   'Would you answer it?'

c | We also use *would* with the verb *mind* (= 'object to' or 'dislike') to make polite requests.

*Would you **mind** switching on the light?*

d | We sometimes make requests by using *would like* as a polite way of saying what we want.

I'd like a glass of water, please.
I'd like to ask you a personal question.

EXERCISE 48A

What are these people asking? Find their questions below.

Example:

Can I close the window?

Could you tell	the TV for me, please?
Would you mind changing	the window?
Would you answer	the menu, please?
May I have	the phone, please?
Can I close	me where the hospital is, please?
Will you switch on	me the cloth, please?
Can you pass	places with me?

Note

–For the form of modal verbs like *can, could, may, will* and *would*, see 35.2.

–Note the meanings of *yes* and *no* after requests with *mind* eg '**Would you mind waiting?**'   '**No, that's all right.** (= I am happy to wait.)/'**Yes, I would!**' (= I am not happy to wait!)

85

49 Offers: *will, shall, can, could, would*

1   We use *will* to say that we are willing to do something or to offer to do something.

I'll help you with your suitcase.
I'll lend you some money if you want.
Are you hungry? I'll make you something to eat.

(*I'll = I will*)

We also use *will you?* in offers and invitations.

*What **will you** have to drink?*
***Will you** have dinner with us?*

2   We use *shall I?* (= do you want me to?) to offer to do something for someone.

***Shall I** help you?*
***Shall I** open the door for you?*
***Shall I** post this letter for you?*

3   We also use *can/could* (= 'ability') to offer to do something for someone.

*I **can** post this letter for you.*
*I **could** lend you some money if you want.*

Sometimes when we use *can* or *could* to 'ask for permission', we are really offering to do something.

***Can** I help you?*
***Could** I carry that bag for you?*

In these uses, *could* is less direct and more polite than *can*.

4   We also use *would* with verbs such as *like, prefer* and *rather* to make polite offers and invitations.

***Would** you **like** to go to a party on Saturday?*
***Would** you **like** me to help you?*
***Would** you **prefer** to stay in or go out this evening?*

EXERCISE 49A

Make offers in these situations using the words below.

Example:

Shall I switch off	something to drink?
I'll help	you an umbrella if you like.
Would you like me to phone	your coat?
Can I take	the light?
Would you like	some bags for you?
Could I carry	for the doctor?
I can lend	you do the washing up.

Would you like something to drink?

Note

–For the form of modal verbs like *will, shall, can, could* and *would*, see 35.2.

50   Suggestions: *shall, let's, why don't we? How/What about? can, could*

1

We use *shall we?* to ask for and make suggestions.

*Where **shall we** go?*
*What time **shall we** leave?*

***Shall we** stay at home?*
***Shall we** play tennis tomorrow?*

2   We can also make suggestions in these ways:

a

> *Let's* (+ infinitive without *to*)

Let's *watch TV.*
Let's *go for a swim.*

(*Let's* = *Let us*)

b

> *Why don't we* (+ infinitive without *to*)?

Why don't we *go for a swim?*
Why don't we *play tennis?*

c

> *How/What about* (+ *-ing* form/noun)?

How about *playing tennis/a game of tennis?*

3   We use *can* and *could* to suggest possible actions.
We **can** *watch TV if you like.*
We **could** *go to the cinema tomorrow.*

In this use, *could* is less direct and more polite than *can*.

EXERCISE 50A

Peter and Sally are trying to decide what to do this evening.

Complete the conversation using the words in the box. Use some words more than once.

> Why don't we   Let's   shall we   How about   could

Peter: So, what *shall we* do this evening?
Sally: Well, we haven't got much money. __1__ staying in and watching TV?
Peter: Oh, no! I'm fed up with watching TV.
Sally: __2__ go out for a drink, then. We can afford one drink each.
Peter: All right. Where __3__ go?
Sally: __4__ go to The Tropical Bar? They have really good music there.
Peter: Yes, but the drinks are very expensive.
Sally: That's true. Well, we __5__ go to the pub on the corner.
Peter: Yes. They have very good videos. __6__ go there.
Sally: I thought you said you were fed up with watching TV!

Note

–For the form of modal verbs like *shall, can* and *could*, see 35.2.

51 Habits: *used to, will, would*

1 **Used to**

a Use

We use *used to* + infinitive to talk about past habits which are now finished.

Robert when he was younger   Robert today

*Robert **used to play** football when he was younger, but he stopped playing 20 years ago.*
(= Robert played football regularly in the past, but he does not play now.)

More examples:

*Kate **used to go** to the cinema a lot, but she doesn't now.*
*When I was a child, I **used to suck** my thumb.*

We also use *used to* for past states and situations which are no longer true.

*Robert **used to be** very slim when he was younger.*
*I **used to live** in London, but I moved in 1980.*

We only use *used to* to talk about the past. When we talk about present habits or present states, we use the present simple.

*Robert never **plays** football now.*
*Kate **goes** to the theatre quite often nowadays.*
*I **live** in Manchester.*
*Robert **is** quite fat.*

We do not use *used to* to say how long something happened.

*I **lived** in London for four years.* (Not: ~~I used to live in London for four years.~~)

b Form

Used to + infinitive takes the same form in all persons.

I You He She etc	***used to***	***play*** football. ***live*** in London. ***be*** very slim.

89

The negative of *used to* is normally *didn't use to* (= *did not use to*).

I **didn't use to live** in London.
You **didn't use to like** classical music.

We also use *never used to* eg You **never used to like** classical music.

We normally form questions with *did . . . use to . . . ?*

Where **did** you **use to live?**
Did you **use to like** classical music?

Note the special pronunciation of *used* / juːst/ and *use* /juːz/ in this structure.

2   **Will and would**

a   We can use *will* to talk about someone's typical behaviour or characteristic habits.

Simon loves music. He'll sit for hours listening to his stereo.
Kate is very kind. She'll always help people if she can.

We use *would* with the same meaning to talk about the past.

*When I was a child my father **would** sometimes take me fishing.*
*My grandmother was very absent-minded. She **would** often buy something and then leave the shop without it.*

Will and *would* are not stressed in this use.

b   If *will* or *would* are stressed ('), it suggests criticism.

*He '**will** leave his clothes all over the floor. It really makes me angry.*
*'She borrowed my camera without asking.'   'She '**would** do a thing like that. That's typical of her.'*

3   **Used to and would**

When we talk about past habits, we can use *used to* or *would*.

*When we were children, we **used to**/**would** play Cowboys and Indians together.*
*When I was a child, my elder brother **used to**/**would** take me to the cinema every Saturday morning.*

When we talk about past states, we can use *used to*, but not *would*.

*My grandfather **used to** be a policeman. (Not: ~~My grandfather would be . . .~~)*
*I **used to** have a moustache, but I shaved it off. (Not: ~~I would have . . .~~)*

EXERCISE 51A

Put one verb in each sentence into the *used to* form and the other verb into the present simple.

Examples:

When Margot first became a doctor, she *used to work* (work) in a small hospital in Brighton, but now she *works* (work) in a large hospital in London.

1 Ken ____ (not | smoke) now, but when he was younger he ____ (smoke) forty cigarettes a day.
2 Nowadays Kate ____ (never | go) dancing, but she ____ (go) a lot before she was married.
3 That shop ____ (be) a grocer's when I was a child. Now it ____ (be) a supermarket.
4 Martin ____ (live) in Manchester now, but he ____ (live) in Newcastle when he was a child.
5 My sister ____ (not | like) fish when she was a child, but now she ____ (love) it.
6 '____ (you | like) history when you were at school?'   'No, I didn't, but now I ____ (find) it quite interesting.'

EXERCISE 51B

Complete the sentences using *will* or *would* and one of the verbs in the box.

Example:

Robert has got a very bad memory. He*'ll often forget* (often) where he's parked his car.

carry on   spend   lend   go   throw   ~~forget~~

1 Kate is very generous. She ____ (always) you money if you need it.
2 Ken's grandfather was very mean. He ____ (never) anything away if he could use it again.
3 Mr Woods is a real chatterbox! He ____ talking for hours and hours if you give him a chance.
4 When Simon was a child, he ____ (often) hours just looking out of the window.
5 'I'm always tired these days.'   'Well, you ____ to bed so late every night, it isn't surprising!'

EXERCISE 51C

Which of these sentences can be completed with either *used to* or *would*? Which of them can only be completed with *used to*?

Examples:

We *used to* live in a village in the North of England.
When Robert was younger, he *used to/would* go running every morning.

1 When Andrew was a small baby he ____ cry a lot.
2 When I was little, I ____ be afraid of the dark.
3 When we were children, we ____ visit my grandmother every Sunday afternoon.
4 When Mrs Woods was younger, she ____ play tennis every weekend.
5 Years ago I ____ have a motorbike.
6 There ____ be quite a lot of cinemas in the town, but now there aren't any.

Note

–For the form of modal verbs like *will* and *would*, see 35.2.
–Do not confuse *used to* + infinitive eg He **used to get** up very early and be used to + -*ing* form eg He**'s used to getting** up early. See 89.

91

52 Refusals: *won't, wouldn't*

> We use *won't* (= *will not*) to say that people or things refuse to do something.
>
> *Annie **won't** do her homework.* (= She refuses to do it.)
> *My car **won't** start.* (= It refuses to start.)
>
> We use *wouldn't* (*would not*) to say that people or things refused to do something in the past.
>
> *My car **wouldn't** start yesterday morning.* (= It refused to start.)

EXERCISE 52A

Replace the words in italics with . . . *won't* . . . or . . . *wouldn't* . . . , as in the examples.

Examples:

I asked my father, but *he refused to lend* me the money.
I asked my father, but *he wouldn't lend* me the money.
I've decided to take the job and *I refuse to change* my mind.
I've decided to take the job and *I won't change* my mind.

1 I pushed hard, but *the window refused to open.*
2 He's proposed to her, but *she refuses to marry* him.
3 I switched on the machine, but *it refused to work.*
4 I've warned her several times about leaving the windows unlocked, but *she refuses to listen* to me.
5 We've asked him, but *he refuses to help* us.
6 We couldn't drive to the country last weekend because *my parents refused to let* me use their car.

53 Promises and threats: *will*

> We can use *will* to express strong intentions, for example in promises and threats.
>
> *I **will** be careful with the car, I promise.*
> *I promise I **won't** be late tomorrow.*
> *Stop making that noise or **I'll** scream!*

EXERCISE 53A

Complete each sentence using *will* or *won't* and a verb from the box. Then say if the sentence is a promise or a threat.

leave   do   tell   ~~hit~~   throw   pay   speak

Example:

Don't touch my camera or I'*ll hit* you!   a threat

1 Don't worry. I ____ you the money tomorrow.
2 It's getting late. If you don't hurry up, I ____ without you.
3 I ____ anyone what you said. Don't worry.
4 I'm very sorry I shouted at you. I ____ it again.
5 Get out of my room or I ____ you out!
6 If you don't help me, I ____ to you ever again.

54   *May/might as well*

> We use *may/might as well* (+ infinitive without *to*) to say that we should do something because there is no strong reason not to do it.
>
> '*Shall we get a taxi or wait for the bus?*'   '*We **might as well** wait for the bus. We're not in a hurry, are we?*'
> '*Why don't we go out for a walk?*'   '*We **may as well**, I suppose. We haven't got anything else to do.*'

EXERCISE 54A

Make sentences from the table to go with these ideas.

Example:

You may as well switch off the TV. Nobody is watching it.

1 ____. It's not very far.
2 ____. I'm too ill to go on holiday.
3 ____. It isn't going to stop raining.
4 ____. No one wants any more to eat.
5 ____. There's a chance I'll get it.

You may as well switch off	to the station.
We might as well stay	the table.
We may as well walk	the hotel bookings.
I might as well apply	the TV.
You might as well cancel	at home today.
I might as well clear	for the job.

55   Other uses of *should*

1

Verb + *should*

We can use *that . . . should* after verbs like *suggest, insist, recommend, agree*; we often leave out *that* in an informal style.

*I **suggest (that)** he **should** see the doctor.*
*She **insisted (that)** I **should** take the money.*
*I **agreed (that)** we **should** tell the police.*

Other structures are possible after these verbs also. For example:

*I **suggest (that)** he **sees** the doctor.* (the present)
*She **insisted (that)** I **took** the money.* (the past)

2

Adjective + *should*

We can use *(that) . . . should* after adjectives which express feelings eg *surprised, sorry, shocked, interesting*.

*I was **surprised (that)** she **should** fail the exam.*
*I am **sorry (that)** he **should** feel so unhappy.*
*It is **interesting (that)** you **should** say that.*

We also use *(that) . . . should* after adjectives such as *important* and *essential*.

*It is **important (that)** we **should** arrive on time.*

Ideas like these can also be expressed without *should*.

*I was **surprised (that)** she **failed** the exam.*
*It is **important (that)** we **arrive** on time.*

EXERCISE 55A

Report these ideas using the verbs in brackets
followed by *(that) . . . should*, as in the example.

Example:

'You must visit us,' they said to me. (insist)
They insisted (that) I should visit them.

1   'Why don't you apply for the job?' she said to me. (suggest)
2   'Stay in bed for a few days,' the doctor said to him. (recommend)
3   'You must help me,' he said to me. (insist)
4   'Let's go to the cinema,' they said to us. (suggest)

EXERCISE 55B

Complete each sentence using *should* and the most suitable verb in the box. Use each verb only once.

Example:

The situation is very difficult, but it is important that everyone *should stay* calm.

come   give up   pass   ~~stay~~   feel

1 The doctor suggested that I ___ smoking.
2 It's essential that Sarah ___ the exams if she wants to go to university.
3 It was embarrassing that Simon ___ into the room just as we were talking about him.
4 I'm sorry that you ___ so angry. I didn't mean to upset you.

Note

–We can use *should* after *if* when a possibility is not very strong eg *If I should see Maria, I'll give her your message.* We can also use *should* instead of *if* eg *Should I see Maria, I'll give her your message.* See 68.3, 73.4.
–We also use *should* with this meaning after *in case* eg *I'll take an umbrella with me when I go out in case it should rain.* See 164.4

56   *Wish* and *if only*

1 | ***Wish* and *if only* + past tense**

We can use *wish* and *if only* with a past tense to express regret about the present (to say that we would like something to be different).

*I **wish** I **had** a car.* (I do not have a car.)
*I **wish** he **wasn't** so horrible to me.* (He is horrible to me.)
*She **wishes** she **could** play the guitar.* (She cannot play the guitar.)
*If only we **knew** Maria's address.* (We do not know Maria's address.)

If only is more emphatic than *wish*.

We often use *were* instead of *was* after *wish* and *if only*, especially in a more formal style.

*I **wish** he **weren't** so horrible to me.*
*If only I **were** better-looking.*

2   **Wish** and *if only* + *would*

*I **wish** it **would** stop raining.*

We use *would* after *wish* and *if only* when we want something to stop happening, or we want something different to happen.

*I **wish** you **would** be quiet. I'm trying to do my homework.*
*I **wish** he **wouldn't** leave his clothes lying all over the bathroom floor.*
*If only you **would** stop complaining!*

3   **Wish** and *if only* + past perfect

To express regret that something happened or did not happen in the past, we can use *wish* and *if only* with the past perfect (*had* + past participle).

*Oh, I'm tired. I **wish** I'd **gone** to bed earlier last night.* (I did not go to bed very early last night.)
*I feel sick. I **wish** I **hadn't eaten** so much chocolate cake.* (I ate too much chocolate cake.)
*If only you **had explained** the situation to me.* (You did not explain the situation to me.)

EXERCISE 56A

Read what this man thinks about himself on the left. Complete what he says on the right.

I'm so shy.   I wish *I weren't so shy.*
I don't know what to say to people.   If only *I knew what to say to people.*

1 I get embarrassed so quickly.   I wish _____
2 I can't relax.   I wish _____
3 I find it so difficult to make friends.   I wish _____
4 I'm not good-looking.   I wish _____
5 My ears are so big.   If only _____

EXERCISE 56B

Some people are complaining about the things they would like other people to do or to stop doing. Complete what they are saying. Use *would/wouldn't* and the words in the box.

Example:

A zoo keeper: 'I wish people *wouldn't feed the animals.*'

take their litter home
pick the flowers
clean the bath after they've used it
do their homework on time
~~feed the animals~~
keep together on a tour

1 A teacher: 'I wish my students ____.'
2 A hotel chambermaid: 'If only guests ____.'
3 A park keeper: 'I wish people ____.'
4 A street cleaner: 'If only people ____.'
5 A travel guide: 'I wish people ____.'

EXERCISE 56C

Each of these people did something yesterday which they now regret.
What does each person wish? Use *He/She wishes . . .* and the words in the box.

Example:

(try) to lift a heavy table on her own
~~(go) out in the rain without an umbrella~~
(eat) less
(drive) more carefully
(stay) in the sun so long

Mrs A has caught a bad cold.
She wishes she hadn't gone out in the rain without an umbrella.

1 Miss B has got very bad sunburn.
2 Mr C has got an awful stomachache.
3 Mr D has hurt his leg in a car crash.
4 Mrs E has hurt her back.

57 *Would rather*

1 *Would rather* means 'would prefer to'. After *would rather*, we use the infinitive without *to*.

> *would rather* + infinitive without *to*

Would you like to go out this evening?'   'I'd rather stay at home.'
Would you rather eat now or later?

We form negatives with *would rather not*.

I'd rather not go out this evening.

Note also the structure *would rather* (do something) *than* (do something else).

I'd rather stay at home than go out this evening.

2 We can also use *would rather* + a past tense to say that one person would prefer someone else to do something.

> *would rather* + subject + past tense

I'd rather you didn't open that window. I'm cold.
'Do you want me to go home?'   'I'd rather you stayed here.'
I'd rather John didn't borrow my car.

We use the past here eg *you didn't open, you stayed, John didn't borrow*, but the meaning is present or future, not past.

EXERCISE 57A

Complete the sentences using *would rather* and the verbs in the box. Use each verb only once.

Example:

What would you like to drink? *Would you rather have* (you) wine or beer?

> listen   do   go   ~~have~~   stay

1 'Shall we go out this evening?'   'I think I ___ at home.'
2 It's a beautiful day. Shall we go to the beach or ___ (you) to the country?
3 'Would you like to watch TV?'   'I ___ to some music.'
4 We could wait for the next bus or walk home. What ___ (you)?

EXERCISE 57B

You are speaking to a friend. Complete the sentences using *I'd rather you* and the past form of the verbs in the box. Use each verb only once.

| come   not tell   ~~stay~~   phone   not turn on |

Example:

You could go now if you want to, but *I'd rather you stayed* a bit longer.

1 This is a secret, so ____ anyone.
2 I could phone the restaurant if you like, but ____ them.
3 ____ the TV if you don't mind. I've got a terrible headache.
4 'Shall I come and see you tomorrow morning?'   '____ in the afternoon. I'll be quite busy in the morning.'

58   *It's time*

---

1 We can use the *to* infinitive after the structure *it's time* (*for* someone).
   It's time *for us* to leave.
   It's time *to go* to bed now.

2 We can also use *it's time* + a past tense when we think that someone should have already done something.
   *Your bedroom is in a terrible mess. Don't you think **it's time** you **cleaned** it?*
   *I'm tired. **It's time** I **went** to bed.*

   We use the past here eg *you cleaned, I went*, but the meaning is present or future, not past.

   We also say *it's about time*.
   *Your bedroom is in a terrible mess. Don't you think **it's about time** you **cleaned** it?*

EXERCISE 58B

Complete the sentences using *it's time* and a past tense.

Andrew's hair looks awful. He hasn't washed it for a long time. He says: *It's time I washed my hair.*

1 You haven't bought any new clothes for a long time. You say: ____.
2 It's nearly lunch time, but Simon hasn't got up yet. His mother asks him: Don't you think ____?
3 You promised to write to a friend three weeks ago, but you still haven't written to him. You say: ____.
4 You haven't had a holiday for a long time. You say: I think ____.

59   The passive: general

1

a   Form

We form passive verbs with the different tenses of *be* (eg *is, was, is being, have been*) + past participle.

Present simple:	*am/are/is* + past participle *The office **is cleaned** every evening.*
Present continuous:	*am/are/is* + *being* + past participle *The house **is being painted** at the moment.*
Past simple:	*was/were* + past participle *My car **was stolen** last night.*
Past continuous:	*was/were* + *being* + past participle *The bridge **was being repaired** last week.*
Present perfect simple:	*have/has* + *been* + past participle *Sarah **has been invited** to the party.*
Past perfect simple:	*had* + *been* + past participle *I thought that you **had been told** the news.*

Perfect continuous passives (*have/has/had* + *been being* + past participle) are very uncommon.

The past participle of regular verbs ends in *-ed* eg *cleaned, painted.* Irregular verbs have different past participle forms eg *steal* → **stolen**, *tell* → **told** (see 190).

When we add *-ed* to verbs, there are sometimes changes in spelling eg *stop* → **stopped**. See 188.3,4,6. For the pronunciation of *-ed*, see 187.2.

b   Compare these active and passive sentences:

Active: *Someone **cleans** the office every evening.*

Passive: *The office **is cleaned** every evening.*

Active: *Someone **has invited** Sarah to the party.*

Passive: *Sarah **has been invited** to the party.*

Note that the object of an active verb (eg *the office, Sarah*) becomes the subject of a passive verb.

c   The rules for choosing tenses in the passive are the same as in the active. For example, to talk about something that is in progress now, we use the present continuous.

*The house **is being painted** at the moment.*

2 | **Use**

a | We often use the passive when we do not know who or what does something.

*My car **was stolen** last night.* (I do not know who stole the car.)

b | We also use the passive when we are not interested in who or what does something.

*This house **was built** in 1795.*
*Sarah **has been invited** to the party.*

In these sentences we are interested in the house and Sarah, not who built the house, or who invited Sarah.

c | We also use the passive when we do not want to say who or what does something. Compare:

Active: *I **made** a mistake.*
Passive: *A mistake **was made**.*

EXERCISE 59A

What is being done in these pictures? Complete the sentences using the present continuous passive of these verbs: *paint, feed, milk, count, repair, cut, clean.*

Example:

1 The road _____
2 The fence _____
3 The cows _____
4 The windows _____
5 The cats _____
6 The money _____

The grass *is being cut.*

EXERCISE 59B

Compare the two pictures. Picture A shows a room some time ago in the past.
Picture B shows the same room as it is now. What is different? Complete the
sentences using the present perfect simple passive of these verbs: *repair, paint,
take out, put up, clean.* Use some verbs more than once.

Example:

In picture B...

The door *has been repaired.*
Some new curtains *have been put up.*

1 The windows ____
2 The carpet ____
3 The walls ____
4 The light ____
5 Some posters ____
6 The old fireplace ____

EXERCISE 59C

Complete the sentences.
(i) Use the present simple passive of the verbs in brackets.

Example:

Bread *is made* (make) from wheat.

1 Football ____ (play) all over the world.
2 Millions of cars ____ (export) from Japan every month.
3 A compass ____ (use) for showing direction.
4 How many languages ____ (speak) in Switzerland?

(ii) Use the past simple passive of the verbs in brackets.

Example:

President John F. Kennedy *was assassinated* (assassinate) in Dallas in 1963.

1 The Tower of London ___ (build) at the beginning of the eleventh century.
2 The 1986 World Cup for soccer ___ (play) in Mexico.
3 When ___ (television | invent)?
4 The first pyramids of Egypt ___ (build) around 3000 BC.

(iii) Use the past continuous passive or the past perfect passive of the verbs in brackets.

Example:

I couldn't wear my suit last Saturday. It *was being cleaned.* (clean).

1 When I got back to the car park, my car wasn't there. It ___ (steal).
2 We couldn't use the photocopier yesterday morning. It ___ (repair).
3 By the time I arrived at the concert hall, there were no tickets left. They ___ (all | sell).
4 We didn't go to the party on Saturday because we ___ (not | invite).

EXERCISE 59D

Choose the correct form: active or passive.

Example:

A valuable painting *stole*/*was stolen* from the Central Art Gallery late last night. The thieves *entered*/*were entered* the gallery through a small upstairs window.

1 Walt Disney *created*/*was created* the cartoon character Mickey Mouse.
2 This problem *discussed*/*was discussed* at the last meeting.
3 In 1964 Martin Luther King *won*/*was won* the Nobel Peace Prize. In 1968 he *assassinated*/*was assassinated* in Memphis, Tennessee.
4 The factory *produces*/*is produced* millions of cars every year and most of them *export*/*are exported.*
5 Teachers *have given*/*have been given* a new pay rise by the government. The news *announced*/*was announced* earlier today.

Note

–For the passive, see also 60–64.

60 The passive: infinitive and *-ing* forms

1 There is a passive infinitive form: *be* + past participle. We use this form after modal verbs (*must, can, will,* etc) and after a number of other structures (eg *going to, have to, want to* and *would like to*).

*This door must **be kept** locked.*
*The job can't **be done**.*
*He's going to **be interviewed** next week.*
*The new motorway will **be opened** next summer.*
*I don't want to **be disturbed**.*

2 There is a passive perfect infinitive form: *have been* + past participle. We can use this form to talk about the past.

*The newspaper may **have been thrown** away last night.*
*We should **have been told** about the dangers.*

3 There is also a passive -ing form: being + past participle.

*I don't like **being kept** waiting.*
*He remembers **being given** the book.*

EXERCISE 60A

Put these sentence into the passive (leaving out *someone, they, we*).

Example:

Someone might steal the car. *The car might be stolen.*

1 Someone will clean the room.
2 They had to cut down that tree.
3 Someone should tell Sally what happened.
4 They're going to build a new hospital.
5 We can solve the problem.

EXERCISE 60B

Complete the sentences using the passive perfect infinitive.

Example:

Why doesn't Kate know about the meeting? She should *have been told* (tell) ages ago.

1 'Sally is late this evening.' 'She might ____ (delay) at work.'
2 Why is all this rubbish still here? It ought to ____ (throw away) yesterday.
3 The sweater I wanted to buy isn't in the shop window any more. It must ____ (sell).
4 It was lucky that you didn't fall off the ladder. You might ____ (kill).
5 You shouldn't have left all that money in your hotel room. It could ____ (steal).

EXERCISE 60C

Put these sentences into the passive, as in the example.

Example:

I don't like people shouting at me.   *I don't like being shouted at.*

1 I don't like people staring at me.
2 I can't stand people telling me what to do.
3 I don't like people interrupting me.
4 I don't usually mind people criticizing me.
5 I enjoy people praising me.

Are these things true for you?

61   Using *get* instead of *be* in the passive

We sometimes use *get* (+ past participle) instead of *be* (+ past participle) to make passive verbs. We do this, for example, when we talk about things that happen by accident or unexpectedly.

*When Annie ran across the road, she nearly **got run** over by a car.*
*I was surprised that I didn't **get invited** to the party.*
*Luckily, nobody **got hurt** in the accident.*

We use *get* mostly in an informal style.

EXERCISE 61A

Billy Palmer was a burglar once. He is speaking about a night some years ago when everything went wrong for him.

Complete Palmer's story using the past simple passive with *get*.

'It was terrible. First of all, my jeans *got ripped* (rip) as I was climbing over the garden wall. Then I ___1___ (stick) climbing through the bathroom window. Then I ___2___ (bit) by a dog inside the house. The dog made so much noise that everyone in the house woke up and I ___3___ (hit) over the head with an umbrella. Then, when I finally got out of the house, there was a police car waiting there. But, to my surprise, I ___4___ (not | caught) that night. Although it wouldn't really have mattered if I had. Two weeks later, I ___5___ (arrest) burgling another house and I ___6___ (sentence) to three years in prison.'

62 Verbs with two objects in the passive

Some verbs eg *give* can have two objects.

Someone gave **Jimmy the money**. (The two objects are *Jimmy* and *the money*.)

In cases like this, we can make two different passive sentences.

Jimmy *was given the money.*   **The money** *was given to Jimmy.*

In general, it is more usual for passive sentences to begin with the person.

Other verbs which can have two objects include *send, offer, show, pay, teach, promise* and *tell*.

I was sent *a telegram.*
She will be told *the news.*

EXERCISE 62A

Put these sentences into the passive, beginning with the words given.

Example:
They promised Robert an interview for the job.   Robert *was promised an interview for the job.*

1 They showed Sarah the photographs.
  Sarah ____.
2 Normally, they pay me my salary every month.   Normally, I ____.
3 I think that they have sent us the wrong tickets.   I think that we ____.
4 I hope that someone will give Sally the message.   I hope that Sally ____.
5 They didn't ask me for my address.   I ____.
6 I thought that someone had told you about the meeting.   I thought that you ____.

63 The passive with *by* and *with*

1 | *By* + *agent*
Compare:
Active: Marconi *invented the radio.*

Passive: *The radio was invented by* **Marconi.**
Active: The strong winds *blew down a number of trees.*

Passive: *A number of trees were blown down by* **the strong winds.**

We sometimes use the subject of an active sentence (eg *Marconi, the strong winds*) as 'the agent' in a passive sentence. When this happens, we use *by* to introduce the agent in the passive.

We only use *by* + agent when it is important to say who or what is responsible for something.

2 | **With + instrument**

We use *with* to talk about an instrument which is used by the agent to do something. Compare:

*He was killed **with a knife**.*   *He was killed **by his wife**.*

3 | **With + material**

We also use *with* to talk about materials or ingredients.

*The room was filled **with smoke**.*
*Irish coffee is made **with whiskey**.*

EXERCISE 63A

Complete the sentences using the past simple passive of the verbs in the box and *by*.

| paint ~~write~~ compose and sing |
| invent   discover   direct |

Example:

The Old Man and the Sea was written by Ernest Hemingway.

1 Radium ____ Pierre and Marie Curie.
2 *The Goldrush* ____ Charlie Chaplin.
3 *Imagine* ____ John Lennon.
4 The safety razor ____ King Camp Gillette.
5 *The Chair* ____ Vincent van Gogh.

EXERCISE 63B

Complete the sentences with *by* or *with*.

My desk was covered *with* papers.

1 These photos were taken ____ a very cheap camera.
2 These photos were taken ____ my sister.
3 I was attacked ____ an old lady.
4 I was attacked ____ an umbrella.
5 The garage was painted ____ a new kind of paint.
6 The garage was painted ____ a friend of mine.

64   *It is said that he .../He is said to ... etc*

1 |
When we talk about what other people say, believe, etc we can use two possible passive forms. Compare:

Active: ***People say that Mr Ross is** a millionaire.*

Passive (1): *It + passive + that-* clause
              ***It is said that Mr Ross is** a millionaire.*

Passive (2): Subject + passive + *to* infinitive
              ***Mr Ross is said to be** a millionaire.*

We often use these passive forms in a formal style and with verbs such as:

say	think	believe	consider	understand	know
report	expect	allege	claim	acknowledge	

It is believed that she is living in Brazil.
She is believed to be living in Brazil.

It is reported that the president is seriously ill.
The president is reported to be seriously ill.

It is expected that a new law will be introduced next year.
A new law is expected to be introduced next year.

When the belief, etc refers to an earlier action, we use the 'perfect infinitive'
(*to have* + past participle). Compare:

It is believed that the fire started late last night.
The fire is believed to have started late last night.

It was thought that two people had died in the accident.
Two people were thought to have died in the accident.

2   **Be supposed to**

We can use *supposed to* to mean 'said to'.

I'd like to read that book. It's supposed to be very good. (= It is said to be very good.)
He's supposed to have been married before. (= He is said to have been married before.)

Supposed to sometimes suggests some doubt about whether something is true or not.

Note that we also use *supposed to* to say what people are expected to do because of an arrangement, a rule, or a duty eg *I'm supposed to see Maria this afternoon.*
See 42.3.

EXERCISE 64A

Read each sentence. Then make two new sentences in the passive, beginning with the words in brackets.

Example:

People expect that the government will win the election. (It)   (The government)
It *is expected that the government will win the election.*
The government *is expected to win the election.*

1 People say that the monument is over 2000 years old.
   (It)   (The monument)
2 People expect that the President will resign.
   (It)   (The President)
3 People think the fire started at about 8 o'clock.
   (It)   (The fire)
4 Journalists reported that seven people had been injured in the fire.
   (It)   (Seven people)

EXERCISE 64B

Read each sentence. Then make a new sentence with *be* + *supposed to*, as in the example.

Example:

People say that Whitby is a very nice town.
Whitby is supposed to be a very nice town.

1 People say that the new film is very violent.
2 People say that those cars are rather unreliable.
3 People say that he moved to New York last year.
4 People say that the new restaurant is very expensive.
5 People say that the concert was very good.

65   *Have something done*

1 **Form**

have + object + past participle

I am **having**	**my house**	***painted*** *at the moment.*
Where do you **have**	***your car***	***serviced?***
I **had**	***these shoes***	***repaired*** *last week.*
Simon has just **had**	***his hair***	***cut.***
You should **have**	***your eyes***	***tested.***
Are you going to **have**	***new carpets***	***fitted*** *in your flat?*

The past participle of regular verbs ends in *-ed* eg *painted, serviced*. Irregular verbs have different past participle forms eg *cut* —➤ **cut**, *build* —➤ **built** (see 190).

When we add *-ed* to verbs, there are sometimes changes in spelling eg *fit* —➤ **fitted**. See 188.6. For the pronunciation of *-ed*, see 187.2.

2 **Use**

a We use the structure *have something done* to talk about something which we arrange for someone else to do for us.

*I'm **having my house painted*** *at the moment.*

Compare:

*I'm **painting my house*** *at the moment.* (I am painting the house myself.)
*I'm **having my house painted*** *at the moment.* (I arranged for someone else to do this for me.)

More examples:

*We **had the carpet cleaned*** *by a professional carpet cleaner. We didn't do it ourselves.*
*I usually **have my car serviced*** *at a garage in East Street.*

b   We can also use *have something done* when we do not arrange for someone else to do something for us.

*I **had my car stolen** last month.*
*Annie **had one of her teeth knocked out** in a fight.*

We often use *have something done* in this way when something unpleasant or unexpected happens to someone.

Note that we can often use *get something done* instead of *have something done*, especially in an informal style eg *I must **get this jacket cleaned**.*

EXERCISE 65A

What are these people having done? Make sentences using the words in the box.

Example:

1 *They're having their flat decorated.*

| a photograph (take)   their flat (decorate) |
| a tooth (take out)   her windows (clean) |
| a suit (make)   her hair (do) |

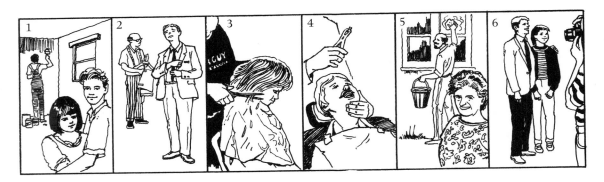

EXERCISE 65B

Complete the sentences using the correct form of *have something done.*

Example:
I haven't *had my central heating serviced* (my central heating | service) since last autumn.

1 Are you going to ____ (these shoes | repair) or shall I throw them away?
2 My neighbours are ____ (an extension | build) onto their house at the moment.
3 I must ____ (my glasses | mend). They keep falling off.
4 Where do you ____ (your hair | do)? It always looks very nice.
5 I ____ (four new tyres | fit) on my car last month.
6 I've just ____ (my suit | dry-clean).

EXERCISE 65C

Something unpleasant happened to each of these people last week. Make sentences using *have something done*.

Example:

Kate *had her wallet stolen* (her wallet | steal) from her bag while she was out shopping.

1 Peter ____ (his flat | burgle) while he was out at work.
2 Mr and Mrs Woods ____ (the roof of their house | damage) in a storm.
3 Lynne ____ (the radio | steal) from her car.
4 My brother ____ (his nose | break) in a football match.

66   *When* and *if*

Compare:

We use *if* for things we are not sure will happen.	We use *when* for things we are sure will happen.
If I see Sarah, I'll invite her to the party. (Perhaps I'll see Sarah, perhaps I won't.)	*When I see Sally, I'll invite her to the party.* (I'm sure I'll see Sally.)
I'll visit Martin if I go to Manchester. (Perhaps I'll go to Manchester, perhaps I won't.)	*I'll visit Martin when I go to Manchester.* (I'm sure I'll go to Manchester.)

EXERCISE 66A

Complete the sentences using *if* or *when*.

Example:

Perhaps I'll go to the USA next year. *If* I go there, I'll visit a friend of mine in New York.

1 I'm seeing Sally tonight. ____ I see her I'll give her your message.
2 I'm going home now. ____ I get home, I'll phone you.
3 We'd like you to come with us on holiday. But ____ you don't want to come, you don't have to.
4 I'll do my homework ____ I finish dinner.
5 ____ it is a nice day tomorrow, I'll go to the beach.
6 We think we'll arrive at 6 o'clock. But ____ we're late, please wait for us.

Note

–When we talk about general truths, we can use *if* or *when(ever)* without much difference of meaning eg *If/When(ever) I have a big lunch, it makes me sleepy.* See 72.
–For *if* sentences, see also 67–74.

67 Conditionals: introduction

1   We can use *if* with many different structures. Here are the most common:

a   **Open present or future conditionals** (see 68)

> *If* + present simple + *will* + infinitive

If he asks me, I'll help him. (Perhaps he will ask me.)

b   **Unreal present or future conditionals** (see 69)

> *If* + past simple + *would* + infinitive

If he asked me I would help him. (But he won't ask me, or he probably won't.)

c   **Unreal past conditionals** (see 71)

> *If* + past perfect + *would have* + past participle

If he had asked me, I would have helped him. (But he didn't ask me.)

d   **General conditionals** (see 72)

> *If* + present simple + present simple

If he asks me, I always help him. (= Whenever he asks me . . .)

2   An *if*-clause can go at the beginning or the end of a sentence.
If it rains, I'll stay at home.
I'll stay at home if it rains.

We often write a comma (,) after the *if*-clause when we begin with this clause.

3   We can use conditional clauses without *if* (see 73).
Unless we hurry, we'll be late.
Suppose you won a lot of money, what would you do?

68   Open present or future conditionals

1 | **Basic form** (See also **3** below.)

IF-CLAUSE	MAIN CLAUSE
If it **rains**,	*I'll stay* at home.
If you **don't study**,	you **won't pass** your exam.
If they **offer** you the job,	what **will** you **do**?

if + present simple + *will* + infinitive without *to*

This structure is often called the 'first conditional'.

2 | **Use**

We use this structure when there is a possibility that the situation in the *if*-clause will happen in the future.

*If it **rains**, I'll **stay** at home.* (Perhaps it will rain, perhaps it won't.)
*If we **have** enough time, we'll **visit** Robert.* (Perhaps we will have enough time, perhaps we won't.)

We also use this structure when there is a possibility that the situation in the *if*-clause is true in the present.

*If you're hungry, I'll **make** you something to eat.* (Perhaps you are hungry, perhaps you aren't.)

3 | **Other forms**

a | We can also use *shall* instead of *will* with *I* and *we* in the main clause.

*If I fail the exam, **I shall** take it again.*

b | In this structure, we can use a modal verb eg *can, may* instead of *will* in the main clause.

*If we have enough time, we **can** visit Robert.*

c | We can also use the imperative in the main clause.

*If you see Maria, **give** her a message for me, please.*

d | We can use the present perfect or present continuous instead of the present simple in the *if*-clause.

*If it **has stopped** raining, I'll go out for a walk.*
*I'll come back later if you're **working** now.*

e | We can also use *should* after *if* when we are less sure about a possibility. Compare:

If I see Maria, I'll give her your message. (Perhaps I will see Maria.)	*If I should see Maria*, I'll give her your message. (I am less sure that I will see Maria.)

We can also begin with *should* when we are less sure.

***Should** I see Maria, I'll give her your message.*

EXERCISE 68A

Put the verbs into the correct form: *will/won't* or the present simple.

Example:

If I *have* (have) time, I*'ll go* (go) shopping this afternoon.

1 I'm sure you ____ (enjoy) the film if you ____ (see) it.
2 If we ____ (leave) now, we ____ (not be) late.
3 If we ____ (miss) the bus, we ____ (take) a taxi.
4 What ____ (she | do) if she ____ (fail) the exam?
5 If you ____ (need) any help, ____ (you | tell) me?
6 If Simon ____ (not apologize) to me, I ____ (not speak) to him any more.

EXERCISE 68B

Complete the sentences using the words in the box.

Example:

If I don't leave now, I *might be* late.

have finished can lend ~~might be~~ should need
are feeling may go should phone

1 If you need any more money I ____ you some.
2 You can go now if you ____ .
3 If the weather is fine tomorrow, we ____ for a picnic.
4 Just ask me if you ____ any help.
5 If anyone ____ for me while I am out, tell them I'll be back at 4 o'clock.
6 Go to bed now if you ____ tired.

69   Unreal present or future conditionals

1   **Basic form** (See also **3** below.)

IF-CLAUSE	MAIN CLAUSE
If I **had** a lot of money,	I**'d travel** round the world.
If he **got** up earlier,	he **wouldn't be** late for work.
If you **didn't pass** the exam,	**would** you **take** it again?

if + past simple + *would* + infinitive without *to*

This structure is often called the 'second conditional'.

2   **Use**

We use this structure to talk about unreal present or future situations.

*If I **had** a lot of money, I**'d travel** round the world.* (But I do not have a lot of money.)
*If I **didn't feel** so tired, I**'d come** out with you.* (But I feel very tired.)
*If the weather **was** nice, I**'d go** to the beach.* (But the weather is not nice.)

We also use sentences like these to talk about unlikely present or future situations.

*If she really **loved** you, she **wouldn't be** so horrible to you.*
*If I **won** a lot of money, I**'d take** a long holiday.*

The past form eg *had, loved* does not have a past meaning in sentences like these; it has a hypothetical present or future meaning.

3 | **Other forms**

a | We often use *were* instead of *was* after *if*, especially in a more formal style.

*If the weather **were** nice, I'd go to the beach.*
*I'd go to the party, if I **weren't** so tired.*
*That watch wouldn't be so cheap if it **were** really made of gold.*

We often use *if I were you* to give advice and *if you were me* to ask for advice.

***If I were you**, I'd apply for the job.*
*What would you do **if you were me**?*

b | We can use the modal verbs *might* or *could* instead of *would* in the main clause.

*If I won a lot of money, I **might** stop working.* (= . . . I would perhaps stop working.)
*I **could** repair the car, if I had the right tools.* (= I would be able to repair the car . . .)

EXERCISE 69A

Put the verbs into the correct form: the past simple or *would* . . . .

Example:

Simon would like to buy some new clothes, but he hasn't got much money. He says: 'If I *had* (have) more money, I *would buy* (buy) some new clothes.'

1 Sarah would like to write to her friend, Alan, but she has lost Alan's address.
She says: 'If I ____ (know) Alan's address, I ____ (write) to him.'
2 You would like to buy some shoes, but you think they are too expensive. You say: 'I ____ (buy) them if they ____ (not be) so expensive.'
3 Peter is thinking of buying a new record. Sally thinks the record isn't very good.
She says: 'I ____ (not buy) it if I ____ (be) you.'
4 Andrew's elder brother, Simon, still lives at home. Andrew says: 'If I ____ (be) Simon's age, I ____ (not live) at home.
5 You see a competition in a magazine with a first prize of a million pounds. You ask a friend: 'What ____ (do) if you ____ (win) a million pounds?'

70 Open and unreal present or future conditionals

We use 'open' conditionals (see 68) to talk about possible present or future situations.

*If you **need** the money, **I'll lend** it to you.* (Perhaps you need the money.)
*If we **leave** at 1.30, **we'll arrive** at 2.30.* (Perhaps we will leave at 1.30.)

We use 'unreal' conditionals (see 69) to talk about unreal or unlikely present or future situations.

*If you **needed** the money, **I'd lend** it to you.* (But you don't need the money, or you probably don't need it.)
*If we **left** at 2.00, **we'd arrive** late.* (But we won't leave at 2.00, or we probably won't leave then.)

EXERCISE 70A

Put the verbs in brackets into the correct form.

Example:

We'll go out later on if it *stops* (stop) raining.

1 Do you want to watch the TV? I ___ (switch) it on if you do.
2 What ___ (you | do) if you were the President of the USA?
3 If she ___ (have) time, she'll phone me this evening.
4 If I ___ (be) you, I'd go to the doctor.
5 ___ (you | buy) a new car if you could afford one?
6 We'll have a picnic tomorrow if the weather ___ (be) fine.

71   Unreal past conditionals

1

Basic form (See also **3** below.)

IF-CLAUSE	MAIN CLAUSE
If the weather **had been** nice yesterday,	I **would have gone** to the beach.
If I **had studied** hard,	I **would have passed** the exam.
If you **hadn't missed** your bus,	you **wouldn't have been** late for school.
If I **hadn't helped** you,	what **would** you **have done**?

if + past perfect + *would have* + past participle

This structure is often called the 'third conditional'.

The contraction of both *had* and *would* is *'d*.

If I'd (= had) studied hard, I'd (= would) have passed the exam.

2

Use

We use this structure to talk about unreal past situations.

*If the weather **had been** nice yesterday, I **would have gone** to the beach.* (But the weather was not nice.)
*If I'd studied hard, I **would have passed** the exam.* (But I did not study hard.)
*If you **hadn't missed** your bus, you **wouldn't have been** late for school.* (But you missed your bus.)

3

Other forms

We can use the modal verbs *might* and *could* instead of *would* in the main clause.

*If you had taken the exam, you **might** have passed it.* (= ... you would perhaps have passed it.)
*I **could** have repaired the car, if I'd had the right tools.* (= I would have been able to repair the car ...)

EXERCISE 71A

Put the verbs into the correct form: the past perfect, or *would(n't) have* + past participle.

Example:

She would have spoken to you if she *had seen* (see) you.

1 If I _____ (not | be) so busy yesterday, I would have visited you.
2 If you had seen the film, you _____ (enjoy) it.
3 She would have gone to university if she _____ (have) the opportunity.
4 If he had been more careful, he _____ (not | have) an accident.

EXERCISE 71B

Read the situation. Then make a sentence with *if*.

Example:

I didn't have time. I didn't go shopping.
If I'd had time, I would have gone shopping.

1 She was ill. She didn't go to work.
2 It rained all morning. We didn't go out.
3 She didn't have enough money. She couldn't buy the shoes.
4 I wasn't hungry. I didn't have breakfast.

72   General conditionals

1   **Form**

	IF-CLAUSE	MAIN CLAUSE
	If I **have** a big lunch,	it **makes** me sleepy.
	If you **mix** yellow and blue,	you **get** green.

if + present simple + present simple

2   **Use**

We use this structure to talk about general truths; here *if* has the same meaning as *whenever*.

If I **have** a big lunch, it **makes** me sleepy. (= Whenever I have a big lunch . . .)
If you **mix** yellow and blue, you **get** green. (= Whenever you mix yellow and blue . . .)

EXERCISE 72A

Join each idea in **A** with the most suitable idea from **B**.

Example:

1 *If I get a headache, I usually take some aspirin.*

A
1 If I get a headache,
2 I feel terrible,
3 If I drink too much coffee,
4 If flowers don't get any water,
5 You put on weight

B
they die
it makes me feel nervous
if you don't get enough exercise
I usually take some aspirin
if I don't get 8 hours' sleep a night

73 Conditional clauses without *if*

We can use other words instead of *if* in conditional clauses:

1 *Unless*

We can use *unless* to mean 'if . . . not'.

Unless I hurry, I'll miss the train. (= If I do not hurry . . .)
*I won't go to the party **unless** you go too.* (= . . . if you do not go too.)

We often use *unless* in threats eg ***Unless** you stop making that noise, I'll scream!* and
warnings *You'll be late **unless** you go now.*

Compare *if* and *unless*:

If I hurry, I won't miss the train.	***Unless** I hurry, I'll miss the train.*
*I'll go to the party **if** you go too.*	*I won't go to the party **unless** you go too.*

2 *As/So long as, provided/providing (that)*

We use *as/so long as* and *provided/providing (that)* to mean 'if but only if'.

*You can borrow my camera **as long as** you're careful with it.* (= . . . if but only if
you're careful with it.)
*I'll go to the party **provided** you go too.* (= . . . if but only if you go too.)

3 *And* and *or(else)*

a We sometimes use *and* to join two ideas instead of using an *if*- clause.

*Stay in bed for a few days **and** you'll be fine.* (= If you stay in bed for a few days,
you'll be fine.)

b We can use *or (else)* to mean 'if not' or 'otherwise'.

*Don't try to lift that box **or (else)** you'll hurt yourself.* (= If you try to lift that box,
you'll hurt yourself.)

4 *Should*

We can use *should* instead of *if* when we are less sure about a possibility. Compare:

If we have enough time, we'll visit Robert. (Perhaps we will have enough time.)	***Should** we have enough time, we'll visit Robert.* (I am less sure that we will have enough time.)

We can also use *should* after *if* with this meaning eg *If we **should have** enough time,
we'll visit Robert.* See 69.3.

5 *Suppose/supposing*

We can also use *suppose* or *supposing* instead of *if*, especially in unreal conditions.
***Suppose/Supposing** you won a lot of money, what would you do?*

EXERCISE 73A

Rephrase the sentences using *unless*.

Example:

If we don't leave now, we'll miss the start of the film.
Unless we leave now, we'll miss the start of the film.

1 If you don't wear your coat, you'll be cold.
2 We'll play tennis tomorrow if it doesn't rain.
3 He won't receive the letter tomorrow if you don't post it before 1 o'clock today.
4 If I don't get a pay rise at work, I'll start looking for another job.
5 I won't lend you the car if you don't promise to drive carefully.
6 Your cough won't get better if you don't stop smoking.

EXERCISE 73B

Choose the correct word or expression.

Example:

We'll have a picnic tomorrow *unless*/~~provided~~ it rains.

1 *Unless/Provided* you tell the truth, everything will be all right.
2 In Britain you can marry at the age of sixteen *unless/providing* you have your parents' permission.
3 He won't forgive you *unless/as long as* you say you're sorry.
4 *Unless/Providing* you lend me the money, I won't be able to go on holiday.
5 I'll buy the car *unless/as long as* it's not too expensive.

EXERCISE 73C

Read the sentence. Make a new sentence with the same meaning using the word(s) in brackets.

Example:

If you don't hurry up, you'll be late. (or)
Hurry up or you'll be late.
If you do as I say, everything will be all right. (and)
Do as I say and everything will be all right.

1 If you don't stop making that noise, I'll hit you. (or)
2 If you take this umbrella, you won't get wet. (and)
3 If you don't drive more carefully, you'll have an accident. (or else)
4 If you help me, I'll help you. (and)

EXERCISE 73D

Complete the sentences using *should I/he/she* and the verbs in the box.

Example:

I think I'll arrive at the meeting on time, but *should I be* late, please start without me.

| miss   change   ~~be~~   need   fail |

1 I think I've got enough money, but ____ any more, I'll borrow some.
2 I'm sure he'll pass the exam, but ____, he can always take it again.
3 I don't think I'll go to the party, but ____ my mind I'll let you know.
4 She expects to catch the last bus, but ____ it, she'll take a taxi.

EXERCISE 73E

Join each idea in **A** with the most suitable idea from **B**. Make sentences beginning *Suppose/Supposing* . . . .

Example:

1 *Suppose/Supposing I moved to Scotland, would you come and visit me?*

A   **B**

1 I moved to Scotland,   would you have taken it?
2 someone finds my wallet,   what would the prize have been?
3 they had stayed at our house, do you think they will take it to the police?
4 they had offered you the job, would you come and visit me?
5 you had won the competition,   where would they have slept?

74 Review of conditionals

EXERCISE 74A

Complete the sentences using the correct form of the verbs in brackets: the present simple, past simple, past perfect, *will/won't* . . . , *would(n't)* . . . or *would(n't) have* . . . .

Examples:

My father would have died if the doctors *hadn't operated* (not | operate) on him straight away.
Don't worry about getting home. If you *miss* (miss) the last bus, I'll give you a lift in my car.
My friend *would get* (get) better marks at school if she did more homework.
If she doesn't have much time, she normally *has* (have) a sandwich for lunch.

1 I ____ (wear) some warm clothes today, if I were you. It's quite cold outside.
2 You ____ (not | have) the accident if you'd been more careful.
3 If I ____ (know) more people, I wouldn't feel so lonely.
4 If you ____ (wait) for a few minutes. I'll come into town with you.
5 I would have told you if I ____ (know).
6 People ____ (like) Robert more if he didn't always talk about himself.
7 I ____ (speak) to my boss about my holidays today if I get the chance.
8 If he ____ (make) a promise, he always keeps it.

9 I'd go to the cinema more often if it ____ (not | be) so expensive.
10 I ____ (not | leave) my last job if the wages had been better.
11 He always ____ (get) angry if you talk to him about politics.
12 If you eat all those cakes, you ____ (make) yourself sick.
13 If you ____ (ask) me, I would have helped you.
14 What ____ (you | do) if you saw someone drowning in the sea?

75 Direct and reported speech: introduction

When we want to report what someone said, we can use 'direct speech' or 'reported speech':

I'm hungry.

ANNIE

In direct speech, we give the exact words that the person said, and we use quotation marks ('...' or "...").

Direct speech: *Annie said, 'I'm hungry.'*

In reported speech, we change some of the words that the person said and we do not use quotation marks.

Reported speech: *Annie said (that) she was hungry.*
        or: *Annie says (that) she's hungry.*

When we use a past reporting verb (eg *Annie said*), the tense in reported speech normally changes (eg *I'm* changes to the past: *she was*).

But when we use a present reporting verb (eg *Annie says*), the tense does not change (eg *I'm* stays in the present: *she's*).

For reported speech, see 77–80.

76 *Say* and *tell*

1   After *tell* we normally use a personal object (eg *Sarah, me, us*) to say who is told. We normally use *say* without a personal object. Compare:

    └ *say* + something   *tell* + someone + something

I said I was going home.   *I told Sarah I was going home.*
He says he can speak French.   *He tells me he can speak French.*

2   If we want to put a personal object with *say*, we use *to*.

I said to Sarah that I was going home.

3   In a few expressions we can use *tell* without a personal object eg *tell a story, tell the time, tell the truth, tell a lie.*

EXERCISE 76A

Complete the sentences using the correct form of *say* or *tell*.

Examples:
I'll *tell* you all about my holiday when I see you.

1 Could you ____ me how to get to Paris?
2 Do you think she's ____ us the truth?
3 Have you ____ goodbye to everyone?

4 They ____ the plane was going to be late.
5 Did he ____ you that he could play chess?
6 Why didn't you ____ what you wanted?

77   Reported statements

1   **Tenses**

*He said he **was going** home.*

a   When the reporting verb is in the past (eg *he said, you told me*), the tense in reported speech normally 'moves back':

■ Verbs in the present change into the past.

SPEAKER'S WORDS	REPORTED SPEECH
'I'm going home.'	*He said he **was going** home.*
'I want to stop.'	*You told me you **wanted** to stop.*
'I don't like tea.'	*She said she **didn't like** tea.*
'Sally has finished.'	*You said that Sally **had finished**.*

■ Verbs already in the past, change into the past perfect or they do not change.

'I spoke to them.'	*I said I **had spoken** to them./I said I **spoke** to them.*
'We arrived late.'	*They said they **had arrived** late./They said they **arrived** late.*

■ Verbs already in the past perfect, do not change.

'I had seen the film before.'	*I told you I **had seen** the film before.*

Modal verbs

Note the past forms of these modal verbs: *can* → *could*; *will* → *would*; *shall* → *should*; *may* → *might*.

SPEAKER'S WORDS	REPORTED SPEECH
*'I **can** swim.'*	*He said he **could** swim.*
*'I **will** be at home.'*	*She said that she **would** be at home.*
*'We **may** go by train.'*	*They told me they **might** go by train.*

The past modals *could, would, should* and *might* do not change in reported speech.

*'You **could** be right.'*	*I said you **could** be right.*
*'You **should** see the film.'*	*They told me I **should** see the film.*

Must either does not change or it takes the past form (of *have to*) *had to* .

*'I **must** go.'*	*He said he **must** go./He said he **had to** go.*

b We do not always change tenses in reported speech when we use a past reporting verb. If we report something that is still true now, we sometimes use the same tense as the speaker.

SPEAKER'S WORDS	REPORTED SPEECH
*'The population of London **is** around 9 million.'*	*He said that the population of London **is** around 9 million.*
*'I **live** in Brighton.'*	*She told me that she **lives** in Brighton.*

But even when something is still true, we often change the tense in reported speech.

*He said that the population of London **was** around 9 million.*

We always change the tense when there is a difference between what was said and what is really true.

*She said that she **was** 18 years old, but in fact she's only 16.*

2 **Pronouns, adjectives, adverbs, etc**

a Pronouns (eg *I, me*) and possessive adjectives (eg *my, your*) often change in reported speech. Compare:

Direct speech: Sue said, *'I'm on holiday with **my** friend'.*
Reported speech: Sue said (*that*) **she** was on holiday with **her** friend.

When we talk about Sue, we say *she*, not *I*, and when we talk about Sue's friend, we say *her* friend, not *my* friend.

b   People use words like *here, now, today* to talk about the place where they are speaking and the time they are speaking. If we report these words in a different place or at a different time, they often change. For example:

SPEAKER'S WORDS	REPORTED SPEECH
here	*there*
this	*that/the*
now	*then*
today	*that day*
tonight	*that night*
tomorrow	*the next day/the following day*
yesterday	*the day before/the previous day*
next Monday	*the following Monday*
last Monday	*the previous Monday*

Compare:

'I'm **here** on holiday.'   She said she was **there** on holiday.
'I'll see you **tomorrow**.'   He said he would see me **the next day**.

The way these words change depends on the situation. For example, if someone was speaking yesterday and they said *'I'll see you **tomorrow**.'*, we could now say *He said he would see me **today**.*

3   ***That***

We often use *that* to join a reported speech clause to the rest of the sentence.

*I said **that** I was feeling tired.*
*You told me **that** you would be careful.*

After *say* and *tell* (+ person), we often leave out *that*, especially in an informal style.

*I **said** I was feeling tired.*
*You **told me** you would be careful.*

EXERCISE 77A

Put these statements into reported speech, as in the examples.

Examples:

'I'm tired,' she said. *She said (that) she was tired.*
'I need to borrow some money,' my brother told me. *My brother told me (that) he needed to borrow some money.*

1   'I can't swim very well,' I told her.
2   'Mr Mason has gone out,' the secretary told me.
3   'I don't want to go swimming,' Andrew said.
4   'We're leaving on Friday,' we said.
5   'We had lunch in Luigi's restaurant,' they said.
6   'I'll phone you later,' Sarah told Simon.

EXERCISE 77B

This is what some people said to Sally today:

The manager of the bank where Sally works: 'You'll get a pay rise later in the year.'
Sally's doctor: 'You're slightly anaemic. You should eat more salads and fresh vegetables.'
Sally's boyfriend, Peter: 'I'd like a big family. I want at least five children.'
Sally's father: 'I've done the shopping. I'll be home at about seven.'
Sally's driving instructor: 'You drove very well. You're making good progress.'
A man who works in a dry-cleaner's: 'Your skirt will be ready on Saturday.'

It is evening now and Sally is telling her mother about her day. Complete what
Sally says using reported speech.

Sally: I went to the dry-cleaner's at lunchtime. The man there said *my skirt would
be ready on Saturday.*
Mother: And what about the doctor? What did she say?
Sally: Oh, it's nothing too serious. She told me __1__ and that I __2__ and fresh vegetables.
Mother: That's right. You eat too much fast food. And what about your driving
lesson? How did that go?
Sally: Oh, fine. My instructor told me that I __3__ and that I __4__ progress.
Mother: That's very good. And what about Peter? Did you see him today?
Sally: No, but he phoned me at work. He made me laugh. He said he __5__ and
that he __6__ children.
Mother: Five! Well, I hope you can afford them.
Sally: Oh, yes. That reminds me. I was speaking to the manager at work and she
said that I __7__.
Mother: Oh, that's good.
Sally: Yes. Oh, and before I forget. Dad phoned. He said he __8__ and that he __9__ seven.

78   Reported questions

*The policeman asked the men **what they were doing**.*

1 | Tenses, adjectives, pronouns, etc in reported questions change in the same way as in reported statements (see 77).

SPEAKER'S WORDS	REPORTED QUESTION
'What **are you** doing?'	The policeman asked the men what **they were** doing.
'How **is your** brother?'	She asked how **my** brother **was**.

In reported questions, the word order is the same as in statements (eg *they were doing, my brother was*), and we do not use a question mark(?).

2 | In reported questions, we do not use the auxiliary verb *do* (*do, does* or *did*).

SPEAKER'S WORDS	REPORTED QUESTION
'What **do you want?**'	I asked what she **wanted**.
'Where **does he live?**'	They asked where he **lived**.
'Why **did you say** that?'	He asked why I'**d said** that.

3 | When there is no question word (eg *what, where, why*), we can use *if* or *whether* to introduce a reported question.

SPEAKER'S WORDS	REPORTED QUESTION
'Are you cold?'	I asked **if** he was cold.
'Do you want a drink?'	She asked **if** I wanted a drink.
'Can you speak German?'	They wanted to know **whether** I could speak German.

4 | After *ask*, we often use an object (eg *Ken, me*) to say who was asked.

*I **asked Ken** if he was cold.*
*He **asked me** why I'd said that.*

EXERCISE 78A

Which questions would you ask to which people?

1	'Will it take long to repair the car?'	a hotel receptionist
2	'Can I park my car in West Street?'	a doctor
3	'What time does the film finish?'	a policeman
4	'Have you got a double room?'	~~a mechanic~~
5	'How many times a day should I take the medicine?'	a waiter
6	'What's the soup of the day?'	a cinema attendant

Report the questions. Begin: *I asked the . . . .*

Example:

1 *I asked the mechanic if it would take long to repair the car.*

EXERCISE 78B

Andrew had a frightening experience recently while on holiday. He was out walking in the countryside when suddenly he was surrounded by a group of soldiers.

Here are the questions which one of the soldiers asked Andrew.

1 'What are you doing here?'
2 'Why are you carrying a camera?'
3 'Did you see the signs warning people not to enter the area?'
4 'Have you been taking photos of the army base?'
5 'What's your name?'
6 'Can I see some proof of your identity?'

After the holiday, Andrew told some friends what had happened. Complete Andrew's story using reported speech.

'I was about seven miles from the youth hostel in the middle of nowhere when suddenly a jeep roared up to me and I was surrounded by soldiers pointing guns! An officer asked me 1 *what I was doing there*. Then he pointed at my Kodak and asked me ___2___. I tried to explain that I was on holiday there, but then he wanted to know ___3___. I told him I hadn't. Then he asked me ___4___. I said that I didn't even know there was an army base there. Then he wanted to know ___5___ and ___6___. Then, just because I couldn't prove who I was, they put me in the jeep and drove me to some kind of underground army base. They kept me there while they phoned the youth hostel to check up on me.'

79   Using the *to* infinitive in reported speech

1

We often report orders, requests, warnings, advice and invitations using the structure verb + object + *to* infinitive.

SPEAKER'S WORDS	REPORTED SPEECH
'Get out of my room,'	*She **told the man to get** out of her room.*
'Could you help me, John?'	*I **asked John to help** me.*
'Stay away from me.'	*He **warned them to stay** away from him.*
'You should phone the police.'	*She **advised him to phone** the police.*
'Would you like to have dinner with us?'	*They **invited me to have** dinner with them.*

2 We often report offers, promises and threats using the structure verb + *to* infinitive.

SPEAKER'S WORDS	REPORTED SPEECH
'Can I help you?'	*The woman **offered to help** me.*
'I'll be careful.'	*You **promised to be** careful.*
'I'll hit you!'	*She **threatened to hit** me.*

3 In negative orders, promises etc we use *not to* + infinitive.

'Don't touch my camera.'	*He told me **not to touch** his camera.*
'I won't be late.'	*You promised **not to be** late.*

EXERCISE 79A

Report these sentences using the *to* infinitive form.

Examples:

'I'll pay back the money.' (she promised)   *She promised to pay back the money.*
'Hurry up.' (he told me)   *He told me to hurry up.*

1 'Can I do the washing up?' (I offered)
2 'I'll phone the police!' (she threatened)
3 'You should stop smoking.' (the doctor advised my brother)
4 'Could you post a letter for me?' (he asked me)
5 'Don't be stupid.' (she told me)
6 'Would you like to come to my party?' (he invited her)
7 'I won't tell anyone.' (I promised)
8 'Don't leave the door unlocked.' (she warned them)

80   Review of reported speech

EXERCISE 80A

Report these sentences. Sometimes two answers are possible.

Examples:

'I'm tired,' he said.
He said (that) he was tired.
'Did you enjoy the film?' I asked her.
I asked her if she had enjoyed the film./
I asked her if she enjoyed the film.
'Switch off the TV,' she told me.
She told me to switch off the TV.
Can you lend me some money? he asked me.
He asked me if I could lend him some money./
He asked me to lend him some money.

1 'I can't type,' I told them.
2 'Are you English?' they asked me.
3 'Where are you going?' I asked her.
4 'We're going into town,' they said.
5 'I haven't got any money,' he told me.
6 'Could you speak more slowly?' he asked her.
7 'Don't touch the wire,' he warned me.
8 'I was on holiday in July,' he told her.
9 'What time did you get home?' they asked him.

10 'Can you do me a favour?' she asked me.
11 'We won't be home late,' we told them.
12 'I've posted the letters,' I said.
13 'My sister doesn't know,' he said.
14 'My parents had gone to bed,' she said.
15 'You should go to the doctor,' she told him.
16 'We'll do the dishes,' they promised.
17 'Where do you work?' I asked her.
18 'Can you phone the doctor for me?' she asked him.
19 'I passed my driving test in 1986,' he told his boss.
20 'I don't know what to do,' I said.

81   *-ing* form: participle or gerund

1   We use the *-ing* form eg *playing, walking, worrying* as a verb in the continuous forms.

'Where's Sally?'   'She's **playing** tennis.'
When I was **walking** along Western Road, I saw Maria.
He's been **worrying** a lot recently.

When we use the *-ing* form in this way, it is called a 'present participle'.

We also use present participles as adjectives (see 99).

It's a **worrying** problem.

We can use a participle to introduce a participle clause (see 100).

I hurt my leg **playing** tennis.
Who is that girl **walking** towards us?

2   We also use the *-ing* form as a noun.

Playing tennis isn't expensive in England.
I enjoy **walking** in the countryside.

When we use the *-ing* form as a noun, it is called a 'gerund'. (For the *-ing* form used in this way, see 82–83, 87–90, 92–94, 98.)

3   When we add *-ing* to verbs, there are sometimes changes in spelling eg *swim* → *swimming* (see 188.3–6).

82 Verb + *-ing* form or infinitive: introduction

1 We often use one verb after another verb.

*I **enjoy playing** tennis.   I **hope to play** tennis tomorrow.*

After some verbs eg *enjoy*, the second verb is the *-ing* form eg *playing* (see 83). After other verbs eg *hope*, the second verb is the *to* infinitive eg *to play* (see 84).

2 After some verbs eg *start* we can use the *-ing* form or the *to* infinitive, without much difference of meaning (see 87).

*Look. It's **started raining/to rain** again.*

But after some other verbs eg *stop*, we can use the *-ing* form or the *to* infinitive with a big difference of meaning (see 88).

*I'm a vegetarian. I **stopped eating** meat 5 years ago. (= I ate meat up to 5 years ago, then I stopped.)*	*After I'd been working for 3 hours, I **stopped to eat** lunch. (= I stopped in order to eat lunch.)*

3 After modal verbs such as *can, must, should* and some other verbs, we use the infinitive without *to* eg *play, eat* (see 91).

*I **can play** the guitar.*
*You **must eat** something.*

83 Verb + *-ing* form

1 If these verbs are followed by another verb, the second verb is normally the *-ing* form.

admit	enjoy	imagine	practise
avoid	fancy	involve	put off (= postpone)
consider	feel like (= want)	keep on (= continue)	risk
delay	finish	mind	stand (= bear)
deny	give up (= stop)	miss	suggest
dislike	can't help (= can't avoid)	postpone	

verb + *-ing* form

*He **admitted stealing** the money.*
*I **enjoy getting** up early in the summer.*
*Have you **finished doing** your homework?*
*They **suggested going** to the cinema.*

Note the negative: *not + -ing* form.

*He admitted **not paying** for the ticket.*

After *mind* we can also use an *if*-clause eg *Would you mind if I closed the window?*

After some of the above verbs, we can also use a *that*-clause.

He admitted (that) he'd stolen the money.
They suggested (that) we went to the cinema.

2   We use *do + the/some/* etc + *-ing* form to talk, for example, about jobs.
You do the cooking. I'll do the washing up.
We're going to do some shopping this afternoon.

(Note that the *-ing* form here is used as a noun, and like any other noun can have *the*, *some*, etc in front of it.)

3   We can use *go* and *come* with the *-ing* form, especially to talk about sports and free time activities.
I'd like to go swimming tomorrow.

EXERCISE 83A

Complete the sentences using the *-ing* form of the verbs in the box.

| do   have   ~~listen~~   play   be   read   go |
| not make   borrow   swim   drive |

Example:

I enjoy *listening* to the radio in the mornings.

1 I'll lend you the book when I've finished ___ it.
2 Do you ever go ___ in the sea?
3 They suggested ___ dinner in an Indian restaurant.
4 Robert gave up ___ football years ago.
5 The man admitted ___ the car dangerously.
6 I really don't mind ___ the housework.
7 I didn't feel like ___ out last night, so I stayed at home.
8 Would you mind ___ so much noise? I'm trying to study.
9 I normally try to avoid ___ money.
10 Since she moved from London, she misses ___ able to see all her friends there.

Note

–After some other verbs we can use the *-ing* form or the *to* infinitive, often with a difference of meaning. See 87–88.

84   Verb + *to* infinitive

If these verbs are followed by another verb, the second verb is normally the *to* infinitive.

afford	fail	pretend
agree	help	promise
appear	hope	refuse
arrange	learn (how)	seem
ask	manage	threaten
attempt	mean (= intend)	want
decide	offer	wish
expect	prepare	

verb + *to* infinitive

*I can't **afford to go** on holiday this summer.*
*The policeman **asked to see** my driving licence.*
*She **decided to stay** at home last night.*
*I **expect to be** late this evening.*
*He's going to **learn to drive.***

Note the negative: *not to* + infinitive.

*You promised **not to be late.***
*She seemed **not to notice** me.*

After *help* we can use the infinitive with or without *to*.

*I'll **help (to) carry** your bags.*

Note also that after *can't help* (= 'can't avoid') we use an *-ing* form eg *I **can't help thinking** we've made a mistake.*

After some of the above verbs, we can also use a *that*-clause.

*She **decided (that)** she would stay at home last night.*
*I **expect (that)** I'll be late this evening.*

After some of the above verbs we can use an object + *to* infinitive, eg *He **asked me to help** him. See 86.*

EXERCISE 84A

Robert is talking about the day he bought a
second-hand car.

Complete Robert's story using the *to* infinitive
form of the verbs in the boxes.

buy   be   not like   ~~have~~   test-drive

'When I got to the garage, I managed *to have* a quick look at the car before the
salesman came out of his office. It seemed __1__ in very good condition and was
worth about £1000, although the garage was asking £1400 for it. When the
salesman came out, I arranged __2__ the car straight away. The salesman and I
got in and we drove off. I liked the car immediately and I decided that I wanted
__3__ it, but, of course, I didn't say this to the salesman. Instead, I pretended
__4__ the car very much.'

try   get   accept   pay

'When we had finished the test-drive and had pulled up outside the garage, I told
the salesman that I couldn't afford __5__ more than £750. The salesman, of
course, refused __6__ such a miserable little offer. He told me that he expected
__7__ at least £1200 for the car. I tried offering £800, £850, £875, but he
wouldn't change his mind. Then I decided __8__ something different.'

give   be   sell   accept

'I thanked the salesman politely, said goodbye, got out of the car and started to
walk away. It worked! The salesman got out of the car too and hurried after me.
He told me that he wanted __9__ fair and was prepared __10__ a reasonable
offer for the car. In the end, he agreed __11__ it to me for £1000. He even agreed
__12__ me £200 for my old car!'

Note

–After some other verbs we can use the *to* infinitive or the *-ing* form, often with a
  difference of meaning. See 97.
–We also use the *to* infinitive in these structures: *ought to* eg *You **ought to stop**
  smoking.* (see 42.1); *have (got) to* eg *I **have to be** home by 10 o'clock.* (see 38.2), and
  used to eg *I **used to smoke**, but I stopped 10 years ago.* (see 51).
–We also use the *to* infinitive after passive verbs eg *She **is believed to be** living in
  Brazil.* See 64.
–We sometimes leave out the verb after *to* to avoid repetition when the meaning is
  clear eg *I didn't go to the party because I didn't want to.* (= because I didn't want **to
  go to the party**).

85 Verb + question word + *to* infinitive

1   After some verbs we can use a question word eg *what, how, where* (but not *why*) + *to* infinitive.

> verb + question word + *to* infinitive

*I don't **know what to** say.*
*Could you **explain how to get** to the station, please?*
*We can't **decide where to go** on our holidays.*
*I don't **know whether to apply** for the job or not.*

2   We often use this structure with an object + question word + *to* infinitive.

> verb + object + question word + *to* infinitive

*Could you **tell me how to get** to the station, please?*
*Will you **show me what to do**.*

EXERCISE 85A

Complete the sentences using the most suitable words in the box.

> what | do   how | make   what | wear
> ~~how | get~~   whether | stay   how | use

Example:
'Could you tell me *how to get* to Western Road, please?'   'Yes. Go down this road and it's second on the left.'

1   'Have you decided ＿＿ to the interview?'   'Yes. I'm going to wear my new blue suit.'
2   Do you think you could show me ＿＿ this machine? I've never used it before.
3   'What are you going to do this evening?'   'I can't decide ＿＿ at home or go out.'
4   Do you know ＿＿ a Spanish omelette?
5   I felt very embarrassed when she started shouting. I didn't know ＿＿, so I just stood there.

86 Verb + object + *to* infinitive

1   After the verbs below, we normally use an object (eg *Sue, me, you*) before the
to infinitive.

force	*order*	*teach* (how)
get (= persuade)	*persuade*	*tell*
invite	*remind*	*warn*

verb + object + *to* infinitive

*We **invited Sue to have** dinner with us.*
*She **persuaded me to go** to the party.*
*He **warned you not to be** late again.*

Note that after these verbs in the passive, we can use the *to* infinitive without an
object eg *Sue **was invited to have** dinner with us.*

2   We can also use an object + *to* infinitive after these verbs:

ask	*help*	*want*
expect	*mean* (= intend)	

*He **asked me to help** him.*
*I didn't **expect Maria to write** to me.*
*I don't **want you to go**.*

After *help* we can use an object + the infinitive with or without *to*.

*I'll **help you (to) carry** your bags.*

After these verbs, we can also use the *to* infinitive without an object eg *I **expect to
see** Simon tomorrow.* See 84.

Note that after *want*, we cannot use a *that*-clause. For example, we cannot say
*I don't **want that you go***.

3   After the verbs *advise, allow, encourage, permit* and *recommend*, we can use an *-ing*
form, or an object + *to* infinitive. Compare:

verb + *-ing* form	verb + object + *to* infinitive
*I wouldn't **advise going** there.*	*I wouldn't **advise you to go** there.*
*They don't **allow smoking** in that room.*	*They don't **allow people to smoke** in that room.*

EXERCISE 86A

Complete the sentences.

Example:

I couldn't do the job on my own, so I | ask | Simon | help me.

I couldn't do the job on my own, so I asked Simon to help me.

1 I was surprised that my brother failed his driving test. I | expect | him | pass | easily.
2 Annie wanted to stay up late, but her parents | tell | her | go to bed at 9 o'clock.
3 Simon phoned Sarah yesterday. He | invite | her | go to a party on Saturday.
4 I was going to buy the car, but a friend of mine | persuade | me | change my mind.
5 Don't tell Sue what I've done. I | not | want | her | know.

EXERCISE 86B

What did they say? Complete the sentences using an object + *to* infinitive . . .

Examples:

'Remember to phone Chris,' Sue told Peter.
Sue reminded *Peter to phone Chris.*
'Can you lend me some money?' I asked him.
I asked *him to lend me some money.*

1 'Close the door,' Ken told Andrew. Ken told ____.
2 'Can you help me?' I asked her. I asked ____.
3 'Would you like to go to a party?' they asked us. They invited ____.
4 'Please don't be late home,' Kate said to Sally. Kate asked ____.
5 'Get out of your car,' the policeman told the woman. The policeman ordered ____.
6 'Don't be late for work again,' my boss told me. My boss warned ____.

EXERCISE 86C

Put the verbs into the correct form: the *-ing* form or the *to* infinitive.

Example:

She doesn't allow anyone *to drive* (drive) her car.

1 She doesn't allow ____ (smoke) in her car.
2 He's always encouraged me ____ (have) confidence in myself.
3 I'd recommend you ____ (see) the film. It's very good.
4 I wouldn't recommend ____ (drive) through the city centre now. The traffic is terrible at this time of the day.
5 What would you advise me ____ (do)?
6 I wouldn't advise ____ (tell) anyone what's happened.

87 Verb + *ing* form or *to* infinitive (1)

1 After the verbs below, we can use the *-ing* form or the *to* infinitive normally without much difference of meaning.

begin	*can't bear*	*like*	*prefer*
continue	*hate*	*love*	*start*

He **began looking/to look** for a job 6 months ago.
I **like swimming/to swim** in the sea.
She **prefers working/to work** at night.

But see 2–4 below.

2 *Like*

a In British English, we often use *like* + *-ing* form to say that we 'enjoy' something.
I **like going** to the cinema. (= I enjoy it.)

We use *like* + *to* infinitive to say that we choose to do something because we think it is a good idea.
I **like to go** to the dentist's for a check-up every 6 months. (= I think it is a good thing to do, although I may not enjoy it.)

b After *would like*, *would love*, *would hate* and *would prefer*, we use the *to* infinitive.
'**Would** you **like to go** out this evening?'   '**I'd prefer to stay** at home.'
We'**d love to see** you at the weekend.

c Compare *like* and *would like*:

Do you like playing tennis? (= Do you enjoy playing, generally?)	**Would you like to play** tennis this afternoon? (= Do you want to play this afternoon?)

3 *Prefer*

Note these structures:

prefer + *-ing* form + *to* + *-ing* form

I **prefer going** to the cinema **to watching** films on TV.

would prefer + *to* infinitive + *rather than* + infinitive without *to*

I **would prefer to stay** in this evening **rather than go** out.

4 | ***Begin, start, continue***

a | We do not normally use the *-ing* form after the continuous forms of *begin, start, continue* (to avoid having two *-ing* endings).

It's beginning to rain. (Not normally: *It's beginning raining.*)

b | After *begin, continue* and *start*, we normally use the verbs *understand, know* and *realize* in the *to* infinitive, not the *-ing* form.

I began to understand. (Not normally: *I began understanding.*)

EXERCISE 87A

Put the verbs into the correct form. Sometimes two answers are possible.

Examples:

I quite enjoy *driving* (drive) at night.
Do you like *getting up/to get up* (get up) early?

 1 Would you like ____ (listen) to some music?
 2 Simon and Sally have started ____ (cook) the dinner.
 3 I prefer ____ (windsurf) to ____ (sail).
 4 I'd prefer ____ (walk) home rather than ____ (go) by taxi.

 5 My sister loves ____ (go) shopping.
 6 I'd love ____ (visit) Australia one day.
 7 My brother hates ____ (have to) work at weekends.
 8 Do you like ____ (play) chess?
 9 I try to look after my car. I like ____ (take) it to the garage to be serviced regularly.
 10 Shh! The orchestra is starting ____ (play).

88   Verb + *ing* form or *to* infinitive (2)

After the verbs below we can use the *-ing* form or the *to* infinitive with a different meaning.

remember   forget   try   stop   go on   regret

1 | ***Remember/forget doing*** and ***remember/forget to do***

We use *remember/forget +-ing* form when we remember or forget something after we do it.

ACTION←————————REMEMBER

I remember going to Paris in 1970. (I went there in 1970 and now I remember this.)

Have you forgotten giving me the money? (You gave me the money.)

We use *remember/forget + to* infinitive when we remember or forget something before we have to do it.

REMEMBER————————→ACTION

I remembered to go to the chemist's for you. Here's your medicine.
(I remembered, then I went there.)

Don't forget to give me the money.

2 | ***Try doing*** **and** ***try to do***

We use *try* + *-ing* form to mean 'make an experiment' – do something and see what happens.

*'The car won't start.' 'Why don't we try **pushing** it?*

We use *try* + *to* infinitive to mean 'make an effort' – see if you can do something.

*I **tried to push** the car up the hill, but I couldn't move it.*

3 | ***Stop doing*** **and** ***stop to do***

We use *stop* + *-ing* form to say what we do before we stop.

*I'm a vegetarian. I **stopped eating** meat 5 years ago.* (= I ate meat up to 5 years ago, then I stopped.)

We use *stop* + *to* infinitive to say why we stop (see 95).

*After I'd been working for 3 hours, I **stopped to eat** lunch.* (= I stopped in order to eat lunch.)

4 | ***Go on doing*** **and** ***go on to do***

We use *go on* + *-ing* form to talk about something that continues.

*She **went on talking** about her holiday all evening.* (= She continued talking . . .)

We use *go on* + *to* infinitive to talk about a change to something different.

*She spoke about her son, then she **went on to talk** about her daughter.*

5 | ***Regret doing*** **and** ***regret to do***

We use *regret* + *-ing* form to say we regret something that we have already done.

*I **regret saying** that he was an idiot.* (I said that he was an idiot.)

We use *regret* + *to* infinitive to say we regret something that we have to do now.

*I **regret to say** that I won't be able to come to the meeting on Monday.*

Note that *regret* + *to* infinitive is rather formal.

EXERCISE 88A

Put the verbs in brackets into the *-ing* form or to the *to* infinitive.

Example:

'I introduced you to Sue last month.' 'Really? I don't remember *meeting* (meet) her.'

1 If you see Martin, remember ____ (say) hello from me.
2 I'll never forget ____ (visit) Istanbul in 1983.
3 'Did you remember ____ (post) those letters I gave you yesterday?' 'Oh, no. I forgot.'
4 Please remember ____ (lock) the front door when you go out. And don't forget ____ (close) all the windows.

EXERCISE 88B

Put the verbs in brackets into the -*ing* form or the *to* infinitive.

Example:

'I've got a headache,'   'Why don't you try *taking* (take) some aspirin?'

1 I'll try ____ (come) to the meeting, but I'm not sure if I'll be able to.
2 If you get hiccups, you should try ____ (drink) a glass of water. If that doesn't work, try ____ (hold) your breath.
3 You can borrow my camera, but please try ____ (be) careful with it.
4 'This soup doesn't taste very good.'   'Try ____ (put) in some more salt.'

EXERCISE 88C

Complete the sentences using the -*ing* form or the *to* infinitive of the verbs in the box. Use each verb only once.

Example:

Could you stop *working* for a moment? I'd like to speak to you.

ask   not learn   tell   ~~work~~   make

1 He went on ____ a noise even though I'd asked him to stop.
2 She started by talking about her job. Then she went on ____ me about her family.
3 He stopped reading ____ me a question.
4 I regret ____ to play a musical instrument when I was younger.

89   *Be used to* + -*ing* form and *used to* + infinitive

1 | **Compare:**

We use *be used to* + -*ing* form to mean 'be accustomed to'.

I'm used to driving my new car now, but I found it very strange at first. (= I'm accustomed to driving the car now, it is no longer strange to me.)

We use *used to* + infinitive to talk about past habits which are now finished.

I used to drive a Mercedes, but now I drive a Citroen. (= I drove a Mercedes regularly in the past, but I do not drive a Mercedes now.)

2 | We can use *get* (= become) *used to* + -*ing* form, eg *I've got used to driving my new car.*

3 | After *be/get used to* we can also use a noun phrase eg *this cold weather, my new glasses.*
*He **isn't used to** this cold weather.*
*I haven't **got used to** my new glasses yet.*

EXERCISE 89A

Put the verbs in brackets into the correct form: *to* + -*ing* form or *to* + infinitive.

Examples:

When I was younger, I used *to play* (play) a lot of football. Now I never play.

1 It won't take you long to get used ____ (work) with your new word processor.

2 My parents used ____ (live) in London, but now they live in Bristol.
3 Bruno is Italian, but he has lived in London for over 5 years. He has got used
   ____ (eat) English food now, but when he first arrived in England he didn't like it
   very much.
4 Bruno found driving in England strange at first. He wasn't used ____ (drive) on the left.
5 I normally go to bed at about 10 o'clock. I'm not used ____ (stay) up late.
6 I used ____ (work) on a farm once and had to get up at 5 o'clock every morning.
   It was difficult at first because I wasn't used ____ (get up) so early.

Note

–For *used to*, see also 51.

90   *Need + -ing* form or *to* infinitive

1	After the full verb *need*, we can use the *to* infinitive.
	*I'm tired. I **need to get** some sleep.*
	*We've got plenty of time. We **don't need to hurry**.*
2	After the full verb *need*, we can also use the *-ing* form in a passive meaning.
	*My car **needs servicing**.*
	*These trousers **need cleaning**.*
	After *need*, we can also use *to be* + past participle in the same passive meaning.
	*My car **needs to be serviced**.*
	*These trousers **need to be cleaned**.*

EXERCISE 90A

Complete each sentence using the correct form of the most suitable verb in the box.
Sometimes two forms are possible.

Examples:

This carpet is quite dirty. It needs *cleaning/to be cleaned*.
Tomorrow is a holiday, so I don't need *to get up* early in the morning.

buy	adjust	~~get up~~	ask
cut	study	feed	~~clean~~

1 My hair is quite long. It needs ____.
2 You really need ____ harder if you want to pass your exam.
3 The brakes on my car aren't working very well. I think they need ____.
4 The cat is hungry. It needs ____.
5 We've got plenty of milk. We don't need ____ any more.
6 I went to see her because I needed ____ her some questions.

91 Infinitive without *to*

1 We use the infinitive without *to* after modal verbs eg *can, must, should* (see 35).

*I **can speak** Italian.*
*We **must go** now.*

Exception: after the modal verb *ought*, we use the *to* infinitive, eg *You **ought to be** careful.*

2 We use the infinitive without *to* after *let's* (= let us) and *why don't we/you . . .?* to make suggestions (see 30,50.2).

'What shall we do this afternoon?'   *'**Let's go** to the cinema.'*
*'**Why don't we have** a party next Saturday?*
*'**Why don't you apply** for the job?*

We also use the infinitive without *to* after *would rather* (see 57.1) and *had better* (see 42.2).

'Would you like to go out this evening?'   *'I**'d rather stay** at home.'*
*I think it's going to rain. You**'d better take** an umbrella with you when you go out.*

3 After the verbs *let* (= 'allow') and *make* (= 'force' or 'cause'), we use an object eg *their children, me, us* + infinitive without *to.*

> *let/make* + object + infinitive without *to*

*They **let their children stay** up late at weekends.* (= allow their children to stay up)
*Will you **let me use** your camera?* (= allow me to use)
*You can't **make us go** if we don't want to.* (= force us to go)
*The film **made me cry**.* (= caused me to cry)

EXERCISE 91A

Complete each sentence using the most suitable verb in the box. Use each verb only once.

Example:

'Would you like a cup of tea?'   'I'd rather *have* coffee.'

> eat   hurry   tell   type   wear   lend
> sit   promise   cry   wait   use   ~~have~~

1 It's very cold today. You'd better ____ a coat when you go out.
2 'I haven't got any money.'   'Let me ____ you some'.
3 Chopping onions makes me ____.
4 'I'm tired of walking.'   'Let's ____ down for a while, then.'
5 I can't ____ you what Sally said. She made me ____ that I wouldn't tell anyone.
6 'Why don't we ____ dinner now?'   'I think I'd rather ____ until later.'
7 It's getting late. We'd better ____.
8 I couldn't ____ the letter because my brother wouldn't let me ____ his typewriter.

EXERCISE 91B

2

Sally is speaking about her boyfriend, Peter.

Complete what Sally says using the correct form of *make* or *let* and the verbs in the box.

have   understand   ~~laugh~~   feel   go

'Peter's very funny. He *makes* me *laugh* a lot. We usually get on very well together, but sometimes I get really angry with him because he's so jealous and won't 1___ me ___ out on my own. He 2___ me ___ jealous, too, when he talks about his ex-girlfriends! But I always 3___ him ___ his own friends and never ask him who he is going out with. I've talked to him about this, but I can't 4___ him ___ that his attitude is unfair.'

Note

–After verbs such as *see, hear, feel* we can use an object + infinitive without *to* or -*ing* form. See 97.
–When we join two *to* infinitive structures using *or* or *and*, we often use the second infinitive without *to* eg *I'd like **to go and see** that film.*

92   Preposition + -*ing* form

1

When there is a verb after a preposition (eg *in, of, about, before, after*), it is always in the -*ing* form.

*Are you interested **in playing** tennis tomorrow?*
*I'm thinking **of changing** my job.*
*How **about going** to the cinema this evening?*

2   *To*

Sometimes *to* is part of the infinitive verb form.

*We've decided **to go** on holiday next month.*
*Would you like **to eat** now or later?*

Sometimes *to* is a preposition.

*She's travelling **to** Greece tomorrow.*
*We're looking forward **to** our holiday.*
*Carlos isn't used **to** English food.*

If you can put a noun after *to*, it is a preposition. If *to* is a preposition, we use the -*ing* form of verbs after it.

*We're looking forward **to going** on holiday.*
*Carlos isn't used **to eating** English food.*

EXERCISE 92A

Complete the sentences. Use a preposition from the box and the -*ing* form of the verbs in brackets. Use some prepositions more than once.

> for   at   ~~about~~   in   to   of   after

Example:
'What shall we do this evening?'   'How *about going* (go) to the cinema?'

1 Annie isn't looking forward ____ (go) to the dentist tomorrow.
2 Are you interested ____ (learn) to play the guitar?
3 ____ (have) breakfast, I did the washing up.
4 I'm not used ____ (eat) such spicy food.
5 Did she apologize ____ (be) late?
6 I'm tired ____ (hear) her complain.
7 We thanked her ____ (give) us a lift in her car.
8 She's very good ____ (paint) and (draw).

93   Person + -*ing* form

1 | In informal English, we normally use an object form eg *me, you, Simon* + -*ing* form.
Do you mind **me asking** *you a question?*
They were angry about **Simon arriving** *late.*

In formal English, we can use a possessive eg *my, your, Simon's* + -*ing* form instead.
Do you mind **my asking** *you a question?*
They were angry about **Simon's arriving** *late.*

2 | After verbs such as *see, hear* and *feel*, we normally use the object form (not the possessive) + -*ing* (see 97).
You saw **me arriving**. (Not: ~~You saw **my arriving**.~~)

EXERCISE 93A

Complete the sentences using (i) the object form + -*ing* form, and (ii) the possessive + -*ing* form.

Example:
Do you mind ____ (I | open) the window?
(i) *Do you mind me opening the window?*   (ii) *Do you mind my opening the window?*

1 I don't mind ____ (you | borrow) my car.
2 Do you mind ____ (I | switch on) the TV?
3 They insisted on ____ (we | stay) for dinner with them.
4 How do you feel about ____ (they | get) married?
5 Annie's parents don't like ____ (she | go) to bed late.
6 I was surprised about ____ (Sue | forget) to come to the meeting.

94 -ing form and to infinitive as subjects

1 | We can use the -ing form as a subject.
Smoking is a terrible habit.
Knowing how to drive is useful.
Playing tennis in England isn't expensive.

2 | We can also use the *to* infinitive as a subject (eg *To know how to drive is useful*) but this is unusual. When we use the *to* infinitive as a subject, it is more usual to begin the sentence with *it* (as a 'preparatory subject').
It is useful to know how to drive.
It isn't expensive to play tennis in England.

EXERCISE 94A

What does *it* mean in each of these sentences? Use the -ing form of the words in the box in your answers.

Example:

It can be dangerous, especially at midday. *Sunbathing can be dangerous, especially at midday.*

live on your own   babysit   ~~sunbathe~~   smoke
read English   swim   watch late night horror films

1 It is a big responsibility, especially with very young children.
2 It is a very good way of keeping fit.
3 It can give you nightmares.
4 It is quite difficult if you are used to being with a lot of people.
5 It is much easier than speaking it.
6 It can cause lung cancer.

EXERCISE 94B

Join each idea in **A** with the most suitable idea in **B**. Make sentences using the *to* infinitive form, as in the example.

Example:

1 *It is very strange to see yourself on video.*

A	**B**
1 It is very strange	eat well
2 It isn't necessary	live on a pension
3 It can be dangerous	see yourself on video
4 It doesn't have to be expensive	have your car serviced every month
5 It is difficult for old people	leave medicine lying around

145

95 *To* infinitive of purpose

1 We can use a *to* infinitive to talk about a person's purpose – why someone does something.

*I'm going out **to do** some shopping.*
*She's saving up **to buy** a motor bike.*
*I went to Paris **to learn** French.*

In a more formal style, we use *in order to* or *so as to*.

*I went to Paris **in order to learn** French.*
*We left early **so as to have** plenty of time.*

2 In negative sentences, we normally use *in order not to* or *so as not to* (not *not to* alone).

*We left early **so as not to be** late./We left early **in order not to be** late.* (Not: ~~We left early **not to be** late.~~)

For purpose, see also 163–164.

EXERCISE 95A

Where did you go yesterday, and why did you go to each place?

1 Chemist's   2 Post Office   3 Cinema
4 Hairdresser's   5 Car Rental Agency   6 Park

Make sentences using *I went to the* (place) *to* . . . and the words in the box.

hire	a haircut
buy	tennis
have	a film
play	some letters
post	a car
see	some medicine

Example:

1 *I went to the chemist's to buy some medicine.*

EXERCISE 95B

Join each idea in **A** with an idea from **B**. Make sentences using (i) *in order (not) to*, and (ii) *so as (not) to*.

Example:

1 (i) *He drank lots of black coffee in order to keep awake.*
   (ii) *He drank lots of black coffee so as to keep awake.*

A
1 He drank lots of black coffee
2 I often write things down
3 She took an umbrella
4 We'll use the computer
5 I want to pass the exams
6 We turned down the music

B
disturb the neighbours
save time
get a better job
forget them
keep awake
get wet

146

96 Noun/pronoun/adjective + *to* infinitive

1   **Noun/pronoun + *to* infinitive**

We can use the *to* infinitive after some nouns and pronouns (often to say what is to be done with them).

*I've got some **letters to write**.*
*There is a lot of **work to do**.*
*Would you like **something to eat?***

We can also use this structure with adjective + noun + *to* infinitive.

*That's an **impossible question to answer**.*

2   **Adjective + *to* infinitive**

a   We can use the *to* infinitive after a number of adjectives.

*I'm very **pleased to see** you.*
*I was **disappointed to hear** that you didn't pass the exam.*
*He'll be **surprised to get** your letter.*
*She isn't always **easy to understand**.*

b   We can use the structure *of* (someone) + *to* infinitive after adjectives such as these:

> *nice   kind   generous   polite   good   mean*
> *silly   careless   clever   wrong   stupid*

*It's **kind of you to help***.
*It was **stupid of me to say** that.*

c   We can use the structure *for* + object + *to* infinitive after adjectives such as these:

> *easy   important   essential   (un)usual   (un)necessary*
> *common   normal   rare*

*It won't be **easy for us to get** tickets for the concert now.*
*It's **important for everyone to be** here on time.*

We can also use this structure after some nouns and verbs.

*It was a **mistake for me to come** here.*
*I'm **waiting for my sister to phone** me.*

EXERCISE 96A

Complete the sentences using the *to* infinitive form of the verbs in the box.

Example:

Are you hungry? Would you like something *to eat?*

| say   unlock   catch   carry   ~~eat~~   write   tell |

1 Have you got a key ___ this door?
2 Can we meet today? I've got something important ___ you.
3 I'm staying at home this evening. I've got some letters ___.
4 'Why are you so quiet?'   'I haven't got anything ___.'
5 I need a bag ___ these books in.
6 I really must go now. I've got a train ___.

EXERCISE 96B

Complete the sentences using the correct form of the words in the box.

Example:

Goodbye. It was very *nice to meet* you.

| impossible | finish   please | hear   safe | go
~~nice | meet~~   easy | use   interesting | plan |

1 My new video recorder looks complicated, but it's actually very ___.
2 That is a very dangerous part of the city. It isn't ___ out there at night.
3 I was ___ that you had passed your exam.
4 I don't like package holidays. I think it's much more ___ your own holiday.
5 It's ___ all that work today. There just isn't enough time.

EXERCISE 96C

Make sentences beginning with the words in brackets, as in the examples.

Examples:

You lent me the money. (It was kind)
It was kind of you to lend me the money.
I forgot my keys. (It was stupid)
It was stupid of me to forget my keys.

1 She sent me a birthday card. (It was nice)
2 He opened your letter. (It was wrong)
3 You found the answer. (It was clever)
4 I made the same mistake twice. (It was careless)

EXERCISE 96D

Rephrase the sentences. Use the words in brackets + *for* + object + *to* infinitive, as in the examples.

Examples:

You needn't explain. (It isn't necessary)
It isn't necessary for you to explain.
She isn't normally late for work. (It's unusual)
It's unusual for her to be late for work.

1 You needn't pay me back the money. (It's unnecessary)
2 We must leave immediately. (It's essential)
3 Everyone should try to keep calm. (It's important)
4 He doesn't normally complain. (It's unusual)

Note

–For the use of the *to* infinitive with *too* (eg *It's **too** early (for me) **to go** to bed*) and *enough* (eg *Is he old **enough to drive** a car?*), see 138.4–5.

97   *See someone doing* and *see someone do*, etc

After the verbs *see, hear, feel, watch, listen to* and *notice* we can use an object +
...-*ing* or the infinitive without *to*.

verb + object + ...-*ing*	verb + object + infinitive without *to*

We saw Peter leaving.
I heard them going out.

We saw Peter leave.
I heard them go out.

There is often a difference of meaning. Compare:

We use the -*ing* form when we see,
hear, etc only part of an action in
progress.

When I looked out of the window, I saw
Sally walking down the street. (= She
was in the middle of walking down the
street.)

We use the infinitive without *to* when
we see, hear, etc. the whole action from
beginning to end.

I saw Sally walk down the street and go
round the corner. (= I saw the whole
thing.)

EXERCISE 97A

Put the verbs in brackets into the -*ing* form or the infinitive without *to*.

Example:
I saw him *get* (get) into his car and drive off.

1 As I walked past the room, I heard two people
____ (argue).
2 We stopped for a moment and watched them
____ (build) the new hospital.
3 Did you see the accident ____ (happen)?

4 We watched them ____ (climb) up to the top
of the hill and then come down again.
5 As I drove past the park I saw some people
____ (play) football.
6 Last week I went to London and saw England
____ (play) Brazil in the big football match.

98   Review of -*ing* form and infinitive

EXERCISE 98A

Complete the sentences using the verbs in brackets in the -*ing* form, the *to*
infinitive, or the infinitive without *to*. Sometimes two answers are possible.

Examples:
You really should *try* (try) to stop *smoking* (smoke).

1 I hate ____ (work) at weekends.
2 Would you like ____ (come) to a disco this
evening?
3 Can I help you ____ (move) your things?

4 I had hoped ____ (see) the musical *Rainbow*,
but I couldn't ____ (get) any tickets.
5 Stop ____ (make) so much noise. People are
trying ____ (sleep).

149

6 Would you like something ____ (drink)?

7 You should ____ (try) to avoid ____ (drive) through the city centre at the rush hour.

8 I want a few days ____ (think) about their offer before ____ (make) a decision.

9 What time do you need ____ (leave) ____ (catch) your bus?

10 It's unusual for him ____ (be) ill.

11 It was horrible to work as an au pair. My family expected me ____ (work) seven days a week.

12 Do you prefer ____ (ski) to ____ (ice-skate)?

13 I'm very fond of ____ (walk) by the sea.

14 I rang the doorbell, but no one seemed ____ (be) at home.

15 It was good of you ____ (explain) everything to me.

16 I'd advise you ____ (not | walk) alone in that part of the city. It can be very dangerous there at night.

17 I remember ____ (meet) her once, but I can't remember her name.

18 I'd like ____ (make) a copy of a letter. Could you ____ (show) me how ____ (use) the photocopier? I've never used it before.

19 I feel like ____ (not | do) anything at all this evening.

20 We're very much looking forward to ____ (see) you next week.

21 I mustn't ____ (forget) ____ (phone) the doctor tomorrow morning.

22 The customs officer made me ____ (empty) my suitcases.

23 ____ (eat) too many sweets is bad for your teeth.

24 Sarah has decided ____ (not | go) away on holiday this summer.

25 They stopped ____ (work) at one o'clock ____ (have) something ____ (eat).

EXERCISE 98B

Complete each sentence using the correct form of one of the verbs in the box. Use each verb only once.

Example:

I phoned my bank manager and I arranged *to meet* him next Tuesday.

| repair | open | have | travel | not study |
| meet | fall | eat | lend | wait | switch off |

1 It was very kind of her ____ you the money.

2 I can't stand ____ by Underground.

3 These shoes need ____. They've got holes in them.

4 I wouldn't recommend ____ in that restaurant. It's very expensive and the food isn't very good.

5 Would you mind ____ the door for me, please?

6 When you leave the room, don't forget ____ all the lights.

7 They saw Maria ____ at the bus stop as they drove past.

8 Autumn is coming. The leaves are starting ____ from the trees.

9 I regret ____ harder for the exam.

10 I like ____ my eyes tested regularly.

99 Participle (*-ing* and *-ed*) adjectives

Compare adjectives ending in *-ed* and *-ing*:

-ed

*He's **bored**.*

Adjectives ending in *-ed* describe someone's feelings.

*I'm **interested** in photography.*
*She feels **tired**.*
*We were all **surprised**.*

-ing

*The film is **boring**.*

Adjectives ending in *-ing* describe the thing or person that produces those feelings.

*I think photography is **interesting**.*
*She's had a **tiring** day.*
*The news was **surprising**.*

EXERCISE 99A

Choose the correct form.

Example:

I enjoyed the book. It was very ~~interested~~/ *interesting*.

1 Are you *interested/interesting* in art?
2 They were *shocked/shocking* when they heard the news.
3 I thought the story was quite *amused/ amusing*.
4 We were all very *worried/worrying* when he didn't come home.
5 It was *surprised/surprising* that she didn't come to the meeting.

EXERCISE 99B

Complete the sentences. Use adjectives formed by adding *-ing* or *-ed* to the words in brackets.

Example:

I don't get *embarrassed* very easily. (embarrass)

1 I find it quite ____ to talk in front of a group of people. (embarrass)
2 I think wet weather is ____. (depress)
3 I'm not very ____ in politics. (interest)
4 I find walking in the countryside very ____. (relax)
5 I think learning a language is very ____. (interest)
6 I get ____ when people smoke in restaurants. (annoy)
7 I don't normally get ____ when I watch horror films. (frighten)

Are these things true for you?

100 Participle (-ing) clauses

1 We can use a present participle eg *sitting, playing* to introduce a 'participle clause'.

*Simon is the boy **sitting in the corner**.*
*I hurt my leg **playing tennis**.*

2 Some participle clauses are like adjectives: they give more information about nouns.

*Simon is the boy **sitting in the corner**.*
*The girl **talking to Simon** is Sarah.*

3 Other participle clauses are like adverbs: they can express ideas such as time or reason:

a When one action happens in the middle of another, longer action, we can use an *-ing* clause for the longer action.

*I hurt my leg **playing tennis**.* (= I hurt my leg while I was playing tennis.)

b When two actions happen at the same time, we can use an *-ing* clause for one of the actions.

*I walked out of the room **smiling to myself**.* (= When I walked out of the room I was smiling to myself.)

c When one action happens before another action, we can use *having* + past participle for the first action.

***Having finished** breakfast, I went out for a walk.* (= I finished breakfast, then I went out for a walk.)

When one action happens immediately after another action, we can often use an *-ing* clause for the first action.

***Taking a book out of his pocket**, he started to read.* (= He took a book out of his pocket and immediately started to read.)

d We can also use an *-ing* clause to say the reason why something happens.

***Knowing you wanted to go to the concert**, I bought a ticket for you.* (= Because I knew you wanted to go to the concert . . .)
***Having failed the exam the first time**, he decided to take it again.* (= Because he had failed the exam the first time . . .)

EXERCISE 100A

Join the sentences using an -ing clause, as in the examples.

Examples:

Who is that man? He's playing tennis with Maria.
Who is that man playing tennis with Maria?
That woman is my boss. She's talking to Peter.
That woman talking to Peter is my boss.

1 That woman is Kate Robinson. She's wearing the green coat.
2 That boy is Sally's brother. He's sitting over there.
3 Who is that girl? She's looking at us.
4 All those people want to see you. They're waiting outside.

EXERCISE 100B

Peter had a very bad day yesterday. What happened to him?
Complete the sentences using the words in the box as -ing clauses.

Example:

1 *He fell off a ladder changing a light bulb.*

1 He fell off a ladder ____.
2 He burnt himself ____.
3 He ran out of petrol ____.
4 He lost his keys ____.
5 He was almost knocked over ____.

drive to work
get out of his car
cross the street
~~change a light bulb~~
cook his dinner

EXERCISE 100C

Join the sentences using an -ing clause, as in the example.

Example:

I was sitting in the park. I was writing a letter.
I was sitting in the park writing a letter.

1 The woman was driving along. She was listening to her car radio.
2 I arrived at the examination hall. I was feeling very nervous.
3 He came into the room. He was carrying a suitcase.
4 They were walking down the street. They were holding hands.

EXERCISE 100D

Rephrase the sentences using *Having* + past participle, as in the example.

Example:

I finished the washing up, then I sat down and watched TV.
Having finished the washing up, I sat down and watched TV.

1 He typed the letters, then he put them all in envelopes.
2 I did all the housework, then I went out for a walk.
3 They finished all their shopping, then they went for a drink.
4 She stopped to look at the map, then she continued on her journey.

EXERCISE 100E

Rephrase the sentences using an -ing clause, as in the examples.

Examples:

Because she didn't want to miss the train, she ran all the way to the station.
Not wanting to miss the train, she ran all the way to the station.
Because I had just eaten, I wasn't hungry. *Having just eaten, I wasn't hungry.*

1 Because I felt hungry, I made myself something to eat.
2 Because he doesn't have much money, he can't afford a car.
3 Because she is rich, she can afford expensive holidays.
4 Because I had finished the book, I decided to take it back to the library.
5 Because they had gone to bed so late the night before, they felt quite tired the next day.

Note

–We normally expect the subject of an -ing clause to be the same as the subject of
the main clause eg *Having just eaten, I wasn't hungry.* (= Because *I* had just eaten,
I wasn't hungry.) It is normally a mistake to make sentences where the subjects
are different. For example, we would not normally say *Running down the street, the
envelope fell out of my hand* (because this makes it sound as if the envelope was
running down the street!)

101   Singular and plural nouns (1)

1 | **Regular plurals**

		SINGULAR NOUN	PLURAL NOUN
a	Most nouns form their plural by adding -s to the singular noun.	*book* *day* *girl*	*books* *days* *girls*
b	We add -es if the singular noun ends in -ch, -sh, -s or -x.	*church* *dish* *bus* *box*	*churches* *dishes* *buses* *boxes*
c	Some nouns ending in -o (*tomato, potato, echo, hero, negro* are the most common), add -es in the plural.	*tomato* *potato* *hero*	*tomatoes* *potatoes* *heroes*
	Other nouns ending in -o, add -s only.	*piano* *radio*	*pianos* *radios*
d	Nouns ending in a consonant + -y, change the -y to i and add -es.	*baby* *factory*	*babies* *factories*

2 | **Irregular plurals**

	SINGULAR	PLURAL

a   Some nouns ending in -*f*/-*fe* drop the -*f*/-*fe* and add -*ves* in the plural eg *half, thief, leaf, loaf, self, shelf, wolf, knife, wife, life.*

SINGULAR	PLURAL
half	*halves*
thief	*thieves*
leaf	*leaves*
knife	*knives*
wife	*wives*
life	*lives*

b   Some nouns form the plural by changing their vowel(s).

SINGULAR	PLURAL
foot	*feet*
tooth	*teeth*
goose	*geese*
man	*men*
woman	*women* /ˈwɪmɪn/
mouse	*mice*

The plural of *mouse* is *mice*.

c   A few nouns form the plural with -*en*.

SINGULAR	PLURAL
child	*children* /ˈtʃɪldrən/
ox	*oxen*

d   Some nouns have the same form in the singular and the plural.

SINGULAR	PLURAL
sheep	*sheep*
deer	*deer*
fish	*fish**
aircraft	*aircraft*
hovercraft	*hovercraft*
spacecraft	*spacecraft*
series	*series*
species	*species*

e   Some nouns borrowed from Greek and Latin have Greek or Latin plural endings.

SINGULAR	PLURAL
crisis	*crises*
phenomenon	*phenomena*
cactus	*cacti*

f   The usual plural of *person* is *people* (not *persons*).

SINGULAR	PLURAL
person	*people*

* *fish* is the normal plural of *fish*; *fishes* is also possible, but less usual.

For the pronunciation of the -(*e*)*s* ending, see 187.1.

EXERCISE 101A

Complete the sentences using the plurals of the nouns in brackets.

Example:

I like *oranges, apples, peaches* and *strawberries.* (orange | apple | peach | strawberry).

1 They've got five ____, three ____ and two ____, (child | girl | boy)
2 London has many different ____, ____, ____ and ____.
   (restaurant | theatre | cinema | disco)

3 When he fell over, he broke two of his ____. (tooth)
4 We've got enough ____, but we need some more ____ and ____.
   (plate | knife | fork)
5 On their tour of Europe, they visited seven ____ in six ____. (country | day)
6 ____ hunt ____. (cat | mouse)
7 Do you know those ____ over there? (person)
8 These ____ are too small for me. They hurt my ____. (shoe | foot)
9 We've got some ____ and ____, but we haven't got any ____.
   (egg | tomato | potato)
10 Autumn is coming. The ____ are starting to all from the ____. (leaf | tree)

102   Singular and plural nouns (2)

1 Normally, we use singular nouns with singular verbs and pronouns, and plural nouns with plural verbs and pronouns.

'Where's the key?' *'It's on the table.'* | *'Where are the keys?'* *'They're on the table.'*

But see 2–9 below.

2 With group nouns eg *family, team, group, crowd, class, company, government* we can use singular or plural verbs and pronouns:

a We use plural verbs and pronouns when we think of these groups as a number of people.

*My **family are** on holiday.*
*The **government think they** can solve the problem.*

b We use singular verbs and pronouns when we think of the group as an impersonal unit.

*The **family is** a very important part of society.*

3 We always use plural words with the nouns *people, (the) police* and *cattle*.

People are** strange, **aren't they?
***The police have** arrested a man.*

4 We use plural nouns, verbs and pronouns with *a number of* and *a group of*.

***A number of my friends are** planning a holiday together. **They hope** to go to Greece and Turkey.*

For *a lot of*, see 116.

5 After expressions with *one of my/his/her* etc we use a plural noun and a singular verb.

***One of my friends is** coming to see me.*

6 When we talk about an amount or a quantity, we often use singular verbs and pronouns with plural nouns.

***Ten thousand pounds is** a lot of money.*
*'The nearest town is **five kilometres** from here.'* *'**That isn't** very far.'*

7 | Some nouns have only a plural form eg *trousers, jeans, pyjamas, shorts, tights, glasses, scissors.*

*Are those your new **trousers**?*
*There **are** some **scissors** in the kitchen.*

We can also use a singular verb + *a pair of* with these nouns.

*There **is a pair of scissors** in the kitchen.*

8 | Some nouns end in *-s,* but are singular eg *news, politics, mathematics, physics, economics, athletics, billiards, rabies.*

*The **news is** depressing.*
*Mathematics **is** an interesting subject.*

9 | Uncountable nouns, the names of things which we cannot count, eg *milk, money,* normally have no plural form.

*There **is** some **milk** in the fridge.*
*Money **isn't** the most important thing in life, **is it**?*

For uncountable nouns, see 107.

EXERCISE 102A

Choose the correct form. In one sentence either answer is possible.

Example:

There *were/~~was~~* a lot of people at the party.

1 Economics *is/are* an interesting subject.
2 My trousers *have/has* got a hole in *it/them.*
3 Rabies *isn't/aren't* a very common disease in Britain.
4 My family *lives/live* in the North of England.
5 The news *was/were* quite surprising.

6 '*Is this/Are these* your scissors?'   'Yes, *they are/it is.*'
7 Two weeks *isn't/aren't* a very long time, *is it/ are they*?
8 My hair *is/are* quite greasy. *It needs/They need* washing.

103   Compound nouns

1 | A compound noun is a noun that is made of two (or more) parts:

*a **toothbrush**   a **tin-opener***

a | Many compound nouns are formed by using one noun (as an adjective) in front of another noun. When this happens, the first noun is almost always singular (even if the meaning is plural).

*a **toothbrush** (a brush for cleaning teeth)*
*a **shoe shop** (a shop which sells shoes)*
*a **taxi driver** (a person who drives a taxi)*

There are a few exceptions eg *clothes, sports, men, women.*

a clothes shop　　**a sports car**　　**women doctors**

b Some compound nouns are written as one word eg *toothbrush*, some are written with a hyphen (-) eg *tin-opener*, and some are written as two words eg *shoe shop.*

Some compound nouns can be written as one word, or with a hyphen, or as two words eg *babysitter, baby-sitter, baby sitter* (but there are no clear rules about this).

c Some compound nouns are formed with an *-ing* form + noun, or an adjective + noun.

a shopping bag　　**a waiting room**　　**drinking water**
a greenhouse (= a building made of glass, used for growing plants)

2 We normally form plurals of compound nouns by adding *-(e)s* to the second word.

a shoe shop	*shoe shops*
a toothbrush	*two toothbrushes*

But note that compounds ending in *-in-law* add *-s* to the first word.

one brother-in-law	*two brothers-in-law*
my mother-in-law	*some mothers-in-law*

A few other compound nouns also add *-s* to the first word eg *passer-by* (= person who happens 'by chance' to pass by a place).

a passer-by	*some passers-by*

EXERCISE 103A

Make compound nouns from the words in the box to describe the objects in the pictures.

Examples:

1　*alarm clock*　　2　*T-shirts*　　3　*crossroads*

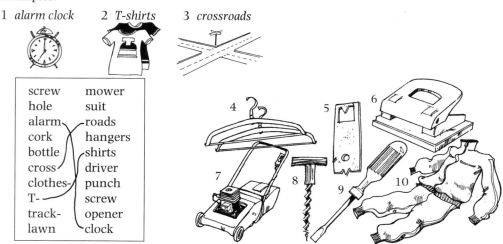

screw	mower
hole	suit
alarm	roads
cork	hangers
bottle	shirts
cross	driver
clothes-	punch
T-	screw
track-	opener
lawn	clock

104 Possessive 's (genitive)

1 | **Use**

Sally's motorbike   *Andrew's bedroom*

a We often add the possessive 's to personal nouns (eg *Sally, Andrew*) to show the relationship of the person to something or someone else.

Sally's motorbike (a motorbike which belongs to Sally)
Andrew's bedroom (the bedroom where Andrew sleeps)
my sister's school (the school which my sister goes to)

We also use the possessive 's with personal indefinite pronouns eg *someone, nobody*.

someone's passport   *nobody's problem*

b We can also use the possessive 's with the names of animals

a dog's life   *the cat's milk*

c We can use the possessive 's with a group of people or with a place where people live, work, etc.

the company's office   *the club's rules*
the world's problems   *London's traffic*

d We also use the possessive 's in some expressions of time.

yesterday's newspaper   *last week's football match*
next year's plans

We use the possessive 's with periods of time.

a week's holiday   *two days' work*

2 | **Form**

a After a singular noun, we add 's.

> *my father's car*
> *Sally's room*

b After a plural noun ending in -s, we add only '.

> *my parents' car*
> *the ladies' room*

c After a plural noun not ending in -s, we add 's.

> *the men's car*
> *the children's room*

d | We sometimes just add ' to a singular noun ending in -s.

Sherlock Holmes' best friend   Archimedes' Law

But it is more common to add 's.

Mrs Jones's husband   Chris's idea

e | We can add the possessive 's to a whole phrase.

Sue and Frank's *daughter*

But with a longer phrase, we often use *... of ...* instead eg *the daughter of the Australian couple who live next door* (see 105).

f | We can also use the possessive 's without a following noun (when it is clear what or who we are talking about).

*My car is next to **Ken's**. (= ... next to Ken's car.)*

We often talk about shops, surgeries, etc in this way.

*She has just been to the **hairdresser's**.*
*I went to the **doctor's** yesterday.*

For the pronunciation of the 's ending, see 187.1.

EXERCISE 104A

Look at the family tree. Make sentences using the possessive 's and the words in the box.

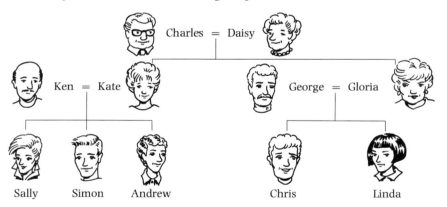

Examples:

Kate–Ken
Kate is Ken's wife.
Simon and Andrew–Sally
Simon and Andrew are Sally's brothers.
Gloria–Ken
Gloria is Ken's sister-in-law.

1 Gloria–Chris and Linda
2 Linda–Chris
3 George–Chris and Linda
4 Chris–George and Gloria
5 Charles–Ken
6 Daisy–Linda and Chris
7 Kate–Chris and Linda
8 Sally, Simon and Andrew–Chris and Linda

~~wife~~	mother	father
sister	~~brother~~	son
aunt	grandmother	
cousin	sister-in-law	
father-in-law		

EXERCISE 104B

Complete the sentences using the correct form of the possessive 's.

Example:

What is your friend's name?

1 Sarah found somebody ____ credit cards in the street.
2 The Eiffel Tower is Paris ____ most famous landmark.
3 The boys ____ bedroom has just been painted.
4 I read about a murder in this morning ____ newspaper.
5 Can you borrow your parents ____ car at the weekend?
6 I need to get some medicine. Is there a chemist ____ near here?

105   Possessive 's or . . . of . . .

1	We normally use 's when the first noun is a person or an animal.	We normally use . . . of . . . with things.
	Andrew's bedroom *Sarah's* book *my parents'* car *the cat's* food	*the door **of the room*** *the middle **of the book*** *the front **of the car*** *the smell **of the food***

2	Also, we often use . . . of . . . instead of 's with longer phrases. *Yesterday I met the daughter **of the Australian couple who live next door**.* (Instead of: *Yesterday I met **the Australian couple who live next door's** daughter.*)

EXERCISE 105A

Complete the sentences. Use the words in brackets with the possessive 's or . . . of . . ., as in the examples.

Examples:

Have you seen *Steven Spielberg's new film?* (the new film | Steven Spielberg)
The roof of the house was badly damaged in the storm. (the roof | the house)

1 We had to leave the cinema early so we didn't see ____. (the end | the film)
2 We met Sue and Frank at ____. (the party | Sarah)
3 My flat is on ____. (the top floor | the house)
4 The bus crashed into ____. (the back | my car)
5 We heard the news from ____. (a friend | the woman who works in the post office)
6 There's a hospital at ____. (the end | this road)
7 I've spoken to ____. (the parents | the girls)
8 The police want to interview ____. (the manager | the Black Cat Club)

106 Double possessive

We can use ... *of* ... and a possessive form in a 'double possessive'.

> ... *of* ... + possessive

*Sarah is **a friend of Simon's**.* (= one of Simon's friends)
***A cousin of mine** is coming to visit me.* (= one of my cousins)
*Sue is having lunch with **some colleagues of hers**.* (= some of her colleagues)

Note that after *of* we can use a possessive pronoun eg *mine, hers*, etc, not a personal pronoun eg *me, her*, etc.

EXERCISE 106A

Make a new sentence using ... *of* ... + possessive, as in the example.

Example:

I met one of my friends in London.   *I met a friend of mine in London.*

1 Robert visited one of his relatives.
2 One of our neighbours is going to babysit for us.
3 Sally is going on holiday with some of her friends.
4 Simon has borrowed some of Sarah's records.
5 Two of my colleagues are ill at the moment.

107 Countable and uncountable nouns

1

a **Nouns can be countable or uncountable:**

Countable nouns are the names of separate objects, people, etc which we can count; they have singular and plural forms.

*one **book**   two **books***   *a **man**   some **men***

Uncountable nouns are the names of things which we do not see as separate, and which we cannot count; they do not have plural forms.

milk   rice   music

b Countable nouns can take singular or plural verbs.

*This **book is** expensive.*   *These **books are** expensive.*
*That **man lives** next door.*   *Those **men live** next door.*

Uncountable nouns always take singular verbs.

***Milk is** good for you.*
*The **music was** very good.*

c   Before countable nouns, we can use *a/an* and numbers.

a man   *one book*   *two books*

We do not normally use *a/an* or a number directly before uncountable nouns. For example, we do not say ~~a music~~, ~~two musics~~, etc. But we sometimes use *a/an* and numbers with eg *coffee, tea, beer,* etc when we order these things by the cup or glass in a restaurant.

*Excuse me, waiter. Could we have **two coffees** and **a tea**, please?*

We use *a* before consonant sounds eg *a book, a man,* and *an* before vowel sounds eg *an apple, an egg* (see 108.1).

d   We use *some* before plural countable nouns and uncountable nouns (see 115).

some books   *some music*
some men   *some milk*

2   Some nouns can be used as countable or uncountable, with a difference of meaning. For example:

COUNTABLE   UNCOUNTABLE

a glass

glass (= the material)

a hair

her hair (= all the hair on her head)

a paper (= a newspaper)

some paper (= the writing material)

an iron

iron (= the metal)

some potatoes

some potato

3 | Some nouns are uncountable in English, but countable in other languages. Here are some of the most common of these uncountable nouns, together with some related countable expressions:

UNCOUNTABLE	COUNTABLE
accommodation	*a place to live/stay*
advice	*a piece of advice*
bread	*a loaf/slice/piece (of bread) a (bread) roll*
furniture	*a piece of furniture*
information	*a piece of information*
luggage	*a piece of luggage; a suitcase/bag*
money	*a note/coin; a sum (of money)*
news	*a piece of news*
traffic	*a car/bus etc*
travel	*a journey/trip*
work	*a job; a piece of work*

Compare:

*I'll give you some **advice**.*	*I'll give you **a piece of advice**.*
*Where is your **luggage**?*	*Where are your **suitcases**?*
*He's looking for **work**.*	*He's looking for **a job**.*

Instead of *a piece of* here, we can use *a bit of* in a more informal style eg *a bit of advice*.

4 | We can use both countable and uncountable nouns in phrases of quantity with *of*.

*a box **of** matches*	*a bottle **of** water*
*two tins **of** tomatoes*	*two loaves **of** bread*

EXERCISE 107A

(i) Look at the things in the pictures. Are they countable (C) or uncountable (U) here?

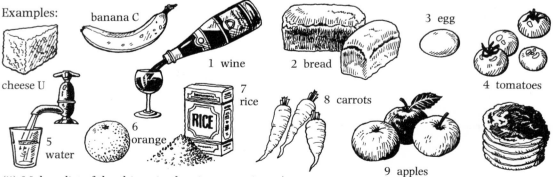

Examples: banana C

cheese U   1 wine   2 bread   3 egg   4 tomatoes

5 water   6 orange   7 rice   8 carrots   9 apples   10 meat

(ii) Make a list of the things in the pictures using *a/an* or *some*.

Examples:

Some cheese, a banana . . .

EXERCISE 107B

Choose the correct form.

Example:

I'd like some *information/~~informations~~* about hotels in London.

1   Sue is the woman with blonde *hair/hairs* who lives opposite.
2   Did you have a good *travel/journey* from Switzerland?
3   I've got a problem and I'd like some *advice/advices*.
4   Don't forget to buy *a bread/some bread* when you go shopping.
5   I'd like to find out what's on TV this evening. Have you got *a paper/some paper*?
6   There *is/are* usually a lot of *traffic/traffics* in the city at this time of the day.
7   He's trying to find a *work/job* at the moment, but there *isn't/aren't* much *work/ works* available.
8   *Is/Are* good *accommodation/accommodations* difficult to find in the city centre?

108   Articles: *a/an* and *the*

1

a   Form and pronunciation

We use *a* /ə/ before words beginning with a consonant sound.

> *a book* /ə bʊk/
> *a car* /ə kɑː/
> *a day* /ə deɪ/
> *a friend* /ə frend/
> *a girl*/ə gɜːl/

We use *an* /ən/ before words beginning with a vowel sound.

> *an apple* /ən æpl/
> *an egg* /ən eg/
> *an interview* /ən ˈɪntəvjuː/
> *an old coat* /ən əʊld kəʊt/
> *an umbrella* /ən ʌmˈbrelə/

b   We say *the* /ðə/ before words beginning with a consonant sound.

> *the book* /ðə bʊk/
> *the car* /ðə kɑː/
> *the day* /ðə deɪ/

We say *the* /ði:/ before words beginning with a vowel sound.

> *the apple* /ði: ˈæpl/
> *the egg* /ði: eg/
> *the interview* /ði: ˈɪntəvjuː/

c   We use *a* and *the* /ðə/ before *u* when it has the consonant sound /j/.

> *a university* /ə ˌjuːnɪˈvɜːsətɪ/
> *the university* /ðə ˌjuːnɪˈvɜːsətɪ/

We use *an* and *the* /ði:/ before *h* when it is not sounded.

> *an hour* /ən ˈaʊə(r)/
> *the hour* /ði: ˈaʊə(r)/

2   **Use of *a/an***

For countable and uncountable nouns, see 107.

a   We use *a/an* before singular countable nouns.

a student   *a book*   *an idea*

We do not use *a/an* before plural countable nouns. For example, we cannot say ~~*a students*~~ or ~~*an ideas*~~. We do not normally use *a/an* before uncountable nouns. For example, we cannot say ~~*a water*~~ or ~~*a music*~~ (but see 107.1–2).

We do not use singular countable nouns alone, without *a/an, the, my, this*, etc.

I'm a student. (Not: ~~*I'm student.*~~)

b   We use *a/an* when the listener or reader does not know exactly which person or thing we mean.

*There is **a** book on the table.* (We don't know which book.)
*He met **a** girl last night. She works in **a** bank.* (We don't know which girl, or which bank.)

We use *a/an* when we say what someone or something is.

*I'm **an** architect*   *He's **a** vegetarian.*   *It was **a** good film.*

3   **Use of *the***

For countable and uncountable nouns, see 107.

a   We use *the* with singular countable nouns, plural countable nouns, and uncountable nouns.

the man   *the shoes*   *the water*

b   We use *the* when the listener or reader knows exactly which person or thing we mean:

■ We use *the* to talk about people and things that we have already mentioned.

*I met a girl and a boy. I didn't like **the** boy much, but **the** girl was very nice.*
*My father bought a shirt and some shoes. **The** shoes were quite expensive.*

■ We use *the* when we say which people or things we mean.

*Who is **the** man over there talking to Sue?*

■ We use *the* when it is clear from the situation which people or things we mean.

*'Where's Simon?' 'He's in **the** bathroom.'* (= the bathroom in this house)
*Could you switch on **the** light?* (= the light in this room)
*I got into a taxi. **The** driver asked me where I wanted to go.* (= the driver of the taxi that I got into)

■ We use *the* when there is only one of something eg *the sun, the moon, the sky, the earth, the world.*

*I enjoy lying in **the** sun.*
*Would you like to travel round **the** world?*

EXERCISE 108A

Put the words in the correct column: **A** or **B**.

A	B
a and *the* /ðə/	*an* and *the* /ði:/
clock	orange

~~clock~~	aunt	sandwich	house	school	examination
~~orange~~	old car	dog	hospital	onion	ice-cream
envelope	university	game	hour	umbrella	

EXERCISE 108B

Add *a* or *an* where necessary.

Examples:

I'd like *a* hamburger, please.
Sarah and Simon are —— students.

1 There's ____ post office in West Street.
2 I've got ____ envelope, but I haven't got ____ stamp.
3 We ate ____ cheese and drank ____ wine.
4 Can you see those two men? They're ____ policemen.
5 Would you like ____ cup of tea?
6 I saw ____ very good film on TV last night.

EXERCISE 108C

Complete the sentences using *a*, *an* or *the*.

Examples:

The Queen of England lives in Buckingham Palace in London.

1 Who is ____ best footballer in ____ world?
2 My brother works in ____ large garage in Brighton. He's ____ engineer.
3 Did you enjoy ____ party you went to on Saturday?
4 ____ earth moves round ____ sun.
5 I had ____ cup of coffee and some toast for breakfast this morning. ____ coffee was delicious.
6 Could you switch off ____ TV? Nobody is watching it.
7 'What's ____ capital of India?'   'Delhi.'
8 'What do you think of Lynne?'   'She's ____ extremely nice person.'

109   Talking in general: no article and *a/an*

1 When we talk about something in general, we use plural or uncountable nouns without *the*.

Shoes *are expensive.* (= shoes in general)
Milk *is good for you.* (= milk in general)

When we talk about something in particular, we use *the*.

*These are **the shoes** which I bought last week.* (= the particular shoes which I bought last week)
*Could you pass **the milk**, please?* (= the particular milk on the table)

More examples:

GENERAL	PARTICULAR
*I like **horses**.*	*Look at **the horses** in that field.*
***Life** isn't easy.*	*I've got a book about **the life** of J. F. Kennedy.*
*He only cares about **money**.*	*Where is **the money** I gave you yesterday?*

It is not always easy to know if something is general or particular. For example:

GENERAL	PARTICULAR
*I enjoy talking to **old people**.* (= old people in general)	*Do you know **the old people** sitting over there?* (= the particular old people sitting over there)

2   We can also talk about something in general by using *a/an* (meaning 'any') with a singular countable noun.

*A **vegetarian** doesn't eat meat.*
*An **architect** designs buildings.*

EXERCISE 109A

Add *the* where necessary.

I find ⸻ history an interesting subject.
We studied *the* history of the Spanish Civil War at school.

1 Andrew hates ⸻ examinations.
2 How did you get on in ⸻ examination yesterday?
3 Do you take ⸻ sugar in ⸻ coffee?
4 Could you pass me ⸻ sugar, please?
5 I'm a vegetarian, I don't eat ⸻ meat or ⸻ fish.
6 I'll put ⸻ shopping away. Shall I put ⸻ meat into ⸻ freezer?
7 Do you like ⸻ English beer?
8 Do you think ⸻ love is the most important thing in ⸻ life?

EXERCISE 109B

Rephrase these general statements using *a/an*, as in the example.

Example:

Carpenters make things from wood.
A carpenter makes things from wood.

1 Florists sell flowers.
2 Children need love.
3 Corkscrews take corks out of bottles.
4 Large cars are expensive to run.
5 Teetotallers don't drink alcohol.

110 Talking in general: *the*

1 *The* + noun

a We sometimes use *the* with a singular countable noun to talk about something in general. This happens, for example, with the names of animals, flowers and plants.

The dolphin is an intelligent animal.
The orchid is a beautiful flower.

(*the dolphin* = dolphins in general; *the orchid* = orchids in general)

b We also use *the* in a general sense with the names of musical instruments and scientific inventions.

She can play the guitar and the piano.
Marconi invented the radio.

c Some common expressions with *the* have a general meaning eg *the town, the country(side), the sea(side), the mountains, the rain, the wind, the sun(shine), the snow.*

I enjoy going for long walks in the country.
They often go to the mountains at weekends.
I like the sound of the rain.

d We also use *the cinema* and *the theatre* with a general meaning.

Which do you prefer, the cinema or the theatre?

2 *The* + adjective

a We can use *the* before some adjectives eg *young, old, rich, poor, blind* with a general meaning.

The young should listen to the old.

(*the young* = young people in general; *the old* = old people in general)

b We also use *the* before some nationality words eg *English, Italian, French, Swiss, Japanese* to mean 'the people of that country'.

The English drink a lot of tea.

Note that these words all end in -*sh* (eg *the English, the Irish*), -*ch* (eg *the French, the Dutch*), or -*ese* (eg *the Japanese, the Chinese*).

With other nationalities we use a plural noun ending in -*s* with or without *the* eg *(the) Italians, (the) Germans.*

EXERCISE 110A

Complete each sentence using *the* and the most suitable noun in the box.

Example:

The blue whale is the largest animal in the world.

> piano   radio   cheetah   sea
> ~~blue whale~~   country   rose

1 ___ is a beautiful, sweet-smelling flower.
2 Do you often listen to that programme on ___?
3 My grandmother has lived in a small village in ___ all her life.
4 ___ is the fastest animal in the world.
5 My favourite musical instrument is ___.
6 Do you ever go swimming in ___?

EXERCISE 110B

What do we call these people? Use *the* + the adjectives in the box.

Example:

people who are unable to hear
the deaf

> blind   sick   ~~deaf~~   unemployed   dead

1 people who are no longer alive
2 people who have no jobs
3 people who cannot see
4 people who are unwell

EXERCISE 110C

What do we call the people of these countries?

Example:

China
the Chinese

1 Britain
2 Russia
3 Spain
4 France
5 Switzerland

111 Common expressions without an article

<table>
<tr><td>1</td><td colspan="2">School, the school, hospital, the hospital etc</td></tr>
<tr><td>a</td><td colspan="2">We often use the following nouns without an article.</td></tr>
</table>

1   *School, the school, hospital, the hospital etc*

a   We often use the following nouns without an article.

> school   university   college
> hospital   prison   church   bed

*Maria goes to **school** every morning.*
*I hope to go to **university** next year.*
*Mr Woods has gone into **hospital**.*
*John has been in **prison** for three years.*
*I think I'll go to **bed** early tonight.*

We use these nouns without an article when we think about the main purpose of the place. Compare:

*I think I'll go to **bed** early tonight. (to sleep)*	*There are some shoes under **the bed**.*
*Maria goes to **school** every morning. (to study)*	***The school** was painted last month.*
*Mr Woods has gone into **hospital**. (for medical treatment)*	*Sarah met Simon outside **the hospital**.*

b   We normally use *work* and *home* without an article.

*What time do you usually go to **work**?*
*Would you like to stay at **home** this evening?*

2   **Means of transport**

We use *by car/bus/train/plane* etc, without an article, to talk about how we travel.

*I usually go to work **by car**.*
*We went to Rome **by train**.*

We also say *on foot* (= walking) eg *I came home **on foot**.*

3   **Meals**

We do not normally use an article with the names of meals.

*What time do you usually have **breakfast**?*
*When would you like to have **dinner**?*

But we use *the* when we specify eg *I enjoyed **the dinner** we had last night.*

We can also say *a/the meal* eg *We had **a meal** on the plane.* We also use *a/an* when there is an adjective before *breakfast/lunch/dinner/* etc.

*They had **a large breakfast**.*

EXERCISE 111A

Add *the* where necessary.

Examples:

Mrs Woods goes to ⸺ church every Sunday.
There is a cemetery behind *the* church.

1 What time does Annie normally go to ___ school?
2 Annie's parents went to ___ school to speak to the teachers last week.
3 I went to ___ bed at 10 o'clock last night.
4 I was lying on ___ bed reading a book.
5 Kate arrives ___ home from ___ work at about 6.00 every evening.
6 Did you go to ___ work by ___ bus or on ___ foot yesterday?
7 Sue went to ___ prison to visit John last month.
8 My mother has gone into ___ hospital for an operation.
9 The ABC cinema is opposite ___ hospital.
10 I usually have coffee and toast for ___ breakfast.

Note

–For expressions of time with and without articles eg *in **the** morning, at night, on Monday, in (**the**) summer*, see 169.

112   Place-names with and without *the*

1

a

Place-names without *the*

We do not normally use *the* with the names of:

continents	*Africa Europe Asia*
countries, states, departments, etc	*England Spain Brazil California Hampshire*
cities, towns and villages	*New York Tokyo Bilbao*
individual islands	*Crete Long Island*
lakes	*Lake Michigan Lake Geneva*
individual mountains	*Mount Everest Mount Etna*
streets	*Oxford Street Broadway*

b   But we use *the* with these place-names when they include a countable noun eg *union, republic, states, kingdom, isle.*

the Soviet **Union**   *the* Federal **Republic** *of Germany*   *the* United **States**   *the* United **Kingdom**

c   We also use *the* with plural place-names eg *the Netherlands, the West Indies, the Alps.*

d   We also use *the* with various others of these place-names eg *the North/South Pole, the Arctic/Antarctic, the Middle East, the Far East, the Costa Brava, the Ruhr.*

2   **Place-names with *the***

a   We normally use *the* with the names of:

oceans and seas	*the Atlantic the Mediterranean*
rivers	*the River Thames the Nile*
canals	*the Panama Canal the Suez Canal*
deserts	*the Sahara the Kalahari*
island groups	*the Canaries the West Indies*
hotels, cinemas	*the Plaza Hotel the Odeon Cinema*
museums, clubs	*the Prado Museum the Black Cat Club*
restaurants, pubs	*the Hard Rock Café the Swan (pub)*

b   But we do not use *the* with hotels, restaurants, etc named after the people who started them + the possessive *'s.*

Macy's Hotel (Not: ~~the Macy's Hotel~~)   · *McDonald's* (Not: ~~the McDonald's~~)

These names are often written without an apostrophe (') eg *Lloyds Bank, Woolworths.*

We do not use *the* with churches named after saints + the possessive *'s.*

St Peter's Church   St Paul's Cathedral   (St = Saint)

c   We use *the* before names with *of.*

*the Statue of Liberty   the Bank of Scotland
the University of London* (Or: *London University*)

EXERCISE 112A

Answer the questions using *the* where necessary. You can find the answers in brackets!

Examples:

Which is the largest country in the world? (VOSTIE NOUIN)   *the Soviet Union*
What's the capital of India? (HELDI)   *Delhi*

1 Which is the longest river in the world? (LEIN)
2 Which is the largest continent in the world? (IAAS)
3 Which canal connects the Atlantic Ocean and the Pacific Ocean? (MANAPA NALCA)
4 Which is the largest desert in the world? (HAAARS)
5 In which state of the USA is Los Angeles? (FLIARIACON)
6 Which is the largest lake in the world? (KEAL PERSOIRU)
7 Which is the largest ocean in the world? (CLATINTA)
8 Which is the highest mountain in the world? (TUMON STEERVE)
9 Which are the highest mountains in Europe? (LAPS)

EXERCISE 112B

Add *the* where necessary.

Example:

The Louvre Museum is in ══ Paris.

1 Ron Lewis was born in ____ Manchester, but he lives in ____ Bristol now. He's a lecturer at ____ University of Bristol.
2 ____ Luigi's restaurant is between ____ Albany Hotel and ____ Jimmy's Wine Bar in ____ Cambridge Road.
3 When we were in London we visited ____ National Gallery, ____ Tower of London, ____ St Paul's Cathedral and ____ Madame Tussaud's waxwork museum.

113   Review of articles: *a/an, the* and no article

EXERCISE 113A

Add *a, an* or *the* where necessary.

Examples:

We saw *an* interesting film at *the* cinema last night.
I start ══ work at 9 o'clock every morning.

1 ____ Soviet Union is ____ biggest country in ____ world.
2 Have you ever been to ____ St Peter's Square in ____ Rome?
3 ____ weather was lovely when I woke up yesterday morning; ____ sun was shining and there was ____ beautiful blue sky.
4 My sister works in ____ large hospital in ____ London. She's ____ doctor.
5 Who was ____ woman you were talking to just now?
6 'Where's Kate?'   'She's in ____ living room.'
7 What time do you usually have ____ lunch?
8 Do you prefer cooking with ____ gas or ____ electricity?
9 We visited ____ Prado Museum when we were in ____ Madrid.
10 What time does Andrew finish ____ school?
11 There are 20 classrooms in ____ school.
12 Who invented ____ telescope?
13 How long have you been looking for ____ work?
14 Did you go to ____ Scotland by ____ car or by ____ train?
15 ____ Japanese export a lot of cars.
16 Sue and Frank have got two children; ____ girl and ____ boy. ____ girl is ____ student and ____ boy is ____ engineer.
17 ____ Giovannis' restaurant is next to ____ Midland Bank in ____ Bath Road.
18 Are you interested in ____ politics?
19 ____ Atlantic Ocean is larger than ____ Indian Ocean.
20 ____ Mont Blanc is higher than ____ Mount Etna.
21 Sue's brother is ill in ____ hospital.
22 The government plan to help ____ poor and ____ unemployed.

114 Quantity: general

When we talk about quantity we use words such as:

some, any (see 115)   *all, every, each* (see 118)
much, many, a lot, (a) little, (a) few (see 116)   *both, either, neither* (see 119)
no, none (see 117)   *more, most, half*

1 We can use these words (except *none, a lot* and *half*) directly before a noun.

*There are **some eggs** in the fridge.*
*Have you got **any money?***
*There are **no letters** for you today.*
***Both films** were very good.*

2 We also use these words (except *no* and *every*) before *of* + *the, her, your, this*, etc + noun.

*We knew **some of the people** at the party.*
*Can **either of your parents** speak French?*

We also use these words (except *no* and *every*) with *of* before an object pronoun
eg *them, us, it*.

*Not all of these books are mine. **Some of them** are Peter's.*
***Neither of us** saw the film.*

After *all, half* and *both* we can leave out *of* before *the, her, my, your, this*, etc.

*I switched off **all (of) the lights**.*
***Half (of) my friends** are on holiday at the moment.*
*I enjoyed **both (of) the films**.*

But after *all, half* and *both* we cannot leave out *of* before an object pronoun eg *them, us, it*.

*'Have you read these books?'   'Not **all of them**.'* (Not: ~~… all them~~.)
*He didn't spend all the money, but he spent nearly **half of it**.* (Not: ~~… half it~~.)
*She invited **both of us** to the party.* (Not: ~~… both us …~~)

We can also use *every one of* before *the, her, my*, etc or an object pronoun.

***Every one of the** students passed the exam.*
*I've read some of those books, but not **every one of them**.*

3 We can also use these words (except *no* and *every*) alone, without nouns.

*If you want some coffee, I'll make **some**.*
*'Were there a lot of people on the train?'   'No, not **many**.'*

Instead of *all* and *each* alone, we often use *all of* + object pronoun eg *them, it*, etc
and *each one*.

*I like some Elvis Presley records, but not **all of them**.*
*They've got three children and **each one** goes to a different school.*

We can also use *every one* alone.

*I've read some of these books, but not **every one**.*

EXERCISE 114A

Choose the correct answer.

Example:

I've spent ~~most~~/*most of* the money you gave me.

1 Not *all*/*all of* birds can fly.
2 The teacher interviewed *each*/*each of* student in turn.
3 I've heard *some*/*some of* those records, but not *all*/*all of* them.
4 I can't lend you *any*/*any of* money because I haven't got *any*/*any of*.
5 *Most*/*Most of* people like Kate.
6 *Neither*/*Neither of* my parents will be at home this evening.
7 *Neither*/*Neither of* these jackets fits me properly.
8 'How *much*/*much of* coffee have we got?' 'Not *a lot*/*a lot of*.'
9 *A few*/*A few of* Simon's friends went to the concert, but not *many*/*many of*.
10 Are there *many*/*many of* museums in Brighton?
11 We tried several chemists' and *every*/*every one of* them was closed.
12 He spends *most*/*most of* his time watching TV.
13 My sister has read nearly *every*/*every one of* book in the library.
14 I answered *each*/*each of* question carefully.
15 Do *either*/*either of* these books belong to you?
16 We haven't painted the whole house yet, but we've done about *half*/*half of* it.
17 They've got five children and *each of*/*each one* is quite different.

115   *Some* and *any*

1 We use *some* and *any* before plural nouns and uncountable nouns to talk about an indefinite quantity:

some letters   *any* letters
some money   *any* money

2 In general, we use *some* mostly in affirmative sentences and *any* mostly in negative sentences.

*There are **some** letters for you.*   *There aren't **any** letters for you.*
*I've got **some** money.*   *I haven't got **any** money.*

But see 3, 4 and 6 below.

3 We use *any* after words with a negative meaning eg *without, never, seldom, rarely, hardly.*

*I found a taxi **without any** trouble.*
*You **never** do **any** homework.*
*There are **hardly any** eggs left.*

4 We can use *some* or *any* after *if.*

*If you need **some**/**any** money, tell me.*

5   We normally use *any* in 'open' questions (when we do not expect a particular answer).

*Have you got **any** money?*
*Is there **any** coffee in the cupboard?*

But we often use *some* in questions when we expect people to say 'yes'.

*Have you got **some** money?* (I think you have got some money; I expect you to say 'yes')

We also use *some* in questions when we want to encourage people to say 'yes', for example in requests and offers.

*'Can you lend me **some** money?'   'How much do you want?'*
*'Would you like **some** more coffee?'   'Oh, yes, please.'*

6   We can also use *any* to mean 'it doesn't matter which' or 'whichever you like'.

*You can get the tickets from **any** travel agency.*
*I can come and see you **any** day next week.*

7   We also use *some* (with the strong pronunciation /sʌm/) to make a contrast.

***Some** people like lying in the sun, others don't.*

EXERCISE 115A

Complete the sentences using *some* or *any*. Sometimes either word is possible.

Example:

He hasn't got *any* brothers or sisters.

1 There are ____ people outside who want to see you.
2 I like ____ water sports, but not all of them.
3 Can you buy ____ butter when you go to the shops? There's hardly ____ left.
4 'Could I have ____ more coffee, please?' 'Yes, of course.'
5 'I haven't got ____ money.' 'Would you like me to lend you ____?'
6 If you need ____ more information, please ask me.
7 Phone me ____ time you like tomorrow. I'll be at home all day.
8 I've done ____ revision for the exams, but not much.
9 ____ museums are worth visiting, but others aren't.
10 Tell me if you want ____ help.

Note

–For *some* and *any*, see also 114.
–*Some time* means 'at some indefinite time' eg *Let's meet **some time** next week*; *sometimes* means 'on some occasions' eg *We **sometimes** meet after school*.
–The difference between *something* and *anything*, *somebody/someone* and *anybody/anyone* is the same as the difference between *some* and *any*. See 125.

116 *Much, many, a lot of, (a) little, (a) few*

1 We use *much* and *(a) little* with uncountable nouns, and *many* and *(a) few* with plural countable nouns.

much money **much** milk	**many** books **many** eggs
(a) little time **(a) little** sugar	**(a) few** jobs **(a) few** friends

We use *a lot of, lots of* and *plenty of* with both uncountable nouns and plural countable nouns.

a lot of money	**a lot of** books
lots of milk	**lots of** eggs
plenty of time	**plenty of** jobs

Note: *a lot/lots* = a great quantity or number; *plenty* = more than enough.

2 *Much, many, a lot (of)*

We use *much* and *many* mostly in questions and in negative sentences.

*How **much** money have you got?*	*I haven't got **much** money.*
*Is there **much** milk left?*	*There isn't **much** milk left.*
*Has he got **many** friends?*	*He hasn't got **many** friends.*

In affirmative sentences, we normally use *a lot (of), lots (of)* and *plenty (of)*, not *much* and *many*.

*You've got **a lot of** money.*
*There's **plenty of** milk left.*

Much is especially unusual in affirmative sentences. For example, we do not say ~~You've got **much money**~~ or ~~There's **much milk left**~~.

But we often use *much* and *many* in affirmative sentences after *too, as, so* and *very*.

*I've spent far **too much** money.*
*Take **as much** milk as you want.*
*I've got **so many** jobs to do today.*
*We enjoyed the party **very much**.*

3 *(A) little, (a) few*

A little and *a few* are positive ideas. *A little* means 'a small amount, but some'; *a few* means 'a small number, but some'.

*There's no need to hurry. We still have **a little** time before the train leaves.* (= a small amount of time, but some time)
*The exam was extremely difficult, but **a few** students passed it.* (= a small number of students, but some students)

Little and *few*, without *a*, are more negative ideas. *Little* means 'not much' or 'almost no'; *few* means 'not many' or 'almost no'.

*We really must hurry. There's **little** time left.* (= almost no time)
*The exam was extremely difficult and **few** students passed it.* (= almost no students)

Little and *few* (without *a*) are rather formal. In everyday speech, it is more common to use *not much, not many, only a little, only a few*, or *hardly any* (= almost no).

*There isn't **much** time left.*
***Hardly any** students passed the exam.*

But *very little* and *very few* are quite common in everyday speech.

*I've got **very little** money.*
***Very few** people went to the football match.*

EXERCISE 116A

Complete the sentences using *much, many, a lot (of), a little* or *a few*. Sometimes more than one answer is possible.

Examples:

There are so *many* jobs to do today and we haven't got *much/a lot of* time.
There were only *a few* people in the cinema.

1 I know _____ people in London, but not many.
2 We've got _____ coffee left, but not much.
3 He earns _____ money in his job.
4 She's got _____ classical music records.
5 We had _____ wine with our meal, but not very much.

6 Have we got _____ eggs left?
7 How _____ money did you spend on holiday?
8 I didn't enjoy the party on Saturday very _____. There were far too _____ people there, and there wasn't _____ food or drink, so everybody was hungry and thirsty.

EXERCISE 116B

Choose the correct answer.

Example:

I've got *a little/~~little~~* money, so I could lend you some if you want.

1 I'm sorry, but I've got very *a little/little* money at the moment. I'm afraid I can't lend you any.
2 He has very *a few/few* friends and he gets rather lonely.
3 She has *a few/few* friends in London and she's very happy there.
4 It is an extremely poor country: it has *a few/few* natural resources and *a little/little* good agricultural land.
5 Would you like *a little/little* more wine? There's still *a little/little* left in the bottle.
6 It won't take long to drive into town. There's very *a little/little* traffic on the road at this time of the day.
7 I think Peter went out *a few/few* minutes ago.
8 It's a very boring little town; there's very *a little/little* to do there.

117 *No* and *none*

1 We use *no* (= 'not a' or 'not any') before a noun.

*There's **no lock** on the door.*
*There are **no letters** for you today.*
*We've got **no milk**.*

We can use *no* before singular countable nouns eg *lock*, plural countable nouns eg *letters* and uncountable nouns eg *milk*.

No is more emphatic than *not a* or *not any* eg *There **isn't a** lock on the door. There **aren't any** letters for you today.*

2 *None* is a pronoun; we use it alone, without a noun.

*'Are there any letters for me today?'   'No, **none**, I'm afraid.'*
*'How much milk have we got?'   '**None**.'*

Before *my, this, the,* etc or an object pronoun eg *us, them,* we use *none of.*

***None of my** friends have seen the film.*
***None of the** photographs were very good.*
***None of us** have any money.*

When we use *none of* with a plural noun, the verb can be singular or plural.

*None of my **friends have/has** seen the film.*

A singular verb is more formal.

EXERCISE 117A

Complete the sentences using *no* or *none*.

Example:

We really must hurry. There's *no* time to lose.

1 ＿＿ of my family are rich.
2 Unfortunately, there were ＿＿ tickets left for the concert.
3 He's so serious. He's got ＿＿ sense of humour.
4 I've got ＿＿ idea what I'm going to do when I leave school.
5 ＿＿ of the students failed the examination.
6 I haven't got any money at the moment, ＿＿ at all.
7 My friends and I would all like to go to the concert, but ＿＿ of us has got a ticket.

118 *All, every, everybody, everything, whole*

1   **All** and *every*

Every has a similar meaning to *all*; *every* means 'all without exception'. Compare:
All *the students in the class passed the exam.*
Every *student in the class passed the exam.* (= all the students without exception)

Note that we can use *all* with plural words, but we only use *every* with singular words.
All children like *playing.*   **Every child likes** *playing.*

We can use *all*, but not *every* with uncountable nouns.
*Do you like **all** pop music?* (Not: ~~. . . every pop music?~~)

2   **All, everybody, everything**

a   We do not normally use *all* alone, without a noun, to mean *everybody* or *everyone*.
Compare:

All the people *stopped talking.*	**Everybody** *stopped talking.* (Not: ~~All stopped . . .~~)
*I have invited **all the students** in my class to the party.*	*I have invited **everyone** in my class to the party.* (Not: ~~. . . all in my class . . .~~)

b   We do not often use *all* to mean *everything*.
Everything *is so expensive these days.* (Not: ~~All is so expensive these days.~~)
*Have you got **everything**?* (Not: ~~Have you got all?~~)

But we can use *all* to mean *everything* in the structure *all (that)* + relative clause.
*Have you got **all (that) you need**?*
*He's forgotten **all (that) I told him**.*

We also use *all* in the expression *all about*.
*Tell me **all about** yourself.*

We can also use *all* to mean 'the only thing(s)' or 'nothing more'.
*I'm not hungry. **All** I want is a cup of tea.*

3   **All** and *whole*

a   *Whole* means 'complete' or 'every part of'. We normally use *whole* with singular countable nouns.
*I haven't read the **whole book**.*
*I've spent my **whole life** in London.*

We always use *the, my, this*, etc before *whole* + a singular noun eg *the **whole book***,
*my **whole life***.

We can also use *the, my, this*, etc with *all*, but the word order is different. Compare:

all *the book*	*the **whole** book*
all *my life*	*my **whole** life*

b | We can also use *a whole* before a (singular) noun.
*They drank **a whole bottle** of vodka.*

c | We do not normally use *whole* with uncountable nouns.
*We've finished **all the coffee**.* (Not: ~~... the whole coffee.~~)

4 | **All day, every day, etc**

We use *all* with some singular countable nouns eg *day, morning, week, year* to mean 'the whole of'; we use *every* with *day, morning,* etc to say how often something happens. Compare:

*I work hard **all day**.* (= the whole day)   *I work hard **every day**.* (= Monday, Tuesday, etc)

We can use *the whole day/morning* etc instead of *all day/morning* etc.

*We've been waiting **the whole morning/all morning**.*

The whole is stronger than *all* in this use.

EXERCISE 118A

Complete the sentences using *all, every, everybody* or *everything.* Sometimes two answers are possible.

Example:

Have you spent *all* the money I gave you?

1 The police searched ____ room in the house.
2 ____ enjoyed the film except Peter.
3 I'm really tired. ____ I want to do is go to bed.
4 Listen to me. I can explain ____.
5 Has Sarah told you ____ about her holiday in Austria?
6 It was late when Simon arrived home and ____ was asleep.
7 Did you remember to switch off ____ the lights?
8 I believe ____ word he says.
9 Have you packed ____ into this suitcase?
10 I'll do ____ I can to help you.

EXERCISE 118B

Complete the sentences using *all (the)* or *the whole.* Sometimes more than one answer is possible.

Examples:

We've finished *all the* wine.
I didn't see *all the/the whole* film.

1 ____ family went on holiday together.
2 Have you spent ____ money I gave you?
3 It's been raining ____ week.
4 Did you understand ____ information I gave you?

EXERCISE 118C

Choose the correct answer.

Example:

My favourite TV programme is on at 8.30 ~~all~~/ *every* Tuesday evening.

1 What time do you normally get up *all/every* morning?
2 The weather was terrible yesterday, so we spent *all/every* day at home.
3 Peter was late for work *all/every* day last week.
4 My neighbours had a party last night and the noise kept me awake *all/every* night.

Note

–Compare *every* and *each*: we use *every* when we think of a whole group; we use *each* when we think of the members of a group separately, one at a time.

every	*each*
*I asked **every** person in the room the same question.*	*Each person gave a different answer.*

–For *all, every* and *each*, see also 114.

119   *Both, either, neither*

1   **Both**

We can use *both* (= 'the two together' or 'one and the other') before a plural countable noun.

Both films were very good.
I spoke to both girls.

We use *both of* before *the, your, these,* etc + plural noun; in this case, we often leave out *of.*

Both (of) the films were very good.
Do both (of) your parents like dancing?

We also use *both of* before the plural object pronouns *you, us, them*; in this case, we cannot leave out *of.*

She invited both of us to the party. (Not: ... ~~both us~~ ...)

We can use *both* after an object pronoun.

She invited us both to the party.

2   **Either and neither**

We can use *either* (= 'one or the other') and *neither* (= 'not one and not the other') before a singular countable noun.

*We could meet on Saturday or Sunday. **Either day** is fine with me.*
Neither road goes to the station.

We use *either of* and *neither of* before *your, these, the,* etc + a plural countable noun.

*Can **either of your parents** speak French?*
***Neither of these roads** goes to the station.*

We also use *either of* and *neither of* before the plural object pronouns *you, us, them.*

*Can **either of you** speak French?*
***Neither of us** went to the party.*

After *neither of* we can use a singular or a plural verb.

*Neither of these roads **goes**/**go** to the station.*
*Neither of them **is**/**are** married.*

A singular verb is more common in a formal style.

(N)either has two pronunciations: /ˈnaɪðə(r)/ or /ˈniːðə(r)/.

3 We use *both, either* and *neither* to link ideas in these structures:

> *both . . . and . . .*
> *either . . . or . . .*
> *neither . . . nor . . .*

*I spoke to **both** Sally **and** Peter.*
*John is **both** thoughtful **and** generous.*
*She **both** speaks Japanese **and** writes it.*

*I don't like **either** football **or** rugby very much.*
*We can **either** stay in **or** go out.*

***Neither** Mrs Woods **nor** her husband were at home.*
*He **neither** apologised **nor** explained.*

EXERCISE 119A

Complete the sentences using *both, both of, either, either of, neither, neither of.* In one sentence two answers are possible.

Examples:

The tennis match was very exciting. *Both* players were very good.

1 'Have your parents got a car?' 'No, ____ them can drive.'

2 They don't like each other and I made the mistake of inviting them ____ to my party.

3 'What does "ambidextrous" mean?' 'It means being able to use ____ hand with equal skill.'

4 'Which of these shirts do you prefer?' 'I don't really like ____ them very much.'

5 'What's the capital of Switzerland, Geneva or Zurich?' '____. It's Berne.'

6 Simon had a very bad accident when he was younger. He fell from a tree and broke ____ his legs.

EXERCISE 119B

Link these ideas by completing the sentences.

Example:

Sue plays the piano. And she sings.
Sue both *plays the piano and sings.*

1 We could eat now. Or we could wait until later. We could either ____.
2 My father couldn't read Arabic. And he couldn't write it. My father could neither ____.
3 Ken didn't know the address. And Kate didn't know the address. Neither Ken ____.
4 I didn't see his sister. And I didn't see his brother. I didn't see either ____.
5 Simon passed the exam easily. And Sarah passed the exam easily. Both Simon ____.
6 The journey wasn't very comfortable. And it wasn't very interesting. The journey was neither ____.
7 My new flat is larger than my old flat. And it is closer to my office. My new flat is both ____.

Note

–For *both, either* and *neither*, see also 114; for *Neither do I, I don't either*, etc, see 151.

120   Personal pronouns

1   The personal pronouns are:

	SUBJECT PRONOUNS		OBJECT PRONOUNS	
	SINGULAR	PLURAL	SINGULAR	PLURAL
1st person	*I*	*we*	*me*	*us*
2nd person	*you*	*you*	*you*	*you*
3rd person	*he* *she* *it*	*they*	*him* *her* *it*	*them*

2   We use personal pronouns to replace nouns when it is clear who or what we are talking about:

a   We use subject pronouns as the subjects of verbs.

'Where's Simon?'   '*He*'s in the kitchen.'
Sue didn't go out last night. **She** *stayed at home.*

Note that in English the subject of a sentence is normally always expressed.

'Where's Simon?'   '*He*'s in the kitchen.' (Not: ~~Is in the kitchen.~~)

b   We use object pronouns as the objects of verbs and prepositions.

verb + object pronoun	preposition + object pronoun

Help **me.**
I like **him.**
Can you see **it?**

I've written to **her.**
Look at **them.**
They're waiting for **us.**

We also use object pronouns as indirect objects.

Can you lend **me** *some money?*
I'll send **him** *a postcard.*

We can use object pronouns after *than* and *as* in comparisons.

I'm older than **him**.
She isn't as tall as **me**.

But, in a more formal style, we use a subject pronoun + verb.

I'm older than **he is**.

We can use object pronouns after the verb *be*.

'Who's there?'   'It's **me**.*'

Subject pronouns are also possible after *be* eg *It's* **I**, but these are very formal and not very common.

We also use object pronouns when we use a pronoun alone in an answer.

'Who has got my book?'   'Me.' (Not: ~~I~~)

3   We use:

a   *I/me* for the person speaking

b   *we/us* for the person speaking and another person or other people

c   *you* for the person or people spoken to

d   *he/him* for a male person and for some male animals eg a pet

e   *she/her* for a female person and for some female animals eg a pet

f   *it* for a thing or for an animal when the sex is not known or not important

g   *they/them* for people or things

But see also 4–9 below.

4   We can use *you* to mean 'people in general, including you and me'.

You *can easily lose your way in Rome.*
You *can drive a car in Britain when you're 17.*

We also use *one* with this meaning, especially in a more formal style.

One *can easily lose* **one's** *way in Rome.*

5   We can use *they* to mean 'people in general, excluding you and me'.

They *say she's a good teacher.*

We use *they* to refer to the government or to people in authority.

'What are the government's plans?'   'They're going to increase taxes.'
They *say the new motorway will be finished by next April.*

6   We often use the plural pronouns *they* and *them* with a singular meaning, especially in an informal style.

*Somebody forgot to lock the door, didn't **they**?*
*If anyone phones for me while I'm out, tell **them** I'll phone **them** back later on.*

In sentences like these, we use *they* instead of 'he' or 'she' and *them* instead of 'him' or 'her' (when we do not specify the sex of the person).

7   Sometimes *we* includes the listener; sometimes *we* does not include the listener. Compare:

*Why don't **we** go to the cinema this evening?* (*we* includes the listener)	*We're going to the cinema this evening. Why don't you come with us?* (*we* does not include the listener)

8   We can use *it* for a person when we are asking or saying who the person is.

*'There's someone at the door. Who is **it**?'   'It's Peter.'*

9   We also use *it* as an 'empty' subject in a number of expressions. For example, we use *it* in expressions of time, distance, weather and temperature.

It's 8 o'clock.
It's the first of June.
*How far is **it** to the next town?*
It's usually very warm here in the summer.

10   We often begin a sentence with *it* as a 'preparatory subject' instead of beginning with a *to* infinitive or a *that*-clause.

*It is interesting **to study** a foreign language.* (Instead of: **To study** *a foreign language is interesting.*)
*It was lucky **that** we didn't miss the bus.* (Instead of: **That** *we didn't miss the bus was lucky.*)

EXERCISE 120A

Choose the correct answers.

Example:

We/Us met Sally yesterday afternoon. She/Her came to the cinema with we/us.

1 I phoned Sarah last night and gave *she/her* the message.
2 My brother is older than *I/me*, but *he/him* isn't as tall as *I/me* am.
3 'Who wants a cup of coffee?'   '*I/Me*.'
4 'Have you seen Simon today?'   'Yes. *I/Me* saw *he/him* this morning. *He/Him* was going to the swimming pool.'
5 'What did those people want?'   '*They/Them* asked *I/me* to help *they/them*.'

EXERCISE 120B

Complete the sentences using the pronouns in the box.

Example:

'I'm looking for Andrew. Have you seen *him?*'   'Yes, *he* was here a few minutes ago.'

I	you	he	she	it	we	they
me	you	him	her	it	us	them

1   Peter and I are going out this evening. ____ 're going to the cinema. Would you like to come with ____?
2   Where are my keys? I put ____ on the table a moment ago, but now ____ 've disappeared.
3   ____ 's usually quite cold in New York in the winter.
4   'What did you think of the film, Simon?'   '____ enjoyed ____ very much.'
5   ____ 's strange that Kate didn't come to the meeting.
6   'What do the government plan to do about education?'   '____ say that ____ 're going to build more schools.'
7   ____ aren't allowed to drive a car in Britain until ____ 're 17 years old.
8   If you have any problems, just tell someone and ____ 'll help you.
9   How far is ____ from Madrid to Paris?
10 My sister and I are quite different. ____ 's much more serious than ____ am.

121   Possessive adjectives and pronouns

1 | The possessive adjectives and pronouns are:

	POSSESSIVE ADJECTIVES		POSSESSIVE PRONOUNS	
	SINGULAR	PLURAL	SINGULAR	PLURAL
1st person	*my*	*our*	*mine*	*ours*
2nd person	*your*	*your*	*yours*	*yours*
3rd person	*his* *her* *its*	*their*	*his* *hers* ———	*theirs*

2 | We use a possessive adjective before a noun to say who the noun belongs to.

*I can't find **my** keys.*
*Sally bought **her** motorbike last year.*

3 | We use a possessive pronoun without a noun, when the noun is understood.

*'Is this Peter's book?'   'No, it's **mine**.'* (= my book)
*I've got my coat, but Maria can't find **hers**.* (= her coat)
*Their flat is smaller than **ours**.* (= our flat)

4 | *My own/your own/his own, etc*

We use *my own/your own/his own*, etc to emphasize that something belongs to only one person, it is not shared or borrowed. Compare:

| *This is **my** room.* | *I've got **my own** room now. I don't share with my brother any more.* |
| *This isn't **my** car.* | *This isn't **my own** car. I only borrowed it.* |

We always use *my/your/his/her*, etc before *own*. We cannot say, for example, ~~an own room/book~~ etc.

Note the structure *of my own/of your own/of his own*, etc.

*I've got a room **of my own** now. I don't share with my brother any more.*

We also use *my own/your own*, etc to emphasize that one person does something instead of somebody else doing it for them. Compare:

| *Clean **your** room.* | *Clean **your own** room! I'm not going to do it for you.* |

On my own/on your own, etc can mean 'alone' or 'without help'.

*I don't live **on my own**, I share a flat with two friends.*
*I can't move this table **on my own**. It's too heavy.*

EXERCISE 121A

Choose the correct answers.

Example:

Have you seen *my/~~mine~~* coat?

1 We know *their/theirs* telephone number, but they don't know *our/ours*.
2 *My/Mine* car wasn't as expensive as *her/hers*.
3 'How are *your/yours* children?'   'Fine, thanks. How are *your/yours*?'
4 Maria has got *her/hers* suitcase, but *her/hers* friends haven't got *their/theirs*.
5 *Our/Ours* flat isn't as big as *their/theirs*, but *our/ours* is much more comfortable.

EXERCISE 121B

Complete the sentences using *my own, your own, his own, her own*, etc.

Example:

I don't particularly like working for other people. One day I hope to have *my own* business.

1 Sarah shares a flat with some friends. She would prefer to have a flat of ____, but she can't afford one.
2 'That isn't ____ camera, is it?'   'No, I borrowed it from my father.'
3 You can wash ____ dirty clothes! I'm not going to wash them for you.
4 We helped them move the piano; they couldn't have done it on ____.
5 Sometimes I'm allowed to use my parents' car, but I wish I had a car of ____.
6 He's always using my shampoo. Why doesn't he buy ____?

Note

–We can use *by myself, by yourself*, etc instead of *on my own, on your own*, etc, eg *I don't live **by myself**. See 122.4

122 Reflexive pronouns

1 The reflexive pronouns are:

	SINGULAR	PLURAL
1st person	myself	ourselves
2nd person	yourself	yourselves
3rd person	himself herself itself	themselves

2 We use reflexive pronouns when the subject and the object of a clause are the same.

*I burnt **myself** cooking the dinner.*
***Annie** hurt **herself** when she fell over.*

Note: *enjoy yourself* = have a good time; *help yourself* (to something) = take (something) for yourself.

*Did you **enjoy yourself** at the circus?*
*If you want some more coffee, **help yourselves**.*

3 After prepositions, we use object pronouns eg *me, him* instead of reflexive pronouns when it is clear who we are talking about. Compare:

*I'll take some money with **me**. (I couldn't take some money with somebody else!)* | *I'm very angry with **myself** (I could be angry with somebody else!)*

4 *By myself/by yourself*, etc can mean 'alone' or 'without help'.

*I don't live **by myself**, I share a flat with two friends.*
*I can't move this table **by myself**. It's too heavy.*

We also use *on my own/on your own*, etc with this meaning (see 121.4)

5 We do not normally use reflexive pronouns after *feel, relax* or *concentrate*.

*I **feel** fine. (Not: . . . feel myself fine.)*
*I must try to **relax**. (Not: . . . relax myself.)*
*I can't **concentrate**. (Not: . . . concentrate myself.)*

We do not normally use reflexive pronouns to talk about actions which people usually do to themselves eg *wash, shave, dress*.

*Ken got up. Then he **washed, shaved** and **dressed**. (Not: . . . washed himself, etc.)*

But we say *dry myself/yourself*, etc, eg *I got out of the bath and **dried myself**.*

6 We can also use reflexive pronouns to emphasize 'that person, nobody else'.

*I didn't take the car to a garage. I repaired it **myself**.*
*I'm not going to clean your room for you. You clean it **yourself**!*

When we use reflexive pronouns in this way they usually come at the end of the sentence, but they can also come after the subject.

*The manager **himself** told me the news.*
*I **myself** prefer golf to tennis.*

7   Compare *-selves* (eg *themselves, ourselves*) and *each other*:

*They're looking at **themselves**.*

*They're looking at **each other**.*

More examples:

*Sue and I can take care of **ourselves**.* (= Sue can take care of herself and I can take care of myself.)	*Sue and I can take care of **each other**.* (= Sue can take care of me and I can take care of her.)

We can use *one another* instead of *each other*.

*They're looking at **one another**.*

But note that some people prefer *each other* for two people or things, and *one another* for more than two. Compare:

*Chris and Sue often help **each other**.*   *We should all try to help **one another**.*

EXERCISE 122A

Complete the sentences using *myself, yourself, himself, herself, itself, ourselves, yourselves, themselves.*

Example:

I taught *myself* to play the guitar; I've never had lessons.

1 Sue's children are too young to look after ____.
2 An elephant hurt ____ when it tried to get out of the zoo yesterday.
3 I couldn't borrow my mother's car last night because she was using it ____.
4 I cut ____ shaving this morning.
5 Mr Woods fell over and hurt ____ when he was running for a bus.
6 Would you all like to help ____ to sandwiches and cakes?
7 Sarah and I didn't really enjoy ____ at the disco last night.

EXERCISE 122B

Complete each sentence using *by* + a reflexive pronoun.

Example:

Nobody helped Kate decorate the room. She did it all *by herself.*

1 'Who did you go to the cinema with?'   'Nobody, I went ___.'
2 Since the old lady's husband died, she's been living ___.
3 Did someone help you move all the furniture, or did you do it all ___?
4 They need some help; they can't manage ___.

EXERCISE 122C

Last Wednesday Sarah stayed up very late to revise for an examination.

Sarah is explaining what happened last Wednesday night. Complete what she says by adding *myself* where necessary.

'I was really annoyed with *myself* for leaving all my revision to the last moment, so I decided to stay up and work. At first, I felt __1__ fine and I even started to congratulate __2__ on all the work I was doing. But at about 3 o'clock in the morning I started to feel __3__ tired. I went to the kitchen and made __4__ a strong black coffee. Then I went back to work, but I couldn't concentrate __5__. In the end, I started to feel sorry for __6__, so I went to my bedroom, undressed __7__ and went to bed to get some sleep. Then, of course, I couldn't relax __8__ because I couldn't stop thinking about all the work I had to do!'

EXERCISE 122D

Complete the sentences using a reflexive pronoun.

Example:

Sally didn't buy that sweater, she made it *herself.*

1 I didn't buy the cake from the shop. I made it ___.
2 'Who built your swimming pool for you?'   'Nobody. We built it ___.'
3 Did someone phone the doctor for you? Or did you phone him ___?
4 'Who told you they were moving?'   'They told me ___.'
5 Mr Mason ___ offered me the job.

EXERCISE 122E

Complete the sentences using *each other* or *-selves.*

Example:

My penfriend and I write to *each other* every month.

1 They're good friends. They like ___ very much.
2 Selfish people only care about ___.
3 We all enjoyed ___ at the party.
4 How long have you and Maria known ___?

123 Review of personal pronouns, possessive adjectives and pronouns, and reflexive pronouns

EXERCISE 123A

Complete the table.

PERSONAL PRONOUN SUBJECT	OBJECT	POSSESSIVE ADJECTIVE	PRONOUN	REFLEXIVE PRONOUN
I	me	my	___	___
___	___	___	___	yourself
he	___	___	___	___
___	her	___	___	___
it	___	___	___	___
___	___	___	ours	___
___	you	___	___	___
they	___	___	___	___

EXERCISE 123B

Complete the sentences using the correct pronoun or adjective.

Examples:

Could *you* lend *me* some money? (you | I)
Why didn't *she* ask *us* to help *her*? (she | we | she)
Do *you* ever talk to *yourself* when *you*'re on *your* own? (you | you | you | you)

1 ____ house is much bigger than ____. (they | we)
2 Is this book ____ or ____? (you | I)
3 'Is Lynne going on holiday with ____ friend?' 'No, ____'s going by ____.'
  (she | she | she)
4 How long have ____ been waiting for ____? (they | we)
5 Don't blame ____; ____ wasn't ____ mistake. (you | it | you)
6 ____ was very angry with ____ for being so stupid. (I | I)
7 ____ was very angry with ____ when ____ broke ____ camera. (he | I | I | he)
8 Someone came to see ____ while ____ were out. ____ told ____ that ____ would
  be back at 2 o'clock. (you | you | I | they | you)
9 'Who painted ____ flat?' 'Nobody. ____ painted it ____. (you | we | we)
10 ____'s a coincidence that ____ birthday is on the same day as ____. (it | he | her)

124   One(s)

1   We often use *one* instead of repeating a noun.

*My new flat is much bigger than my old **one**.* (= my old flat)
'Which of those girls is your sister?'   *'She's the **one** with the blonde hair.'* (= the girl with the blonde hair)

There is a plural *ones*.

*I like these shoes more than the other **ones**.* (= the other shoes)

2   We only use *a/an* with *one* if there is an adjective eg *a blue one*, but not *a one*. Compare:

I'm looking for a tie.	*I'm looking for a tie.*
*I want **a blue one**.*	*I want **one** with stripes.*

3   We can use *one* after the demonstrative adjectives *this, that*.

*Which picture do you prefer, **this one** or **that one**?*

But we normally only use the plural *ones* after *these* or *those* when there is an adjective eg *those black ones*. Compare:

I like these shoes more than those.	*I like these brown shoes more than **those black ones**.*

4   We use *which one(s)* in questions.

*I like the green shirt best. **Which one** do you prefer?*

5   We can use *one* after *each*.

*I've got three children, and **each one** goes to a different school.*

6   We only use *one(s)* instead of countable nouns; with uncountable nouns eg *milk, sugar* we either repeat the noun, or we can often leave it out.

*I couldn't get fresh milk, so I got powdered **(milk)**.*

EXERCISE 124A

Complete each sentence using *one* or *ones*. What does *one(s)* mean in each case?

Example:

The best road to the centre of town is the *one* on the left.   *one* = road

1 'Would you like a drink?'   'Oh yes, please, I'd love ____.'
2 My new glasses are much stronger than my old ____.
3 'Which of the women in this photo is your aunt?'   'She's the ____ with the dark hair.'
4 There are two films on TV this evening. Which ____ would you prefer to see?

Note

–In a formal style, we can also use *one* to talk about people in general. See 120.4

125 *Something, anything, somebody, anybody, etc.*

1 We can form compounds by joining *some, any, no* and *every* with *-thing, -body, -one* and *-where*.

	some	any	no	every
-thing	something	anything	nothing	everything
-body	somebody	anybody	nobody	everybody
-one	someone	anyone	no-one	everyone
-where	somewhere	anywhere	nowhere	everywhere

2 The difference between *something/somebody*, etc and *anything/anybody*, etc is the same as the difference between *some* and *any*:

a In general, we use *something, somebody,* etc mainly in affirmative sentences, and *anything, anybody,* etc mainly in negative sentences and questions.

*I've got **something** to ask you.*
*There's **somebody** at the front door.*

*I **don't** want to do **anything** this evening.*
*I **can't** see **anybody** outside.*

*Have you got **anything** to say?*
*Did **anybody** phone for me?*

b But we often use *something, somebody,* etc in questions when we expect or want people to answer 'yes', for example in requests and offers.

*Could I have **something** to eat?*
*Would you like **someone** to help you?*

For more information about the difference between *some* and *any*, see 115.

3 All these compounds *something, anyone, nobody, everywhere,* etc are singular.

***Something is** wrong. What **is** it?*
*There **was nobody** at home when I phoned.*
***Everything is** so expensive these days.*

But we sometimes use the plural words *they, them* and *their* with the compounds ending in *-body* or *-one* eg *somebody/someone, anybody/anyone,* especially in an informal style.

***Somebody** forgot to lock the door, didn't **they**?*
*If **anybody** phones for me while I'm out, tell **them** I'll phone **them** back later on.*
*Look. **Someone** has left **their** bag on this seat.*

In sentences like these, we use *they* instead of 'he' or 'she', *them* instead of 'him' or 'her', and *their* instead of 'his' or 'her' (when we do not specify the sex of the person).

EXERCISE 125A

Complete the sentences using the words in the box.

Example:

Somebody has written in my book.

something	anything	nothing	everything
somebody	anybody	nobody	everybody
somewhere	anywhere	nowhere	everywhere

1 There's ____ in this envelope. It's empty!
2 Why don't we go out ____ for dinner this evening?
3 There's ____ waiting outside to see you. She didn't tell me her name.
4 They've got ____ to live; they're homeless.
5 There isn't ____ watching the TV at the moment.
6 He lost ____ in the fire: his house and all his possessions.
7 Lynne is the only one in the office at the moment. ____ else has gone home.
8 'Shall I make you ____ to eat?' 'Oh, yes, please. I'm really hungry. I've had hardly ____ all day.'
9 It's a secret. ____ knows about it.
10 Have you seen my glasses? I've looked ____ for them, but I can't find them ____.

126 Form, position and order of adjectives

1

Form

Adjectives in English only have one form, which we use with singular and plural nouns.

an **old** man	**old** men
an **old** woman	**old** women
an **old** car	**old** cars

When a noun is used as an adjective, it does not have a plural form. Compare:

five pounds	*a **five-pound** note*
two weeks	*a **two-week** holiday*

2 **Position**

a An adjective can come in two places in a sentence:

■ before a noun

*a **young** man*	***new** shoes*
*an **empty** house*	*a **nice** girl*

■ after the verbs *be, look, appear, seem, feel, taste, smell, sound* (and a few other verbs) when we describe the subject of a sentence.

*He is **young**.*	*These shoes are **new**.*
*The house looks **empty**.*	*She seems **nice**.*
*That soup smells **good**.*	

b A few adjectives eg *asleep, alone, alive, awake, afraid, ill, well* can come after a verb, but not before a noun. For example we can say *he is* **asleep**, but not *an* **asleep** *man*. Before nouns, we use other adjectives eg *sleeping* instead of *asleep, living* instead of *alive, frightened* instead of *afraid, sick* instead of *ill,* and *healthy* instead of *well.*

a **sleeping** *man*   *a* **frightened** *animal*
sick *children*   **healthy** *people*

c In expressions of measurement, the adjective normally comes after the measurement noun.

He's eighteen years **old**.   *I'm 1.80 metres* **tall**.

3 **Order**

a When we use two or more adjectives together, 'opinion' adjectives (eg *nice, beautiful*) normally go before 'fact' adjectives (eg *sunny, blue*).

a **nice sunny** *day*   *a* **beautiful blue** *dress*

b When two or more fact adjectives come before a noun, they normally go in the following order:

size + age + shape + colour + origin + material + purpose + NOUN

a **large wooden** *box* (size + material)
an **old French** *woman* (age + origin)
a **tall thin** *man* (size + shape)
a **white plastic shopping** *bag* (colour + material + purpose)

EXERCISE 126A

What can we call these people and things?

Examples:

a child who is four years old   *a four-year-old child*
a journey which takes six hours   *a six-hour journey*

1 a holiday which lasts for three weeks
2 a man who is fifty years old
3 a delay which lasts for twenty minutes
4 a letter which has ten pages
5 a meeting which lasts for two hours

EXERCISE 126B

Which of these words are adjectives?

Example:

'You look tired.'   'Yes, I don't feel very well.'
Adjectives: *tired, well*

1 It's a very long book, but it's not at all boring.
2 Were you late for work today?
3 You seem sad. Is something wrong?
4 The boss sounded angry when I spoke to him on the phone.
5 He's quite a shy person. He often feels embarrassed when he meets people.

EXERCISE 126C

Put the words in the right order.

Examples:

is | a | generous | Kate | woman | very | .   *Kate is a very generous woman.*
look | very | Simon | angry | did | ?   *Did Simon look very angry?*

1 children | asleep | the | are?
2 very | city | is | a | Sydney | modern | .
3 building | over | old | that | 500 years | is | .
4 don't | happy | very | you | sound | .
5 a | he | very | man | healthy | looks | .
6 bridge | long | is | 1.55 kilometres | the | .
7 blue | seen | have | my | you | T-shirt | ?

EXERCISE 126D

Put the adjectives in the box under the correct headings.

Opinion	Size	Age	Shape	Colour	Origin	Material	Purpose
horrible	*short*	*old*	*round*	*grey*	*English*	*glass*	*shopping*
——	——	——	——	——	——	——	——
——	——	——	——	——	——	——	——

English   old   horrible   grey   glass   round   shopping
short   middle-aged   plastic   Italian   beautiful   sports
ugly   square   leather   red   German   small   young   white
writing   curly   large

EXERCISE 126E

Put the adjectives in brackets into their usual order.

Example:

an (German | interesting | young) woman   *an interesting young German woman*

1 a (fat | short) man
2 a (middle-aged | tall) woman
3 two (round | wooden | large) tables
4 some (Japanese | tiny) TV sets
5 a (young | handsome) doctor
6 a (red | plastic | cheap) raincoat
7 (blonde | long | beautiful) hair
8 a pair of (leather | expensive | black) shoes

Note

–An adjective normally has the same form in the singular and in the plural (see
  126.1), but note that the demonstrative adjectives *this* and *that* change to *these*
  and *those* with plural nouns eg *this man, these men.*

127 Comparative and superlative adjectives

1 Form of comparatives and superlatives

a Short adjectives

We use *-er* for the comparative and *-est* for the superlative of one-syllable adjectives.

ADJECTIVE	COMPARATIVE	SUPERLATIVE
small	smaller	smallest
cheap	cheaper	cheapest
young	younger	youngest
long	longer	longest

When we add *-er* or *-est* to adjectives, there are sometimes changes in spelling eg *big* → *bigger*. See 188.3,4,6.

b Longer adjectives

Adjectives of three or more syllables take *more* in the comparative and *most* in the superlative.

Two-syllable adjectives ending in a consonant +*-y*, change the *-y* to *-i* and add *-er* and *-est*.

A few other two-syllable adjectives also take *-er* and *-est* eg *quiet, clever, simple, narrow, gentle*.

Most other two-syllable adjectives take *more* and *most*.

Some two-syllable adjectives can take either *-er/-est* or *more/most* eg *polite, common, pleasant, stupid*.

ADJECTIVE	COMPARATIVE	SUPERLATIVE
expensive (ex-pen-sive)	**more** expensive	**most** expensive
interesting (in-ter-est-ing)	**more** interesting	**most** interesting
funny (fun-ny)	funnier	funniest
easy (eas-y)	easier	easiest
quiet (qui-et)	quieter	quietest
clever (clev-er)	cleverer	cleverest
boring (bor-ing)	**more** boring	**most** boring
modern (mod-ern)	**more** modern	**most** modern
polite (po-lite)	politer/**more** polite	politest/**most** polite
common (com-mon)	commoner/**more** common	commonest/**most** common

c | Irregular comparatives and superlatives

	ADJECTIVE	COMPARATIVE	SUPERLATIVE
The adjectives *good, bad, far* and *old* have irregular comparatives and superlatives.	*good*	*better*	*best*
	bad	*worse*	*worst*
	far	*farther/ further*	*farthest/ furthest*
	old	*older/ elder*	*oldest/ eldest*
Little and *much/many* also have irregular comparatives and superlatives.	*little*	*less*	*least*
	much/many	*more*	*most*

2 | **Use of comparatives**

a | We use comparatives when we compare one person, thing, etc with another.

*Martin is **taller** than Annie.*

More examples:

*The Amazon is **longer** than the Mississipi.*
*Good health is **more important** than money.*

After a comparative we often use *than* eg taller ***than***, longer ***than***, more important ***than***.

b | We can use comparative + *and* + comparative eg *colder and colder, more and more expensive* to say that something increases or decreases.

*The weather is getting **colder and colder**.*
*Things are becoming **more and more expensive** all the time.*

c | We can use *the* + comparative clause, *the* + comparative clause to say that two things change together or that one thing depends on another thing.

***The smaller** a car is, **the easier** it is to park.*
***The colder** the weather, **the higher** my heating bills are.*

d | Before a comparative, we can use *(very) much, a lot, a little, a (little) bit, rather* or *far* (= very much).

***very much** taller   **a lot** more important   **a little** cheaper*
***a bit** more expensive   **rather** colder   **far more** interesting*

3

a

Use of superlatives

We use superlatives when we compare one person or thing in a group with two or more other people or things in the same group.

Martin

*Martin is the **tallest** of the three children.*

More examples:

*The Nile is the **longest** river in the world.*
*What's the **most interesting** book you've ever read?*

We normally use *the* with superlatives eg **the tallest, the longest, the most interesting.**

b

Before a superlative, we often use *by far* or *easily* eg **by far** the tallest, **easily** the most interesting.

EXERCISE 127A

Complete the sentences using comparatives of the adjectives in brackets + *than*.

Example:

My brother is *younger than* my sister. (young)

1 Today is a lot ____ yesterday. (cold)
2 My new car is much ____ my old one. (comfortable)
3 This restaurant is ____ the one we went to yesterday. (good)
4 I'm a little ____ my father. (tall)
5 The film was much ____ I'd expected. (interesting)

EXERCISE 127B

Maria is a foreign student in London. She is speaking about the problems of learning English.

Complete what Maria says using comparatives of the adjectives in brackets; add *than* where necessary.

'Oh, why is English such a difficult language! I think it's *much more difficult than* (much | difficult) French. Sometimes I feel that my English is getting ___(1)___ (bad), not ___(2)___ (good)! When you first start learning English, it seems ___(3)___ (a lot | easy) other languages and the grammar looks ___(4)___ (much | simple). However, when you become ___(5)___ (a little | advanced), it gets ___(6)___ (a lot | complicated). There are also so many words in English! The dictionary I bought when I first came to Britain is far too small. I'm already looking for something ___(7)___ (rather | big) and ___(8)___ (comprehensive).'

EXERCISE 127C

Complete these sentences about the world today using the structure:
comparative + *and* + comparative.

Example:

Computers are becoming *more and more important* in our lives. (important)

1 The world's population is getting ____. (big)
2 The problem of feeding all the people in the world is getting ____. (bad)
3 Many of the world's seas, rivers and lakes are becoming ____. (polluted)
4 Life is becoming ____. (automated)

EXERCISE 127D

Make sentences using the structure:
the + comparative clause, *the* + comparative clause.

Example:

(small) a house is | (easy) it is to look after
The smaller a house is, the easier it is to look after.

1 (big) a car is | (expensive) it is to run
2 (bad) the weather | (dangerous) it is to drive on the roads
3 (old) he gets | (thoughtful) he becomes
4 (complicated) the problem | (hard) it is to find a solution

EXERCISE 127E

Complete the sentences using *the* and superlatives of the adjectives in brackets.

Example:

What's *the most precious* (precious) metal in the world?

1 Who's ____ (good) footballer in Europe?
2 This was ____ (cheap) watch that they had in the shop.
3 What's ____ (popular) sport in Japan?
4 This is one of ____ (expensive) restaurants in Milan.
5 The blue whale is ____ (large) of all the animals.
6 He's one of ____ (stupid) people I know.
7 ____ (old) university in the world is in Morocco.
8 I think that was one of ____ (bad) days of my life.
9 Sydney Opera House is one of ____ (famous) modern buildings in the world.

Note

–*Further* (but not *farther*) can mean 'more' or 'in addition' eg *Tell me if you have any further problems* (= any more problems).
–We use *older/oldest* (but not *elder/eldest*) in comparisons eg *My sister is older than me.* (Not: *... elder than me.*) We use *elder/eldest* (often before a noun eg *sister, son, brother*) mostly to talk about members of a family eg *my elder sister.*
–After superlatives we use *in* with places eg *Mount Everest is the highest mountain in the world.*
–In an informal style we use object pronouns eg *me, him* after *than* eg *You're taller than me.* In a more formal style we use a subject pronoun eg *I, he* + verb eg *You're taller than I am.* Some people think that the subject form + verb is more 'correct'.
–We sometimes use *most* + adjective to mean 'very' eg *It was most kind of you to lend me the money* (= very kind).

128 *As . . . as*

1 We use *as . . . as* to say that two people, things, etc are the same in some way.

*Judy is **as tall as** Martin.*

> *as* + adjective + *as*

*Judy is **as tall as** Martin*
*I'm **as old as** you are.*
*Was the exam **as difficult as** you'd expected?*

2 After *not*, we can use *as . . . as* or *so . . . as*.

> *not as/so* + adjective + *as*

*Judy **isn't as/so tall as** Carla.*
*Today **isn't as/so cold as** yesterday.*

EXERCISE 128A

Complete the sentences using *as . . . as* and the adjectives in the box.

Example:

'Are you *as old as* Mike?'   'No, I'm younger than he is.'

> far   expensive   ~~old~~   easy   tall

1 Jill is almost ____ her father. She's 164 cm and he's 166 cm.
2 It didn't take long to walk to the station. It wasn't ____ I'd thought it was.
3 'Was the exam ____ you'd expected?'   'No, it was much harder.'
4 Going by coach is almost ____ taking the train. They both cost around £100.

EXERCISE 128B

Make comparisons using *isn't as . . . as* and the adjectives in brackets.

Example:

Japan | India   (large | industrialised)
Japan isn't as large as India.
India isn't as industrialised as Japan.

1 a giraffe | an elephant   (tall | strong | fast)
2 iron | gold   (strong/valuable)
3 a gorilla | a human   (intelligent | strong)
4 a car | a bicycle   (expensive | fast | easy to park)

Note

–In an informal style we use object pronouns eg *me, him* after *as* eg *You aren't as tired as me.* In a more formal style we use a subject pronoun eg *I, he* + verb *You aren't as tired as I am.* Some people think that the subject form + verb is more 'correct'.

129   Review of comparatives, superlatives and *as . . . as*

EXERCISE 129A

Complete the sentences using the correct form of the adjectives in brackets. Add *than, the* or *as* where necessary.

Examples:

A mile is *longer than* a kilometre (long)
Today isn't as *sunny as* yesterday. (sunny)
What's *the best* holiday you've ever had? (good)

1 Baseball is ＿＿ sport in the USA. (popular)
2 She's much ＿＿ her brother. (serious)
3 He wasn't as ＿＿ he usually is. (friendly)
4 That was ＿＿ film I've ever seen. (good)
5 He's much ＿＿ any of his brothers. (generous)
6 You aren't as ＿＿ you think you are. (clever)
7 Where's ＿＿ place in the world? (hot)
8 Debbie is far ＿＿ she used to be. (self-confident)
9 My brother is one of ＿＿ people I know. (strange)
10 Which is ＿＿ building in the world? (tall)
11 Our holiday was much ＿＿ we'd expected. (cheap)
12 That was one of ＿＿ times of my life. (enjoyable)

130   Adjectives and adverbs of manner

1   Adverbs of manner say **how** something happens.

*She sings **beautifully**.*
*I passed the exam **easily**.*

Compare adjectives and adverbs of manner:

An adjective tells us more about a noun eg *singer, worker, exam*.	An adverb of manner tells us more about a verb eg *sings, works, passed*.
*She's a **beautiful** singer.*	*She **sings beautifully**.*
*He's a **slow** worker.*	*He **works slowly**.*
*The **exam** was **easy**.*	*I **passed** the exam **easily**.*

2   We form most adverbs of manner by adding *-ly* to the adjective.

ADJECTIVE	ADVERB
beautiful	*beautiful**ly***
bad	*bad**ly***
serious	*serious**ly***

But note that the adverb of *good* is *well*.
*You're a **good** swimmer.   You swim very **well**.*

And we use *fast, hard* and *late* as both adjectives and adverbs.

*He's a **fast** runner.*	*He runs very **fast**.*
*She's a **hard** worker.*	*She works very **hard**.*
*I was **late**.*	*I got up **late**.*

3   Not all words ending in *-ly* are adverbs. Some adjectives also end in *-ly* eg *friendly, lovely, lonely, silly, ugly*. These adjectives have no adverb forms; instead we use different structures eg *in a . . . way*.

*He said hello **in a friendly way**.* (Not: ~~He said hello friendly/friendily~~.)

4   When we add *-ly* to adjectives, there are sometimes changes in spelling eg *easy* → *easily*. See 188.3,4.

EXERCISE 130A

Choose the correct answers.

Example:

Simon is a *good*/~~well~~ guitarist and he sings quite ~~good~~/*well*, too.

1   She learnt to swim very *easy/easily*.
2   How *fast/fastly* were you driving when the accident happened?
3   He speaks extremely *slow/slowly*, doesn't he?

4   I can't sing very *good/well*.
5   I'm taking some exams next month, so I'm studying very *hard/hardly* at the moment.
6   He felt quite *nervous/nervously* before the interview.
7   This spaghetti tastes *delicious/deliciously*. You're a very *good/well* cook.
8   This is a very *serious/seriously* problem and it needs thinking about *careful/carefully*.

131 Adverbs of manner, place and time

1 An adverb can be one word eg *quickly*, or a phrase (sometimes called an 'adverbial phrase') eg *in the park*.

An adverb that says **how** something happens eg *carefully, well* is an adverb of manner.

An adverb that says **where** something happens eg *here, in the park* is an adverb of place.

An adverb that says **when** something happens eg *now, yesterday* is called an adverb of definite time.

2 **Position**

a Adverbs of manner, place and (definite) time normally go after the direct object.

> direct object + adverb

*I read **the letter carefully**.*
*We saw **Maria in the park**.*
*He bought **a camera yesterday**.*

b If there is no direct object, the adverb normally goes after the verb.

> verb + adverb

*She **drove carefully**.*
*He **lives here**.*

c If there is more than one adverb, the usual order is:

> manner + place + time

*I slept **very well last night**.* (manner + time)
*He lives **here now**.* (place + time)
*We worked **hard at school yesterday**.* (manner + place + time)

d Note that an adverb does not normally go between a verb and its direct object.

> verb + direct object + adverb

*I like **Maria very much**.* (Not: ~~I like **very much** Maria.~~)
*He drank **his coffee quickly**.* (Not: ~~He drank **quickly** his coffee.~~)
*We played **tennis yesterday**.* (Not: ~~We played **yesterday** tennis.~~)

e | Some adverbs of manner, place and time can also go at the beginning of a clause (if we want to give special emphasis to the manner, place or time).

Slowly, he started to walk away.
In London, we went to the zoo.
Tomorrow I have to go to the doctor's.

EXERCISE 131A

Complete the sentences by putting the parts in brackets in the order: object + manner + place + time.

Example:

Annie did ____ (last night | her homework | very quickly)
Annie did her homework very quickly last night.

1 You speak ____ (now | very well | English).
2 I posted ____ (early this morning | in the town centre | your letters)
3 The children have been playing ____ (this afternoon | in the park | football)
4 It snowed ____ (yesterday evening | heavily | in the north of Scotland)
5 They studied ____ (carefully | later on in the day | the map)
6 He walked ____ (out of the room | at the end of the meeting | angrily)
7 She played ____ (at the concert | last night | beautifully | the guitar)

Note

–Some adverbs of manner can go with verbs eg *He **angrily walked** out of the room.*
Some adverbs of indefinite time (eg *still, already, just*) and indefinite frequency eg *always, never* go with verbs eg *I **still love** you, He **always starts** work at 8.00.*
For details of adverb position with verbs, see 132.

132 Adverb position with verbs

We can use some adverbs eg *usually, never, always, probably, certainly, still, already, just, almost, only* with verbs:

1 | An adverb normally goes before a full verb.

> adverb + verb

*They **usually watch** TV in the evenings.*
*I **never eat** sweets.*
*He **probably knows** what to do.*
*We **still live** here.*

2   But an adverb normally goes after the verb *be* or an auxiliary verb eg *have, will, can.*

> be + adverb

*They're **usually** in bed by 11.30.*
*He's **probably** at home now.*
*We're **still** here.*

> auxiliary verb + adverb

*I've **never** eaten Chinese food.*
*We'll **probably** be late this evening.*
*I **can never** remember your phone number.*

3   When there is more than one auxiliary verb eg *have been*, the adverb normally goes after the first auxiliary.

*These curtains **have never** been cleaned.*
***Have** you **ever** been to Australia?*

4   In negative sentences, adverbs of probability eg *probably, certainly,* normally go before the negative *won't, not,* etc.

*We **probably won't** be here tomorrow./We'll **probably not** be here tomorrow.*

EXERCISE 132A

Put the adverb in brackets into the correct place (with the verb).

Example:

He'll be in Paris until next Friday. (probably)
He'll probably be in Paris until next Friday.

1 They've been trying to contact us. (probably)
2 She went to the meeting last week. (probably)
3 They take their summer holidays in May. (normally)
4 Have you lived in a foreign country? (ever)
5 I've eaten Indian food. (never)
6 Do you live in the same flat? (still)
7 He wants to borrow the money. (only)
8 I won't see Martin again until next weekend. (probably)
9 We've finished painting the outside of the house. (almost)
10 I try to go jogging at least three times a week. (always)
11 We haven't got any time to lose. (certainly)
12 I can lend you some money until next week. (certainly)
13 He's complaining about something. (always)
14 I don't watch this TV programme. (usually)

133 Time: *still, yet* and *already*

1 We use *still* (= 'as late as now or then'; 'later than expected') before a full verb, or after *be* or an auxiliary verb (see 132).

*Do you **still live** in the same flat, or have you moved?*
*'Has Andrew woken up?'   'No, he's **still** asleep.'*
*When we left the office, Lynne **was still** working.*

We also use *still* after the subject in negative sentences; in this use *still* can express impatience or surprise.

Oh, no! **It still** *hasn't stopped raining.*
They wrote to me a week ago, but **I still** *haven't received their letter.*

2 We use *yet* (= 'up to now or then') only in questions and negative sentences; *yet* normally goes at the end of a clause.

*Has Peter come back from his holiday **yet**?*
*I wrote to her a week ago, but she **hasn't** answered my letter **yet**.*

We often use *yet* after *not* in negative short answers.

*'Have you finished yet?'   'No, **not yet**.'*

3 We normally use *already* (= 'by now or then'; 'sooner than expected') before a full verb, or after *be* or an auxiliary verb (see 132).

*You don't need to tell Ken the news; he **already knows**.*
*'What time is Sue going to be here?'   'She's **already** here.'*
*'Could you do the washing up?'   'I've **already** done it.'*

We can also use *already* at the end of a clause for emphasis.

*I've seen the film **already**.*
*Have you finished **already**?*

EXERCISE 133A

Complete the sentences using *still, yet* or *already*.

Example:

Is Lynne *still* here, or has she gone home?

1 When we arrived at the cinema, the film had ___ started.
2 Paul has been looking for a job for ages, but he ___ hasn't found one ___.
3 Do you ___ drive the same car or have you sold it?
4 I wrote to them over two weeks ago and I'm ___ waiting for a reply.
5 She only started the book yesterday, but she's finished it ___.
6 'They started the job ages ago. Haven't they finished it ___?'   'No, not ___.'

EXERCISE 133B

Put the word in brackets in the correct place in the sentence. Sometimes two answers are possible.

Example:

The meeting started three hours ago and it *still* hasn't finished. (still)

1 You needn't clean the kitchen; I've done it. (already)
2 You don't need to tell me; I know what to do. (already)
3 Haven't you received your invitation to the party? (yet)
4 I can't decide what to do this evening. (still)
5 I can remember the first time I flew in a plane. (still)
6 Robert works for the same company in London. (still)

134   Time: *any more, any longer* and *no longer*

> We can use *not . . . any more, not . . . any longer* and *no longer* to say that a situation has changed:
>
> 1   *Any more* and *any longer* go at the end of a clause.
> Annie doesn't live here **any more**. She moved last year.
> My father is not a young man **any longer**.
>
> 2   Normally, *no longer* goes before a full verb, or after *be* or an auxiliary verb.
> Annie **no longer lives** here. She moved last year. | My father **is no longer** a young man.
>
> We do not normally use *no more* in this way.

EXERCISE 134A

Put the correct word in brackets in the correct place in the sentence.

Example:

I don't want to stay here. (any more/no longer)
I don't want to stay here any more.

1 Sue works for the same company in London. (any longer/no longer)
2 My brother isn't a young child. (any more/no longer)
3 Her father is unemployed. (any longer/no longer)
4 There is a large ship-building industry in Britain. (any more/no longer)

135 Adverbs of frequency

Adverbs of frequency say **how often** something happens.

Examples:

*always   normally   usually   frequently   often   sometimes
occasionally   rarely   seldom   hardly ever   never   ever*

1   These adverbs normally go before a full verb, but after *be* or an auxiliary verb.

They **usually watch** TV.	They**'re usually** in bed by 11.30
She **never eats** sweets.	She**'s never** eaten Chinese food.
I **always go** to work by bus.	I**'ll always** remember you.

When there is more than one auxiliary verb eg *have been*, the adverb normally goes after the first auxiliary.

*These curtains **have never** been cleaned.*
***Have** you **ever** been to Scotland?*

2   *Sometimes, usually, normally, frequently, often* and *occasionally* can also go at the beginning or end of a clause.

***Sometimes** I walk to work.*
*Do you come here **often**?*

3   Adverb phrases of frequency eg *every evening, once a week* normally go at the end (or the beginning) of a clause.

*They watch TV **every evening**.*
*I go swimming **once a week**.*

4   Adverbs of definite frequency eg *daily, weekly, monthly, yearly* normally go at the end of a clause.

*The post is delivered here twice **daily**.*

EXERCISE 135A

Put the adverbs in order of frequency.

seldom   never   ~~usually~~   often   sometimes not ever   frequently   ~~normally~~   ~~always~~ hardly ever   rarely

all the time   (1) *always*
(2) *normally   usually*
(3) _____   _____
(4) _____
(5) _____   _____
(6) _____
at no time   (7) _____   _____

EXERCISE 135B

Put the adverbs in the correct place in the sentences. Sometimes more than one answer is possible.

Example:

She *always* tries to visit her parents at the weekends.   (always)

1 I've seen that programme on TV.   (never)
2 He's late for appointments.   (hardly ever)
3 They go to the cinema nowadays.   (rarely)
4 Is he bad-tempered?   (often)
5 They listen to the radio.   (every morning)
6 I'm at home before 8 o'clock.   (seldom)
7 Have you had a really serious illness? (ever)
8 I'll forget our holiday together.   (never)
9 She's been interested in music.   (always)
10 I brush my teeth.   (always/three times a day)

136   Adverbs of probability

Adverbs of probability say **how sure** we are about something.

Examples:

certainly   definitely   obviously   probably

1 | These adverbs normally go before a full verb, but after *be* or an auxiliary verb (see 132).

He **probably knows** your address.
They **definitely saw** me.
She **obviously likes** you.

He's **probably** at home now.
They've **definitely** gone out.
She **can obviously** do the job.

2 | In negative sentences, adverbs of probability normally go before the negative *won't, isn't, not,* etc.

She **probably won't** be late.
He **certainly isn't** at home now.
They're **obviously not** very happy.

3 | *Perhaps* and *maybe* normally go at the beginning of a clause.

Perhaps *I'll see you later.*
Maybe *you're right.*

Maybe is quite informal.

EXERCISE 136A

Put the adverbs in the correct place in the sentence.

Example:

In the future, machines will *probably* do many of the jobs that people do today. (probably)

1 Simon is at Sarah's house at the moment. (probably)
2 She won't go to the party on Saturday evening. (probably)
3 We'll play tennis later this afternoon. (perhaps)
4 They enjoyed the film very much. (obviously)

5 You should go and see the doctor. (definitely)
6 I don't want to be home late tonight. (definitely)
7 Computers are becoming more and more important in our lives. (certainly)
8 The bridge has been repaired by now. (probably)

137 *Fairly, quite, rather* and *pretty*

1 | The adverbs *fairly, quite, rather* and *pretty* modify adjectives or other adverbs. They normally go before the adjective or adverb which they modify.

*The film was **quite good**.* (adverb + adjective)
*I know her **fairly well**.* (adverb + adverb)

2 | Compare:

```
_____●_____●_____●_____●____
 fairly     quite   rather/pretty   very
  good       good       good        good
```

a | In general, *quite* is a little stronger than *fairly*.

*I'm **fairly** tired, but I don't think I'll go to bed yet.*
*I'm **quite** tired. I think I'll go to bed now.*

b | *Rather* is stronger than *quite*; we can use *rather* to mean 'more than is usual', 'more than is wanted' or 'more than is expected'.

*It's **rather** cold today. You should wear your coat when you go out.*
*We're **rather** late. We'd better hurry.*
*The concert was **rather** good. I was surprised.*

c | We can use *pretty* with a similar meaning to *rather*; we use *pretty* in a more informal style.

*The exam was **pretty** difficult.*

d | But note that the meanings of *fairly, quite, rather* and *pretty* can depend on stress and intonation.

*He's **quite** 'nice.* (more positive)
*He's '**quite** nice.* (less positive)

213

3 | We use *quite* before *a/an*, but *fairly* and *pretty* after *a*. Compare:

*He's **quite a** young man.* | *He's **a fairly** young man.*
*It was **quite an** interesting film.* | *It was **a pretty** interesting film.*

We can use *rather* before or after *a/an*.

*It was **rather an** interesting film./It was **a rather** interesting film.*

4 | *Quite* and *rather* can also modify verbs; they go before a full verb, but after an auxiliary verb (see 132).

*She **quite enjoyed** the film.*
*I **rather like** driving at night.*
*He's **quite** enjoying himself.*

5 | *Rather*, but not *fairly, quite* or *pretty*, can be used before comparatives.

rather colder   **rather more** expensive

6 | *Quite* can also mean 'completely' with some adjectives.

*The animal was **quite dead**. (= completely dead)*

Quite can only mean 'completely' with 'non-gradable' adjectives such as *dead* (something cannot normally be more or less dead; it is dead or it is not).

More examples:

*The meal was **quite perfect**. (= completely perfect)*
*The story is **quite untrue**. (= completely untrue)*

We also use *quite* meaning 'completely' with some adverbs and verbs.

*She sang **quite perfectly**. (= completely perfectly)*
*I **quite agree** with you. (= completely agree)*

EXERCISE 137A

Complete each sentence using the correct word in brackets. Sometimes either word is possible.

Examples:

She's *quite* a generous woman. (quite/fairly)
It's *rather/fairly* cold in this room. (rather/fairly)

1 I've made ____ a stupid mistake. (pretty/rather)
2 She ____ enjoys working at night. (fairly/quite)
3 It was a ____ boring football match. (pretty/rather)
4 I'm ____ looking forward to the party on Saturday. (pretty/quite)
5 The weather was ____ worse than we'd expected. (quite/rather)
6 My grandfather was ____ an amazing man. (quite/fairly)
7 Maria speaks English ____ well, doesn't she? (quite/pretty)
8 I'm feeling ____ better today. (fairly/rather)

EXERCISE 137B

Complete the sentences using the most suitable expression in the box. Use each expression only once.

Example:

There was nothing in the envelope.
It was *quite empty.*

quite useless   quite sure   quite impossible
quite original   ~~quite empty~~   quite different

1 He's not at all like his sister; they're ____.
2 This clock keeps on breaking down. It's ____ really.
3 I like your idea. It's really ____; I've never heard anything like it before.
4 'What are you going to do this evening?'   'I'm not ____.'
5 We can't finish the job by tomorrow. It's ____.

138   *Too* and *enough*

1 | *Too* goes before adjectives and adverbs; *enough* goes after adjectives and adverbs.

*I don't think I'll go out tonight. I'm **too tired.***
*Slow down! You're driving **too fast.***

*Are you **warm enough**, or do you want me to switch on the heating?*
*He failed the exam because he didn't work **hard enough**.*

2 | We also use *too many, too much* and *enough* before nouns:

a | We use *too many* before countable nouns (eg *eggs*), and *too much* before uncountable nouns (eg *salt*).

*I bought **too many eggs**.*
*There's **too much salt** in this soup.*

b | We use *enough* before both countable and uncountable nouns.

*We can't make an omelette. We haven't got **enough eggs**.*
*There's **enough salt** in the soup. It doesn't need any more.*

We can use *too many, too much* and *enough* alone, without a noun.

*'Is there enough salt in the soup?'   'There's **too much**. I can't eat it'*
*Do you want me to lend you some money, or have you got **enough**?*

3 | After *too* and *enough* we can use *for* + object.

*This jacket is **too small for me**.*
*The flat isn't really **big enough for all of us**.*

4 | After *too* and *enough* we can use the *to* infinitive.

*It's **too early to have** dinner.*
*He isn't **old enough to drive** a car.*

5 | We can also use the structure *too/enough* + *for* + object + *to* infinitive.

*It's **too early for us to have** dinner.*
*The water wasn't **warm enough for me to go** swimming.*

6 | We can modify *too* (but not *enough*) with *much, a lot, far* (= very much), *a little, a bit, rather.*

much too *heavy*   **far too** *cold*   **a bit too** *fast*

7 | Compare *very* and *too*:

Too (but not *very*) has the negative meaning 'more than necessary' or 'more than is good'.

*She's a good worker. She works **very** quickly.*	*He works **too** quickly and makes a lot of mistakes.*
*They arrived at the airport **very** late, but they just caught their plane.*	*They arrived at the airport **too** late and missed their plane.*

EXERCISE 138A

Complete each sentence using *too* or *enough* and an adjective or adverb in the box.

Example:

Annie can't go to school today. She has got a temperature and isn't *well enough* to get up.

warm   dark   ~~well~~   early   quietly   loud

1 We couldn't see what was in the room because it was ____.
2 I couldn't hear everything she said because she spoke ____.
3 They missed their plane because they didn't leave home ____.
4 He told them the music was ____ so they turned it down.
5 We didn't go to the beach yesterday because the weather wasn't ____.

EXERCISE 138B

Complete the sentences using *too much, too many* or *enough*.

Example:

We've been so busy today we didn't even have *enough* time for lunch.

1 I'd like to go to the cinema, but I haven't got ____ money.
2 I can't drink this soup. It's got ____ salt in it.
3 Doctors say that ____ sugar is bad for you.
4 We didn't really enjoy the party; there were far ____ people there.
5 We couldn't make an omelette because we didn't have ____ eggs.

EXERCISE 138C

Join these ideas using *too/enough* + *to* infinitive, or *too/enough* + *for* + object + *to* infinitive.

Examples:

Annie isn't old enough. She can't leave school.
Annie isn't old enough to leave school.
The weather was too bad. We couldn't go out.
The weather was too bad for us to go out.

1 She doesn't feel well enough. She can't go to school.
2 The table was too heavy. I couldn't move it.
3 The children aren't tall enough. They can't reach that shelf.
4 They arrived too late. They didn't see the beginning of the film.
5 Our old flat was much too small. We couldn't live in it.
6 He spoke too quietly. The people at the back of the room couldn't hear.

139 *So* and *such*

1 | We use *such* before a noun, with or without an adjective.

She's such a nice woman.
Don't be such a fool!

We use *so* before an adjective alone, without a noun.

She's so nice.
Don't be so foolish!

We can also use *so* with an adverb.

He works so slowly.

2 | We can use *so* (but not *such*) with *many* and *much*.

There were so many people on the train.
I've got so much to do today. I'm really busy.

We can use *such* (but not *so*) before *a lot (of)*.

There were such a lot of people on the train.
I've got such a lot to do today. I'm really busy.

3 | After *so* and *such*, we can use a *that*-clause to express result (see 162.2).

The table was so heavy that I couldn't move it.
It was such a beautiful afternoon that we went to the beach.

EXERCISE 139A

Complete the sentences using *so* or *such.*

Example:

It was *such* a good film. I really enjoyed it.

1 She's ____ shy. She always gets very nervous when she meets people.
2 You shouldn't eat ____ quickly; you'll give yourself indigestion.
3 It's ____ an interesting town; there really is ____ much to do there.
4 I didn't realize it was ____ far from the town centre to the airport.

5 He felt ____ tired that he decided not to go out.
6 It was ____ a hot day that they had to open all the windows.
7 I've made ____ many mistakes in this letter, I think I'll type it again.
8 He had ____ a lot of luggage that we couldn't get it all into the car.

Note

—We also use *so* to express result eg *I was hungry so I made something to eat.* See 162.2.
—We also use *so that* and *so as to* to express purpose eg *I gave her my address so that she could write to me.* See 163.3.

140   Comparison: adverbs

1

Form of comparative and superlative adverbs

Most adverbs form the comparative with *more* and the superlative with *most.*

| *beautifully* | ***more** beautifully* | ***most** beautifully* |
| *carefully* | ***more** carefully* | ***most** carefully* |

One-syllable adverbs eg *fast, hard, late, long, soon* add *-er* in the comparative and *-est* in the superlative.

| *fast* | *faster* | *fastest* |
| *hard* | *harder* | *hardest* |

But note: *early (ear-ly)* also adds *-er/-est: earlier* → *earliest.*

When we add *-er/-est* to words, there are sometimes changes in spelling eg *early* → *earlier.* See 188.3,4,6.

The adverbs *well, badly* and *far* have irregular comparatives and superlatives.

well	*better*	*best*
badly	*worse*	*worst*
far	*farther/further*	*farthest/furthest*

2 | **Making comparisons using adverbs**

We use the same structures when we make comparisons using adverbs or adjectives:

a | comparatives (see 127.2)
*You should drive **more carefully**.*
*They arrived **later** than I'd expected.*

b | comparative + *and* + comparative (see 127.2)
*It snowed **more and more heavily** as the day went on.*

c | *the* + comparative clause, *the* + comparative clause (see 127.2)
***The sooner** we leave, **the earlier** we'll arrive.*

d | superlatives (see 127.3)
*She tries **the hardest** of all the students in her class.*

e | *as . . . as* (see 128)
*I'm working **as fast as** I can.*
*I can't swim **as/so well as** you can.*

EXERCISE 140A

Complete the sentences using the correct form of the words in brackets. Add *than*, *the* or *as* where necessary.

Examples:

Of all those cars, the Alfa Romeo goes *the fastest*. (fast)
I don't work as *hard as* Sally does. (hard)
We finished the job a lot *more quickly than* we'd expected. (quickly)

1 She always arrives at work much ____ anyone else. (early)
2 The children are behaving far ____ they normally do. (badly)
3 Of all the animals in the world, which one lives ____? (long)
4 Our new central heating system works a lot ____ our old one did. (efficiently)
5 He doesn't speak French as ____ his sister. (fluently)
6 The car went ____ and ____ down the hill. (fast)
7 They normally play much ____ they did last night. (well)
8 Andrew is studying a lot ____ usual now that his exams are getting closer. (hard)

Note

–In an informal style we often use object pronouns eg *me, him* after *than* and *as* eg *You run faster than **me**. I can't swim as well as **him**.* In a more formal style we use a subject pronoun eg *I, he* + verb eg *You run faster than **I do**. I can't swim as well as **he can**.* Some people think that the subject form + verb is more 'correct'.

141 Negative statements

We form negative statements by putting *not* (contraction *n't*) after an auxiliary verb (eg *be, have, can*).

We're leaving. ⟶	We **aren't** leaving.
They've finished. ⟶	They **haven't** finished.
He can swim. ⟶	He **can't** swim.
I may go to the party. ⟶	I **may not** go to the party.

We also form negative statements by putting *not/n't* after the full verb *be*, and after *have* in *have got*.

I'm hungry. ⟶	I'**m not** hungry.
She's got a car. ⟶	She **hasn't** got a car.

In the present simple and past simple there is no auxiliary verb, so we use *do/does* (in the present simple) and *did* (in the past simple) before *not/n't*.

I smoke. ⟶	I **don't** smoke.
She lives in London. ⟶	She **doesn't** live in London.
We went out last night. ⟶	We **didn't** go out last night.

Note that after *do, does* and *did*, the verb is always the infinitive without *to* eg *smoke, live, go*.

If there are two or more auxiliary verbs, *not/n't* goes after the first auxiliary.

He's been working. ⟶	He's **hasn't** been working.

For negative contractions eg *aren't* (= *are not*), *don't* (= *do not*), see 189.

EXERCISE 141A

Make these statements into negatives.

Examples:

I'm going to apply for the job.
I'm not going to apply for the job.
She got up very early this morning.
She didn't get up very early this morning.

1 I like travelling by train.
2 He was late for the appointment.
3 We've got a lot of time.
4 I'm enjoying myself very much.
5 Robert works for a company in Manchester.
6 The weather is very nice today.
7 She can come to the party on Saturday.
8 I've been working too hard recently.
9 She's got a very interesting job.
10 They may have gone home.
11 We saw you at school yesterday.
12 The bank opens on Saturday afternoons.
13 My sister is going to work tomorrow.
14 The telephone has been repaired.
15 We play tennis every weekend.
16 I'll be seeing Martin tomorrow.

Note

–We form negative imperatives by putting *not/n't* after *do* eg **Don't** shout. See 30.1.
–We can use other negative words eg *never* to make negative statements eg *I **never** smoke.*

142   *Yes/No* questions

1   A *Yes/No* question is a question which can be answered with *Yes* or *No*.

'*Is Sue coming?*'   '*Yes.*'/'*No.*'
'*Have they finished?*'   '*Yes.*'/'*No.*'

2   We form questions by changing the position of the subject (eg *Sue, they, he*) and the auxiliary verb (eg *be, have, can*).

Sue is coming. ───────────────→ **Is Sue** coming?
They have finished. ─────────────→ **Have they** finished?
He can swim. ──────────────────→ **Can he** swim?

We form questions with the full verb *be* in the same way.

They are English. ───────────────→ **Are they** English?

We form questions with *have got* by changing the position of the subject and *have*.

He has got a car. ───────────────→ **Has he** got a car?

If there are two or more auxiliary verbs, we change the position of the subject and the first auxiliary.

He has been waiting. ─────────────→ **Has he** been waiting?

In the present simple and past simple there is no auxiliary verb, so we use *do/does* in present simple questions and *did* in past simple questions.

They live here. ──────────────────→ **Do they** live here?
She likes tennis. ─────────────────→ **Does she** like tennis?
He enjoyed the film. ──────────────→ **Did he** enjoy the film?

Note that after *do, does* and *did*, the verb is always the infinitive without *to* eg *live, like, enjoy*.

EXERCISE 142A

Make *Yes/No* questions from these statements.

Examples:

She lives in London.   *Does she live in London?*
You'd like a cup of coffee.   *Would you like a cup of coffee?*

1 They played tennis yesterday.
2 He's doing his homework.
3 She's got a lot to do today.
4 They've bought a new car.
5 You know Simon Robinson.
6 He can play the piano and the guitar.
7 The shop closes at 6 o'clock.
8 You'd like to go swimming.
9 The job will be finished soon.

EXERCISE 142B

Complete the *Yes/No* questions, as in the examples.

Examples:

'I'll be at home this evening.'   '*Will you be* there at 7 o'clock?'
'He likes most sports.'   '*Does he like* tennis?'

1 'They visited Milan.'   '___ Rome?'
2 'She bought some coffee.'   '___ any milk?'
3 'She's got two sisters.'   '___ any brothers?'
4 'I speak Italian.'   '___ Spanish?'

5 'They've gone out.'   '___ into town?'
6 'I can play the guitar.'   '___ the piano?'
7 'He works eight hours a day.'   '___ on Saturdays?'
8 'I'm going to the cinema.'   '___ on your own?

Note

–We sometimes ask a *Yes/No* question using a statement with a rising intonation
  eg *You're ~~English~~?* We often ask in this way when we think we know something
  and we are asking for confirmation. We also ask in this way to express surprise
  eg *You're ~~only 14~~?* I thought you were at least 18!

143   *Wh-* questions

1   A *Wh-* question begins with a question word: *what, where, who, whose, when, why,
    which, how* (see 145).
    What is she reading?
    Where do they live?

2   We form questions by changing the position of the subject (eg *she, they, we*) and
    the auxiliary verb (eg *be, have, can*).

    She is reading. ──────────────→ *What **is she** reading?*
    They have gone. ──────────────→ *Where **have they** gone?*
    We can start. ──────────────→ *When **can we** start?*

    We form questions with the full verb *be* in the same way.

    He is here. ──────────────→ *Why **is he** here?*

    We form questions with *have got* by changing the position of the subject and *have*.

    He has got your key. ──────────────→ *Why **has he** got your key?*

    If there are two or more auxiliary verbs, we change the position of the subject and
    the first auxiliary.

    He has been reading. ──────────────→ *What **has he** been reading?*

    In the present simple and past simple there is no auxiliary verb, so we use *do/does*
    in present simple questions and *did* in past simple questions (but see 144).

They start work. ——————→	*When **do they** start work?*
She goes to school. ——————→	*Where **does she** go to school?*
He arrived. ——————→	*When **did he** arrive?*

Note that after *do, does* and *did* the verb is always the infinitive without *to* eg *start, go, arrive.*

EXERCISE 143A

Complete the questions, as in the examples.

Examples:

'They went to the station.'   'What time *did they go* there?'

'I've got some money.'   'How much *have you got?*'

1 'We're going.'   'Where ____?'
2 'I'm worried.'   'Why ____ worried?'
3 'I was reading.'   'What ____?'
4 'He visits his grandparents.'   'How often ____ them?'
5 'They'll do it.'   'When ____ it?'
6 'She's been waiting outside.'   'How long ____ there?'

7 'I come from Australia.'   'Which part of Australia ____ from?'
8 'I've got a car.'   'What kind of car ____?'
9 'We bought some wine.'   'How much wine ____?'
10 'She likes pop music.'   'What kind of pop music ____?'
11 'We saw a film.'   'Which film ____?'
12 'She was talking to someone.'   'Who ____ to?'

144   Subject and object questions

1   *Who* can ask about the subject or the object. Compare:

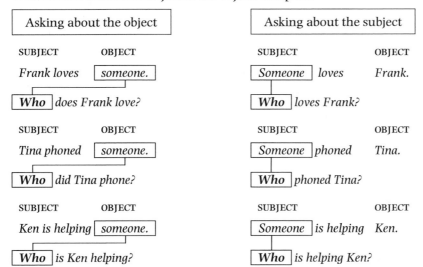

When *who* asks about the subject, the verb has the same form as a statement eg *loves, phoned, is helping,* and we do not use *do, does* in the present simple or *did* in the past simple.

223

2   We can also use *what, which* and *how many* to ask about the subject.

'**What made** that noise?'   'It was the cat.'
'**Which car goes** the fastest?'   'The Mercedes.'
'**How many people went** to the party?'   'About fifty.'

EXERCISE 144

Ask questions with *who* or *what*.

Examples:

She wants to see someone.   *Who does she want to see?*
Someone wants to see her.   *Who wants to see her?*
Someone told me.   *Who told you?*

1 I told someone.
2 Someone wrote to me.
3 I wrote to someone.
4 Something is making that noise.
5 He's making something.
6 Someone makes the decisions.

7 They helped someone.
8 Someone helped them.
9 She was looking for someone.
10 Someone was looking for her.
11 Something happened.
12 Someone lives there.

145   Question words

1   *What, who and which*

a   We use *what* with a noun (eg *what colour, what nationality*) or without a noun to ask mostly about things.

What colour is your car?
What nationality is Maria?
What is Ken doing?
What would you like to drink?

We can sometimes use *what* to ask about people.

What actors do you like?

b   We use *who* without a noun to ask about people.

Who is your favourite actor?
Who told you the news?

c   We use *which* with or without a noun to ask about things or people when there is a restricted choice.

Which colour do you like best – red, blue or yellow?
Which actor do you prefer – Robert de Niro or Dustin Hoffman?
Which would you like – wine or beer?

But we often use *who* even when there is a restricted choice.

Who *do you prefer – Robert de Niro or Dustin Hoffman?*

We often use *which one* instead of *who* or *what* when there is a restricted choice.

Which one *do you prefer – Robert de Niro or Dustin Hoffman?*
Which one *do you want – the red one or the blue one?*

We can also use *which of* . . . .

Which of *these colours do you like best?*

2   ***Whose***

We use *whose* with or without a noun to ask about possession.

*'***Whose** *book is this?'*   *'It's Maria's.'*
*'***Whose** *are these?'*   *'They're mine.'*

3   ***Where, when, why* and *how***

a   We use *where* to ask about place.

*'***Where** *are you going on holiday?'*   *'To Greece.'*
*'***Where** *does Sue live?'*   *'In London.'*

b   We use *when* to ask about time.

*'***When** *were you born?'*   *'In 1970.'*
*'***When** *is she leaving?'*   *'At 2 o'clock.'*

c   We use *why* to ask about reason or purpose.

*'***Why** *are you late?'*   *'Because my car broke down.'*
*'***Why** *did you go out?'*   *'To do some shopping.'*

d   We use *how* to ask 'in what way?'

*'***How** *did you get here?'*   *'I came by bus.'*
*'***How** *do you spell your name?'*   *'D-A-V-I-S.'*

We use *how* in greetings and introductions, and to ask about state of health.

*'***How** *are you?'*   *'I'm fine, thanks. And you?'*
*'***How** *do you do?'*   *'***How** *do you do? I'm pleased to meet you.'*
How *is your mother now? Is she feeling any better?*

We use *how* with adjectives (eg *old, tall*) and adverbs (eg *often, well*), and with *much* and *many*.

*'***How old** *are you?'*   *'I'm 18.'*
*'***How often** *do you go to the cinema?'*   *'About once a week.'*
How much *money have you got with you?*
How many *brothers and sisters have you got?*

EXERCISE 145A

Look at the answers and complete the questions using the question words in the box.

Example:

'*How old* are you?'   'I'm 20.'

> what   who   which   whose   where   when   why   how
> how often   how much   how many   ~~how old~~   how long

1 '____ do you do?'   'I'm a student.'
2 '____ do you live?'   'In London.'
3 '____ have you lived there?'   'For two years.'
4 '____ brothers and sisters have you got?'   'Two brothers and two sisters.'
5 '____ is your favourite pop singer?'   'Michael Jackson.'
6 '____ is your birthday?'   'November the 3rd.'
7 '____ do you play tennis?'   'About once a week.'
8 '____ does it cost to play tennis in Britain?'   'It's not very expensive.'
9 '____ bag is this?'   'I think it's Simon's.'
10 '____ do you usually get to work?'   'By car.'
11 '____ of those girls is your sister?'   'She's the one in the black skirt.'
12 '____ are you smiling?'   'Oh, I've just thought of something funny.'

146   Negative questions

1 We normally form negative questions with the contraction *n't*. We put *n't* after an auxiliary verb (eg *be, have, can*).

Aren't you watching TV?
Haven't they finished yet?
Can't he swim?

We also form negative questions by putting *n't* after the full verb *be*, and *have* in *have got*.

Aren't you Simon Robinson?
Haven't they got any money?

If there are two or more auxiliary verbs, *n't* goes after the first auxiliary.

Haven't you been listening?

In the present simple and past simple there is no auxiliary verb, so we use *do/does* (in the present simple) and *did* (in the past simple) before *n't*.

Don't you smoke?
Doesn't she live here any more?
Didn't they go to the cinema?

2   The word order is different when we use the full form *not* instead of *n't*. Compare:

*Are you **not** watching the TV?* | ***Aren't** you watching the TV?*
*Does she **not** live here any more?* | ***Doesn't** she live here any more?*

The forms with *not* are more formal and not so common.

3   We often use negative questions to express surprise, disappointment or annoyance.

***Don't** you smoke? I thought you did.*
***Hasn't** she finished the letter yet? She's been typing it all morning!*

Negative questions are common in exclamations.

***Isn't** it a terrible day!*

We also use negative questions when we think we know something and we are asking for confirmation.

*'**Aren't** you Simon Robinson?'   'Yes, that's right.'   'I thought you were.'*

4   Notice the meanings of *yes* and *no* in answers to negative questions.

*'**Didn't** they see the film?'   '**Yes**.'* (= Yes, they saw the film.)/*'**No**.'* (= No, they didn't see the film.)

EXERCISE 146A

Make negative questions using the contraction *n't* and the words in brackets.

Example:

I posted the letter to you over a week ago! *Haven't you received* (you | have | received it yet?)

1 Why aren't you eating your dinner? (you | do | like it?)
2 'Look! ____ (that | is | your brother over there?)'   'Oh, yes.'
3 'I really must go now.'   'But it's only half past nine. ____ (you | can | stay a little longer?)
4 '____ (it | is | a beautiful day today!)'   'It's lovely.'
5 ____ (I | have | met you somewhere before?) I'm sure I know your face.
6 'Sally is still in bed.'   '____ (she | is | going to work today?)
7 (____ you | do | want to come to the concert tonight?) I thought you said you did.

147   Question tags

1   Study the examples.

*It's cold today, **isn't it**?*
*You haven't seen my keys, **have you**?*

A question tag is an expression like *isn't it?* and *have you?* put at the end of a statement.

2   We form question tags with an auxiliary verb (eg *be, have, can*) + personal pronoun (eg *it, you*):

*You aren't listening to me, **are you?***
*You haven't seen my keys, **have you?***
*He can swim, **can't he?***

A question tag has the same auxiliary verb that is in the main clause.

If the main clause has the full verb *be*, we use *be* in the question tag.

*It's cold today, **isn't it?***

If the main clause has *have got*, we use *have* in the question tag.

*You **haven't got** a stamp, **have you?***

If there are two or more auxiliary verbs, we use the first auxiliary in the question tag.

*He **hasn't been** waiting long, **has he?***

We use *do/does* in present simple question tags and *did* in past simple question tags.

*You don't like football, **do you?***
*Simon lives in London, **doesn't he?***
*You saw the film, **didn't you?***

3   We normally put a negative question tag with a positive statement, and a positive question tag with a negative statement. Compare:

−	+		+	−

*It **isn't** cold today, **is it?*** | *It's cold today, **isn't** it?*
*You **don't** like football, **do you?*** | *You **like** football, **don't** you?*
*He **can't** swim, **can he?*** | *He **can** swim, **can't** he?*

4   The meaning of a question tag depends on the intonation:

a   If we are asking a real question, we use a rising intonation (the voice goes up).

You haven't seen my keys, ~~have you~~?  (= Have you seen my keys?)

b   But if we are sure of the answer and we are only asking the other person to agree with us, we use a falling intonation (the voice goes down).

It's cold today, ~~isn't it~~?  (= It's cold. Don't you agree?)

c   We often use a negative statement + positive question tag to ask people for things, or to ask for help or information.

−	+

*You **couldn't** lend me some money, **could you?***
*You **don't** know where Peter lives, **do you?***

5 Note:

a The question tag for *I am* is *aren't I?*

*I'm right, **aren't I?***

b After imperatives, we can use the question tags *will/would you?* and *can/can't/ could you?* when we want people to do things.

Shut** the door, **will you?
Help** me with these bags, **could you?

After a negative imperative, we use *will you?*

Don't be** late, **will you?

c After *let's* we use *shall we?* to make suggestions.

Let's** go out, **shall we?

d We use *they* in question tags after *somebody/someone*, *everybody/everyone* and *nobody/no one*.

Somebody** told you, didn't **they?
No one** phoned for me, did **they?

e We use *it* in question tags after *nothing*.

Nothing** is wrong, is **it?

f We can use *there* as a subject in question tags.

There** won't be any problems, will **there?

EXERCISE 147A

Put a question tag at the end of each sentence. Sometimes more than one answer is possible.

Example:

It's a lovely day today.
It's a lovely day today, isn't it?

1 You don't like this music.
2 Robert isn't at work today.
3 I'm too late.
4 You haven't seen the newspaper.
5 Lynne speaks French and German.
6 They didn't go to the concert.
7 You'd like to have something to eat.
8 We're leaving tomorrow.
9 You couldn't do me a favour.
10 You don't know where Sarah is.
11 Switch on the light for me.
12 Don't forget to lock the door.
13 Nobody was watching the TV.
14 Everyone will be here soon.
15 Nothing terrible has happened.
16 There's plenty of time.
17 Pass me that magazine.
18 Let's have a cup of tea.

148   Reply questions

1   Study the examples.

'I'm going to bed now.'   *'**Are you?** Oh, good night, then.'*
'He can't swim.'   *'**Can't he?** I thought he could.'*

We often answer people with 'reply questions' – short questions formed with an auxiliary verb + personal pronoun eg *Are you?* and *Can't he?*

These reply questions are not real questions; they often just show that we are listening. They can also express interest, sympathy, surprise, or anger, depending on the intonation.

2   In reply questions we use the same auxiliary verb that is in the sentence we are answering.

*'I**'m** going to bed now.'*   *'**Are you?** Oh, good night, then.'*
*'We**'ve** finished.'*   *'**Have you?**'*

If the sentence has the full verb *be*, we use *be* in the reply question.

*'I**'m** hungry.'*   *'**Are you?** I'll make you something to eat.'*

If the sentence has *have got*, we use *have* in the reply question.

*'I**'ve got** a headache.'*   *'Oh, **have you?** Do you want some aspirin?'*

If the sentence has two or more auxiliary verbs, we use the first auxiliary in the reply question.

*'I**'ve been** waiting for an hour.'*   *'**Have you?**'*

We use *do/does* in present simple reply questions and *did* in past simple reply questions.

'I like football.'   *'**Do you?**'*
'She lives in Brighton.'   *'**Does she?**'*
'We saw the film.'   *'**Did you?**'*

3   We use positive reply questions to answer positive statements, and negative reply questions to answer negative statements. Compare:

−	−	+	+
*'He **can't** swim.'*	*'**Can't he?**'*	*'He **can** swim.'*	*'**Can he?**'*
*'I **don't** like football.'*	*'**Don't you?**'*	*'I **like** football.'*	*'**Do you?**'*

We can also answer an affirmative sentence using a negative reply question with a falling intonation. This expresses emphatic agreement.

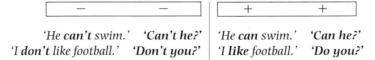

'It was a fantastic film.'   *'Yes, **wasn't it?** I really enjoyed it.'*

EXERCISE 148A

You are sitting on a park bench when a tramp comes up to you and starts a conversation.

React to what the tramp says using reply questions.

Tramp: It's a lovely day.
You: Yes, *isn't it?*
Tramp: This is my bench you know.
You: Oh, *is it?* I'm sorry, I didn't know.
Tramp: It's all right. You can sit here. You may not believe this, but I was very rich once. I was almost a millionaire.
You: ___1___? That's amazing.
Tramp: Yes, but I gave all my money away.
You: ___2___? What, all of it?
Tramp: Yes, every penny. I gave it away to my friends, to my relatives. But they didn't thank me.
You: ___3___?
Tramp: No. Still, I'm much happier now.
You: ___4___?
Tramp: Yes, I like the simple life. I like sleeping in the park under the stars.
You: ___5___ Don't you get cold?
Tramp: No, I don't feel the cold. I'm used to it.
You: ___6___? Really? Even in winter?
Tramp: Yes, I've been sleeping on this bench for over twenty years.
You: ___7___? Really? That's a long time.
Tramp: Yes, the only problem is my health. I've got a bad heart condition.
You: Oh, ___8___?
Tramp: Yes I haven't got long to live.
You: ___9___?
Tramp: No, but I'm going to enjoy my last few weeks. I'm going to eat and drink well . . . But food and drink are so expensive nowadays.
You: Yes, they are, aren't they?
Tramp: Yes, if I had some money, I'd go and have a good meal.
You: ___10___?
Tramp: Yes . . . You couldn't let me have a few pounds, could you?

149 Indirect questions

<table>
<tr>
<td>1</td>
<td colspan="2">When we ask people for information, we sometimes use 'indirect' questions beginning with a phrase like Could you tell me . . .? Do you know . . .? or Can you remember . . .? Compare:</td>
</tr>
<tr>
<td></td>
<td>QUESTION</td>
<td>INDIRECT QUESTION</td>
</tr>
<tr>
<td></td>
<td>Where is the station?
When will she be here?</td>
<td>Could you tell me where the station is?
Do you know when she will be here?</td>
</tr>
<tr>
<td></td>
<td colspan="2">In indirect questions, the word order is the same as in statements eg the station is, she will be.</td>
</tr>
<tr>
<td>2</td>
<td colspan="2">Notice what happens in present simple and past simple indirect questions.</td>
</tr>
<tr>
<td></td>
<td>What time does the film start?
What did she say?</td>
<td>Can you tell me what time the film starts?
Can you remember what she said?</td>
</tr>
<tr>
<td></td>
<td colspan="2">In indirect questions, we do not use the auxiliary verb do (do, does and did).</td>
</tr>
<tr>
<td>3</td>
<td colspan="2">When there is no question word eg what, who, where we can use if or whether to introduce an indirect question.</td>
</tr>
<tr>
<td></td>
<td>Is she at home now?
Can he speak Italian?</td>
<td>Do you know if she is at home now?
I wonder whether he can speak Italian?</td>
</tr>
</table>

EXERCISE 149A

Make these questions into indirect questions, beginning with the words in brackets.

Example:

Where is the Tourist Information office? (Could you tell me)
Could you tell me where the Tourist Information office is?

  1 When does the last bus leave? (Can you tell me)
  2 Is he over 18? (Do you know)
  3 Can she speak French? (Do you know)
  4 How does this machine work? (Can you explain)
  5 Where are you going on holiday? (Have you decided)
  6 What did he tell you? (Do you remember exactly)
  7 Will you be here tomorrow? (Do you know)
  8 Does she like horse riding? (Have you got any idea)
  9 Did you switch off all the lights? (Can you remember)
10 Has everyone gone home? (Do you know)

Note

–We also make the above changes in reported questions, eg '**Where do** you
live?' —> He asked me **where** I **lived**. See 78.

150 Short answers

1 We often answer *Yes/No* questions using 'short answers' – answers made with a subject (eg *you, he, she*) + auxiliary verb (eg *be, have, can*).

'*Are you going out?*' '*Yes, I am.*' (= Yes, I am going out)
'*Has he seen the film?*' '*No, he hasn't.*' (= No, he hasn't seen the film)
'*Can she speak French?*' '*Yes, she can.*' (= Yes, she can speak French)

If the question has the full verb *be*, we use *be* in the short answer.

'*Are you angry?*' '*No, I'm not.*'

If the question has *have got*, we use *have* in the short answer.

'*Have you got a car?*' '*No, I haven't.*'

If there are two or more auxiliary verbs, we use the first auxiliary in the short answer.

'*Have you been working?*' '*Yes, I have.*'

We use *do/does* in present simple short answers, and *did* in past simple short answers.

'*Do you know Kate?*' '*Yes, I do.*'
'*Does Simon smoke?*' '*No, he doesn't.*'
'*Did they see the film?*' '*Yes, they did.*'

2 We can also use short answers in replies to statements.

'*I'm not angry.*' '*Yes, you are.*'
'*Sue lives in Western Road.*' '*No, she doesn't.*'
'*Simon is very helpful.*' '*Yes, he is.*'

EXERCISE 150A

Complete the short answers to these questions, as in the examples.

Examples:
'Have you ever been to the USA?' 'No, *I haven't.*'

1 'Can you play the guitar?' 'No, ____.'
2 'Are you over 21?' 'Yes, ____.'
3 'Did Andrew go to school yesterday?' 'Yes, ____.'
4 'Do you smoke?' 'No, ____.'
5 'Does Sarah like tennis?' 'Yes, ____.'
6 'Have you got time for a coffee?' 'No, ____.'
7 'Is Ken working today?' 'No, ____.'
8 'Were you at home last night?' 'Yes, ____.'
9 'Will you be seeing Martin tonight?' 'Yes, ____.'
10 'Have they been living here very long?' 'No, ____.'
11 'Has Lynne got any brothers or sisters?' 'No, ____.'
12 'Does Simon want to go to university?' 'Yes, ____.'

EXERCISE 150B

All these statements are untrue. Disagree with them using short answers.

Examples:

'Rio de Janeiro is the capital of Brazil.'   *'No, it isn't.'*
'Marconi didn't invent the radio.'   *'Yes, he did.'*

1 'Penguins can fly.'
2 'The earth doesn't move around the sun.'
3 'Shakespeare was born in London.'
4 'The population of the world isn't increasing.'
5 'The Second World War ended in 1940.'
6 'Spaghetti grows on trees.'

151   *So/neither am I, so/neither do I, so/neither can I, etc*

1 | Study these examples.

'*I'm going out later.*'   **'So am I.'** (= I, also, am going out later.)
He can play the guitar, and **so can I.**' (= ... I, also, can play the guitar.)

'*I'm not feeling very well.*'   **'Neither am I.'** (= I, also, am not feeling very well.)
She can't swim, and **neither can I.**' (= ... I, also, can't swim.)

We can use *so* (= 'also') and *neither* (= 'also not') before an auxiliary verb (eg *be, can*) + subject (eg *I, he*).

We also use the full verb *be*, and *have* in *have got*, in this structure.

'*I'm hungry.*'   **'So am I.'**
You haven't got any money and **neither have I.**

If there are two or more auxiliary verbs, we use the first auxiliary after *so* and *neither*.

'*I've been there before.*'   **'So have I.'**

We use *do/does* in the present simple and *did* in the past simple after *so* and *neither*.

'*I like tennis.*'   **'So do I.'**
I don't want anything to eat, and **neither does Sue.**
'*I went to the concert last week.*'   **'So did I.'**

2 | We can use *nor* instead of *neither*.

'*I haven't got a car.*'   **'Nor/Neither have I.'**

3 | We can use *not ... either* instead of *neither* and *nor*.

'*I'm not tired.*'   **'Neither am I./Nor am I./I'm not either.'**
I can't swim, and **neither** *can you./and* **nor** *can you./and you* **can't either.**

4 | *(N)either* has two pronunciations: /'(n)aɪðə(r)/ or /'(n)iːðə(r)/.

EXERCISE 151A

Agree with these statements using *'So . . . I'* or *'Neither . . . I'*.

Examples:

'I don't like noisy people.'   *'Neither do I.'*
'I'm a very tidy person.'   *'So am I.'*

1 'I'm not very interested in football.'
2 'I enjoy travelling.'
3 'I've never been to Australia.'
4 'I'd like to go there one day.'
5 'I haven't got a very good memory.'
6 'I haven't been working very hard recently.'
7 'I often forget things.'
8 'I went to bed quite late last night.'
9 'I should go to bed earlier.'
10 'I always tell the truth.'
11 'I'd rather die than tell a lie.'
12 'I didn't tell lies even when I was a child.'

Note

–For *either* and *neither*, see also 119.2.

152 *I think so, I hope so, I expect so*, etc

1   Study the examples.

'Is she ill?'   *'I think so.'* (= I think she is ill.)
'Do you think the weather will be nice tomorrow?'   *'I hope so.'* (= I hope the weather will be nice.)
'Do you think you'll come to the party?'   *'I expect so.'* (= I expect I will come to the party.)

We use *so* after verbs such as *think, hope, expect, imagine,* and *suppose* to avoid repeating something said before.

We also use *so* in this way with the expression *be afraid*.

'Is she seriously ill?'   *'I'm afraid so.'*

2   With the verbs *suppose, imagine* and *expect* we can make negative forms in two ways:

subject + verb + *not*	subject + *do not* + verb + *so*
I suppose not.	*I don't suppose so.*
I imagine not.	*I don't imagine so.*
I expect not.	*I don't expect so.*

We always use *hope* and *be afraid* with . . . *not* (not *do not . . . so*).

'Do you think it will rain tomorrow?'   *'I hope not.'* (= I hope it won't rain.)
'Did he pass the exam?'   *'I'm afraid not.'* (= I'm afraid he didn't pass.)

We normally use *think* with *do not . . . so*.

'Is she ill?'   *'I don't think so.'* (= I don't think she is ill.)

EXERCISE 152A

Give short answers using the words in brackets. Sometimes two answers are possible.

Examples:

'Do you think it will be a good concert?'   *'Yes, I hope so.'* (Yes | hope)
'Do you think we'll be late?'   *'No, I hope not.'* (No | hope)

  1 'Are you going to sell your car?' (Yes | think)
  2 'Will you give him the money?' (Yes | suppose)
  3 'Have your parents heard the news?' (No | think)
  4 'Will you be able to help us?' (No | afraid)
  5 'Is she going to apply for the job?' (Yes | imagine)
  6 'Do you think they will come with us?' (No | expect)
  7 'Will he have to go into hospital?' (Yes | afraid)
  8 'Will you have time to go shopping this afternoon?' (No | suppose)
  9 'Do you think everything will be all right?' (Yes | expect)
10 'Does he know about the accident yet?' (Yes | imagine)

153   Defining relative clauses with *who*, *that* and *which*

1

Study the examples:

*I spoke to the woman **who lives next door**.*
*Did you see the letter **that came this morning**?*

Who lives next door and *that came this morning* are 'defining relative clauses'. These clauses tell us which person or thing the speaker means (eg *who lives next door* tells us which woman; and *that came this morning* tells us which letter).

2

We use *who* for people. Compare:

*I spoke to the woman. **She** lives next door.* *The man was very nice. **He** interviewed me.*	*I spoke to the woman **who** lives next door.* *The man **who** interviewed me was very nice.*

We use *that* for things. Compare:

*Did you see the letter? **It** came this morning.* *The keys have disappeared. **They** were on this table.*	*Did you see the letter **that** came this morning?* *The keys **that** were on this table have disappeared.*

Note that *who* and *that* replace the pronoun.

*I spoke to the woman **who** lives next door.* (Not: ~~I spoke to the woman who she lives next door.~~)

3 | We can use *which* instead of *that* (to talk about things) in a defining relative clause.
*Did you see the letter **which** came this morning?*
*The keys **which** were on this table have disappeared.*

In an informal style, it is also possible to use *that* instead of *who* (to talk about people).
*I spoke to the woman **that** lives next door.*

4 | Note that we can leave out *who, that* and *which* when they are the objects in defining relative clauses eg *He's the man **(who) we met last night.*** See 154.

EXERCISE 153A

Join each pair of sentences using *who* for people and *that* for things.

Examples:

That's the woman. She works in the post office.
That's the woman who works in the post office.
The man wasn't English. He spoke to us.
The man who spoke to us wasn't English.

1 He's the man. He painted my house.
2 What is the name of the boy? He telephoned you.
3 What's happened to the money? It was on my desk.

4 They're the people. They offered Sue a job.
5 The car has now been found. It was stolen.
6 She's the person. She gives me a lift to work every day.
7 The lock has now been repaired. It was broken.
8 Most of the people are very nice. They work in Peter's office.

154   Leaving out *who, that* and *which* in defining relative clauses

1 | *Who, that* and *which* can be the subject or the object of a defining relative clause. Compare:

Marianne is the girl ⬚ *who* ⬚ *invited us to the party.*

who is the subject: ⬚ *she* ⬚ invited us to the party

Marianne is the girl ⬚ *who* ⬚ *we met last night,*

who is the object: we met ⬚ *her* ⬚ last night

2 | We often leave out *who, that* or *which* when they are the objects in defining relative clauses.
*Marianne is the girl **we met last night**.* (We met *her* last night)
*Have you seen the book **I put on this table?*** (I put *it* on this table)

237

3 But we cannot leave out *who, that* or *which* when they are the subjects in these clauses.

*Marianne is the girl **who invited us to the party**.* (Not: ~~Marianne is the girl **invited us . . .**~~)

*Have you seen the book **that was on this table**.* (Not: ~~Have you seen the book **was on this table?**~~)

4 We can use *whom* instead of *who* (for people) when it is the object of the verb in a relative clause.

*I met a woman **whom I know**.* (I know *her*)

But *whom* is quite formal and not very common in everyday speech. Instead, we use *who* or *that* (or we leave them out).

*I met a woman **(who) I know**.*

EXERCISE 154A

Complete the sentences using *who* for people and *that* for things; if it is possible to leave out *who* or *that*, write *(who)* or *(that)* – in brackets.

Examples:

I can't find the envelopes *(that)* I bought this morning.
Have seen the film *that* is on TV tonight?

1 John Murray is the man ___ owns the Grand Hotel.
2 The man ___ we spoke to wasn't very nice.
3 This is the sweater ___ I bought on Saturday.
4 What is the name of the company ___ you work for?

5 A bi-lingual person is someone ___ can speak two languages equally well.
6 Who's that boy ___ Sally is dancing with?
7 Are these all the letters ___ came in this morning's post?
8 Have you found the money ___ you lost?
9 The people ___ used to live in that house have moved.
10 I don't like films ___ are very violent.

---

155   Defining relative clauses with *whose, where, when* and *why/that*

1 *Whose*

We use *whose* in relative clauses (in place of *his, her, their*, etc) to talk about possession. Compare:

*I've got a friend. **His** brother is an actor.*	*I've got a friend **whose** brother is an actor.*
*Those are the people. **Their** car was stolen.*	*Those are the people **whose** car was stolen.*

Do not confuse *whose* and *who's*; *who's* = *who is* or *who has*.

*I've got a friend **who's** at university.* (= who is at university)

2 | ***Where*, *when* and *why*/*that***

a | We can use *where* (for places) and *when* (for times) in relative clauses.

*The hotel **where we stayed** was very small.*
*Is there a time **when we can meet?***

b | After the word *reason*, we can use *why* or *that* in relative clauses.

*Is there a **reason why/that you don't want to come to the party?***

c | We can leave out *when*, *why* and *that*.

*Is there a time **we can meet?***
*Is there a reason **you don't want to come to the party?***

We can also leave out *where* if we use a preposition.

*The hotel **we stayed at** was very small.*

EXERCISE 155A

Join each pair of sentences using *whose*.

Example:

I know someone. His mother is an opera singer.
I know someone whose mother is an opera singer.

1 She's the woman. Her husband teaches at Annie's school.
2 He's the man. His flat was broken into.
3 They're the couple. Their children were injured in the accident.
4 That's the girl. Her friend lent me the money.
5 I'm the person. My credit cards were stolen.
6 Are you the one? Your mother phoned the police.

EXERCISE 155B

Complete the sentences using *where*, *when* or *why*/*that*.

Example:

Is this the town *where* you were born?

1 Did they tell you the reason ____ they wanted you to do that?
2 What's the name of the restaurant ____ you had lunch?
3 I can remember a time ____ there was no television.
4 The place ____ we spent the weekend was very nice.
5 I don't understand the reason ____ he was late.
6 Do you remember the time ____ your car broke down on the motorway?

156   Defining and non-defining relative clauses

1 | 'Defining' relative clauses identify nouns: these clauses tell us which person, thing, etc the speaker means. See 153 and 154.

*I spoke to the woman **who lives next door**. (who lives next door tells us which woman)*
*The house **which Sue has bought** is over 100 years old. (which Sue has bought tells us which house)*

239

2   'Non-defining' relative clauses do not tell us which person, thing, etc the speaker means; these clauses give more information about a person or thing already identified.

*Ken's mother, **who is 69**, has just passed her driving test.* (*who is 69* does not tell us which woman; we already know that it is *Ken's mother*)
*Sue's house, **which is in the centre of town**, is over 100 years old.* (*which is in the centre of town* does not tell us which house; we already know that it is *Sue's house*)

Non-defining clauses are more common in a formal style, especially in writing. When we write these clauses, we put commas (,) at the beginning of the clause (and often at the end of the clause).

*Last weekend I met Sue, **who told me she was going on holiday soon**.*
*Frank Morris, **who is one of my best friends**, has decided to go and live in France.*

3   In a non-defining clause we always use *who* for people and *which* for things; we cannot use *that*.

*She gave me the key, **which** I put in my pocket.* (Not: ~~She gave me the key, **that I put in my pocket**.~~)

In a non-defining clause we cannot leave out *who* or *which*.

*My uncle John, **who lives in Manchester**, is coming to visit me next week.* (Not: ~~My uncle John, **lives in Manchester, is coming . . .**~~)
*She gave me the key, **which I put in my pocket**.* (Not: ~~She gave me the key, **I put in my pocket**.~~)

EXERCISE 156A

Add commas (,) where necessary.

Example:
Robert's parents __,__ who are both retired __,__ now live in Spain.

1 The people ____ who live next door ____ helped us to move the furniture.
2 Have you still got the money ____ that I gave you?
3 Sydney ____ which has a population of more than three million ____ is Australia's largest city.
4 Peter's sister ____ who I've known for years ____ is a very nice person.
5 We saw Sue last night with that man ____ who works in the library.
6 The chair ____ that was broken ____ has now been repaired.

EXERCISE 156B

Complete the sentences using *who, that* or *which,* but only where necessary – leave a blank if possible. In one sentence two answers are possible.

Example:
Is that the same song ____ we heard yesterday?

1 Maria, ____ has only been in Britain for a few weeks, speaks excellent English.
2 Who was the girl ____ you were speaking to just now?
3 My sister, ____ wasn't feeling very hungry, didn't want to go to the restaurant.
4 I've lost all the money ____ you gave me.
5 This is the letter ____ came in today's post.
6 Mr and Mrs Woods, ____ live next door to us, have gone on holiday.
7 Brighton, ____ is a tourist centre on the south coast of England, is about 85 kilometres from London.

157 Non-defining relative clauses with *whose, where, when* and *whom*

> We can use *whose, where* and *when* (see 155) in non-defining relative clauses.
>
> *Tina Harris, **whose brother is the actor Paul Harris**, is a good friend of mine.*
> *We visited a town called Christchurch, **where we had lunch in an Italian restaurant**.*
> *We're going on holiday in September, **when the weather isn't so hot**.*
>
> We can also use *whom* instead of *who* when it is the object of the verb in a non-defining clause (see 154.4).
>
> *Sarah Ross, **who/whom you met in Madrid last summer**, will be at the party tonight.*

EXERCISE 157A

Peter is going to the United States next year. Complete what he says about his visit using *whose, who/whom, where* and *when.*

'I'm going to the States at the beginning of January *when,* hopefully, it won't be too cold. I'm flying to New York, __(1)__ my friend Brian has been living for the past two years. I'm really looking forward to meeting his American girlfriend Cyndy, __(2)__ I met when they both came over to London last year. Cyndy, __(3)__ brother is quite a famous jazz musician, has promised to take me to Greenwich Village, __(4)__ there are a lot of jazz clubs. After two weeks in New York, I'll take the Greyhound bus to Cleveland, Ohio. I'm going to stay there with my Aunt Jackie, __(5)__ son – my cousin Abe – I met last summer in England. Then, if I have enough money, I'll travel south to New Orleans. I hope to get there by the first two weeks of February, __(6)__ the Mardi Gras Festival takes place.'

158 Relative clauses with prepositions + *which* and *whom*

1	**Defining clauses**

We can use a preposition before *which* and *whom* eg *in which, with whom* in a defining relative clause.

*That's the town **in which he was born**.*
*The people **with whom I stayed** were very kind.*

But, in everyday speech, it is more usual to put the preposition at the end of the clause and to leave out the pronoun *which, whom,* etc.

*That's the town **he was born in**.*
*The people **I stayed with** were very kind.*

2   **Non-defining clauses**

a   In a formal style, we can also use a preposition before *which* and *whom* in a non-defining relative clause.

*She's studying chemistry, **about which I know very little**.*
*Mr and Mrs Morris, **with whom we went on holiday**, live in Bristol.*

But, in everyday speech, it is more usual to put the preposition at the end of the clause and to use *who* instead of *whom*.

*She's studying chemistry, **which I know very little about**.*
*Mr and Mrs Morris, **who we went on holiday with**, live in Bristol.*

Note that we cannot leave out the pronoun *which*, *who*, etc in a non-defining clause.

b   Note the structure *some of/many of/much of/none of/all of/* etc + *which/whom*.

*A number of my friends, **some of whom** you've met before, will be at the party.*
*He gave me a lot of advice, **much of which** was very useful.*

EXERCISE 158A

Join each pair of sentences without using *who*, *whom* or *which*.

Examples:

The restaurant was in West Street. We went to it.
The restaurant we went to was in West Street.
The woman is a good friend of mine. I borrowed the money from her.
The woman I borrowed the money from is a good friend of mine.

1   The man is Sue's cousin. I introduced you to him.
2   The hotel overlooked the sea. We stayed at it.
3   The shop is closed. I bought the shoes from it.
4   The people like him very much. He works with them.

EXERCISE 158B

Join each pair of sentences using (i) *who* or *which*, and (ii) a preposition + *whom* or *which*, as in the example.

Example:

Mr Jones is a teacher at Annie's school. I was talking to him a moment ago.
 (i) *Mr Jones, who I was talking to a moment ago, is a teacher at Annie's school.*
 (ii) *Mr Jones, to whom I was talking a moment ago, is a teacher at Annie's school.*

1   Peter's party is next Saturday evening. We are all invited to it.
2   Mr Mason apologized for the mistake. We complained to him.
3   The film *Family Life* is showing next week. I've heard good reports about it.

EXERCISE 158C

A woman is complaining about a man she really dislikes. Complete what the woman says using the words in brackets and *of which* or *of whom*.

'He's always giving people lots of advice, *much of which* (much) is complete nonsense. He also talks about all the famous people he says he knows, ___(1)___ (most) I'm sure he's never even met. He boasts about the hundreds of books he says he's read, ___(2)___ (many) I'm sure he's never opened in his life. He talks about his 'three lovely children', ___(3)___ (all) are, in fact, as horrible as their father. He talks constantly about what a good son he is, and how often he visits his parents, ___(4)___ (neither) ever actually see him. And what else? Well, he spends lots of money, ___(5)___ (none) is his, and drives two big cars, ___(6)___ (both) belong to his wife!'

159   *Which* referring to a whole clause

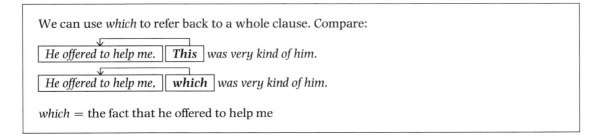

We can use *which* to refer back to a whole clause. Compare:

| He offered to help me. | **This** | was very kind of him. |

| He offered to help me, | **which** | was very kind of him. |

which = the fact that he offered to help me

EXERCISE 159A

Join each idea in **A** with the most suitable idea in **B** using *which*.

Example:

1 *She lent me the money, which was very generous of her.*

A
1 She lent me the money.
2 They had to wait for over an hour.
3 There was a lot of snow on the roads.
4 I knew you didn't want to go to the concert.
5 There was a bus strike.
6 There was a delicious smell coming from the kitchen.

B
This made driving dangerous.
It made us all feel very hungry.
That is why I didn't buy you a ticket.
It meant I had to take a taxi.
This annoyed them very much.
This was very generous of her.

160 Time: *when, as, while, as soon as, before, after, until*

1 When we want to say that things happen at the same time, we can use *when, as, while*.

When I was watching TV, the telephone rang.
As they were walking down the street, they saw Sue.
I often listen to the radio while I'm having breakfast.

Note that we normally use *when, as* or *while* + a continuous form (eg *when I was watching, as they were walking, while I'm having*) for longer actions.

We often use *(just) as* for two short actions that happen at the same time, eg *The doorbell rang (just) as I sat down.*

2 When we want to say that things happen one after the other, we can use *when, as soon as, before, after*.

When I had finished breakfast, I went out.
I'll phone you as soon as I get home.
The train had left before they arrived at the station.
After he left school, he started working in a bank.

Note that when we talk about the future, we normally use the present simple after *when, as soon as, before,* etc, eg *I'll phone you as soon as I get home.* See 22.

3 *When* can have the same meaning as *while/as, before* or *after*.

When/While/As I was watching TV, the telephone rang.
The train had left when/before they arrived at the station.
When/After he left school, he started working in a bank.

4 We use *until* (or *till*) to mean 'up to the time when'.

We waited until she arrived.
I knew nothing about it until you told me.

EXERCISE 160A

Choose the correct answer.

Example:

I'm not going out now. I'll wait *until/~~when~~* it stops raining.

1 *While/When* I had locked all the doors, I went to bed.
2 I burnt my hand *while/until* I was cooking the dinner.
3 They waited *when/until* everybody was there *before/until* they started the meeting.
4 My grandfather worked hard all his life *until/when* he retired.
5 I usually get up *before/as soon as* I wake up.
6 It started to rain *until/just as* we got to the park.
7 He dropped his shopping bag *as soon as/when* he was running for the bus.
8 The film had already started *when/just as* we sat down in the cinema.

161 Contrast: *although, even though, though, in spite of, despite, while, whereas, however*

1　We can use *although* and *even though* to introduce a contrast. After *although* and *even though* we use a clause, with a subject and a verb.

***Although** he hadn't eaten all day, he wasn't very hungry.*
*She passed the exam, **although** she hadn't studied for it.*
***Even though** the weather was bad, we had a very good holiday.*

Even though is more emphatic than *although*.

We can use *though* instead of *although*, especially in a more informal style.

***Though** I didn't feel well, I went to work.*

We also use *though*, to mean 'however' (see 5 below) at the end of a sentence.

*The room is very small. It's quite comfortable **though**.*

2　We can use *in spite of* or *despite* to talk about contrast. After *in spite of/despite* we can use a noun, or an *-ing* form.

***In spite of** the bad weather, we had a very good holiday.*
*She came to the meeting **despite** feeling ill.*

We also say *in spite of/despite the fact (that) . . . .*

***In spite of the fact that** the weather was bad, we had a very good holiday.*
*She came to the meeting **despite the fact that** she was feeling ill.*

3　Compare *in spite of/despite* and *although*:

***In spite of/Despite** the rain*, we went out for a walk.	***Although it was raining**, we went out for a walk.*

4　We can introduce a contrast between two ideas using *while* and *whereas*.

*He is quiet and shy, **while**/**whereas** his sister is lively and talkative.*

5　We can also express a contrast by using the adverb *however* with two sentences.

*She said she didn't want to change her job. **However**, she may change her mind.*

EXERCISE 161A

Rephrase the sentences beginning with the words in brackets.

Example:

She has plenty of money, but she is very mean. (although)
Although she has plenty of money, she is very mean.

1　They have a car, but they rarely use it. (though)
2　It was late and I was tired, but I didn't feel like sleeping. (although)
3　He has a number of relatives living nearby, but he never visits them. (even though)
4　She never takes any kind of exercise, but she is quite fit and healthy. (even though)

EXERCISE 161B

Rephrase the sentences using the words in brackets and a noun, as in the examples.

Examples:

They went out for a walk, even though the weather was bad. (despite)
They went out for a walk despite the bad weather.
She managed to write, even though her hand was injured. (in spite of)
She managed to write in spite of her injured hand.

1   All the trains were on time, even though the snow was heavy. (despite)
2   Our coach didn't arrive late, even though the traffic was terrible. (in spite of)
3   A lot of people buy those houses, even though the prices are high. (despite)

EXERCISE 161C

Rephrase the sentences using the words in brackets and (i) an *-ing* form, and
(ii) *the fact (that)* . . ..

Example:

He stayed up late, even though he was very tired. (despite)
 (i) *He stayed up late despite being very tired.*
(ii) *He stayed up late despite the fact (that) he was very tired.*

1   She didn't apply for the job, even though she had the right qualifications.
    (despite)
2   He stayed outside in the cold weather, even though he felt ill. (despite)
3   People continue to smoke, even though they know the dangers. (in spite of)

EXERCISE 161D

Sally and Peter are good friends, but they are very different.

Compare Sally and Peter. Join each idea in **A** with the most suitable idea in **B**.
Make sentences using *while/whereas.*

Example:

1 *She likes hard work, while/whereas he's quite lazy.*

A	B
1 She likes hard work.	He prefers classical music.
2 She likes jazz and pop music.	He prefers staying at home.
3 She likes going out a lot.	He can be rather mean.
4 She's very practical.	He's quite lazy.
5 She's very generous.	He's quite idealistic.

162 Reason and result: *because, because of, as, since, so, as a result, therefore, so/such ... (that)*

1 | **Reason: *because, because of, as, since***

a | We use *because* before a clause, with a subject and a verb.

*He went to bed early **because** he was tired.*
*We didn't go out **because** it was raining.*

We use *because of* before a noun.

*We didn't go out **because of** the rain.*
*We arrived late **because of** the traffic.*

b | We can use *as* and *since* to mean 'because' before a clause; *as* and *since* often come at the beginning of a sentence.

As it was raining, we didn't go out.
Since you haven't got any money, I'll lend you some.

2 | **Result: *so, as a result, therefore, so/such ... (that)***

a | We can use *so, as a result* and *therefore* to introduce the result of something:

We use *so* (with or without *and*) before a clause.

*He was tired **(and) so** he went to bed early.*

We use *and as a result* and *and therefore* before a clause.

*It was raining hard **and as a result** we didn't go out.*
*I failed my driving test the first time **and therefore** I took it again.*

Therefore can also go before the verb eg ... *and I **therefore took** it again.*

We also use *as a result* and *therefore* at the beginning of a new sentence.

*It was raining hard. **As a result**, we didn't go out.*
*I failed my driving test the first time. **Therefore**, I took it again.*

Therefore is rather formal.

b | We can also use *so/such ... (that) ...* when we talk about the result of something.

*The film was **so** good **(that)** I went to see it again.*
*It was **such** a beautiful afternoon **(that)** we decided to go out for a walk.*

We use *so* before an adjective or adverb eg **so** *good,* **so** *well*, but we use *such* before a noun (with or without an adjective) eg **such** *a beautiful* **afternoon**, **such** *an* **idiot**.
See 139.1.

EXERCISE 162A

Complete the sentences in **A** using *because* or *because of* and an idea from **B**. Use each idea in **B** only once.

Example:

1 *We had to walk home because we missed the last bus.*

A	**B**
1 We had to walk home ___	his bad leg
2 I didn't have any lunch ___	I thought it might rain
3 Our plane was delayed ___	I wasn't hungry
4 He went to Paris ___	~~we missed the last bus~~
5 I took an umbrella ___	the fog
6 He couldn't run very fast ___	he wanted to learn French

EXERCISE 162B

Choose the correct answers.

Example:

I haven't got much money ~~as~~/so I can't afford a new car.

1 *As/As a result* it was such a beautiful day, we decided to have a picnic.
2 It was his birthday *because/so* we decided to buy him a present.
3 *As a result/Since* all the seats on the train were taken, we had to stand.
4 The banks were closed and *as a result/because* we couldn't get any money.
5 I didn't find the book very interesting and *so/as* I didn't finish it.
6 We couldn't drive across the bridge *as a result/because* it was closed.
7 She had the best qualifications and she *so/therefore* got the job.

EXERCISE 162C

Join each pair of sentences using *so/such . . . (that).*

Example:
He's got a very good memory. He never needs to write anything down.
He's got such a good memory (that) he never needs to write anything down.

1 It was a very warm evening. We had dinner outside in the garden.
2 He was very nervous. He couldn't eat anything.
3 Our neighbours' party was very noisy. We couldn't sleep.
4 The restaurant was very crowded. They couldn't find anywhere to sit down.
5 We were all having a good time. We didn't want to stop.

163   Purpose: *to, in order to, so as to, for, so that*

1

We can use the *to* infinitive to talk about a person's purpose – why someone does something.

*I went to Paris **to learn** French.*
*I'm going out **to do** some shopping.*

In a more formal style, we use *in order to* or *so as to*.

*I went to Paris **in order to learn** French.*
*We got up early **so as to have** plenty of time.*

In negative sentences, we normally use *in order not to* or *so as not to* (not *not to* alone).

*We got up early **so as not to be** late./We got up early **in order not to be** late.* (Not: ~~We got up early **not to be** late.~~)

2 We can use *for* to talk about a person's purpose, but only when it is followed by a noun (not by a verb).

*We went to a restaurant **for lunch**.*
*I'm going out **for a walk**.*

We use *for + -ing* form to talk about the purpose or function of a thing.

*A thermometer is used **for measuring** temperature.*
*We use this knife **for cutting** bread.*

3 We also use *so (that)* to talk about purpose. We often use this structure with *can, can't, will* or *won't*.

*I'll give you my address **so (that)** you **can** write to me.*
*We'll leave early **so (that)** we **won't** arrive late.*

We often use *so (that)* with *could(n't)* and *would(n't)* to talk about the past.

*I gave him my address **so (that)** he **could** write to me.*
*We left early **so (that)** we **wouldn't** arrive late.*

EXERCISE 163A

Answer each question in **A** by making a sentence using *to* or *for* and the most suitable idea in **B**.

Examples:

1 *I'm going to the library to return a book.*
2 *She's gone to the greengrocer's for some potatoes.*

A	**B**
1 Why are you going to the library?	go jogging
2 Why has she gone to the greengrocer's?	a drink
3 Why is he taking the car to the garage?	invite me to his party
4 Why did he phone you?	~~some potatoes~~
5 Why do you get up early every day?	~~return a book~~
6 Why have they gone to the pub?	have it serviced

EXERCISE 163B

What are these things used for? Make sentences using the words in the box.

Example:

cut grass   make holes in paper   ~~show direction~~
take corks out of bottles   measure temperature

It's used for showing direction.

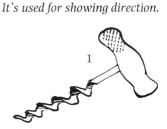

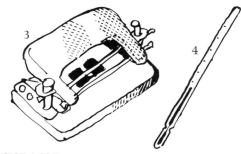

EXERCISE 163C

Join these ideas using the words in brackets.

Example:

I wrote down the number. I didn't want to forget it. (so as not to)
I wrote down the number so as not to forget it.

1 He's started walking to work. He wants to get more exercise. (so as to)
2 The government are going to increase taxes. They want to raise more money. (in order to)
3 We took a map with us on the journey. We didn't want to get lost. (so as not to)
4 They stopped work at 1 o'clock. They wanted to have lunch. (in order to)

EXERCISE 163D

Join the sentences using *so that* and the words in brackets.

Example:

She got up early. She didn't want to be late for work. (wouldn't)
She got up early so that she wouldn't be late for work.

1 He switched on the light. He wanted to see what he was doing. (could)
2 I turned down the music. I didn't want to disturb the neighbours. (wouldn't)
3 She repeated everything. She wanted us to remember it. (would)
4 She's saving money. She wants to buy a new car. (can)

164   Purpose: *in case*

1 We use *in case* to talk about things we do in order to be ready or safe because perhaps something else will happen.

*Take an umbrella with you **in case** it rains.* (... because perhaps it will rain.)
*I'll take some food with me **in case** I'm hungry on the journey.* (... because perhaps I will be hungry on the journey.)
*I'll write down the telephone number **in case** I forget it.* (... because perhaps I will forget it.)

After *in case*, we use the present simple to talk about the future eg *. . . in case I forget it.* See 22.

2   Compare *if* (see 66) and *in case*:

*We'll buy another concert ticket **if** Simon wants to come with us.* (We will wait and see if Simon wants to come before we buy another ticket.)	*We'll buy another concert ticket **in case** Simon wants to come with us.* (We will buy another ticket now. Then we will already have a ticket for Simon if he wants to come.)

3   We can use *in case* to talk about the past.

*I wrote down the phone number **in case** I **forgot** it.*
*We bought another concert ticket **in case** Simon **wanted** to come with us.*

4   After *in case*, we can use *should* when a possibility is less sure. Compare:

*Take an umbrella with you **in case** it **rains**.* (I think perhaps it will rain.)	*Take an umbrella with you **in case** it **should rain**.* (I am less sure it will rain.)

EXERCISE 164A

You are going away on a camping holiday in Britain. Here are some of the things you are taking with you: **1** a raincoat   **2** some warm underwear   **3** a map   **4** a medical kit   **5** a tennis racket   **6** some water

Why are you taking each of these things? Find the reasons in the box and make sentences: *I'm taking . . . in case . . . .*

Example:

1 *I'm taking a raincoat in case it rains.*

> You might become ill.
> It might get cold.
> You might have the chance to play tennis.
> ~~It might rain~~.
> You might get lost.
> You might get thirsty on the journey.

EXERCISE 164B

Complete the sentences using *if* or *in case*.

Example:

I'll write down the address *in case* I forget it.

1 We'll walk home ____ we miss the last bus.
2 Go and see the doctor ____ you don't feel well.
3 You should carry some kind of identification with you ____ you have an accident.
4 I'll come and see you later today ____ I have enough time.
5 We'll close all the windows ____ it rains while we're out.

Note

–The expression *in case of* is different to *in case*. *In case of*, which is often found in notices, means 'if something happens' eg **In case of** *fire, press the alarm.* (= If there is a fire . . .).

165　Place: *in, at, on*

1　We use *in* when we think of a place as three-dimensional.

Simon is **in** his room.
*Do you like swimming **in** the sea?*

We also use *in* when we think of a place as an area.

*We went for a walk **in** the park.*
*He's got a flat **in** Milan.*

2　We use *at* when we think a a place as a point.

*I waited **at** the bus stop for twenty minutes.*
*I'll meet you **at** the station.* (a meeting point)

3　We use *on* when we think of a place as a surface.

*What's that **on** the floor?*
*I'll put this picture **on** the wall.*

We also use *on* when we think of a place as a line.

*Memphis is **on** the Mississippi River.*
*Brighton is **on** the south coast of England.*

4　With cities, towns and villages, we use *at* when we think of the place as a point eg a point on a journey.

*Our train stops **at** Brighton.*

But we use *in* when we think of the place itself eg *He's got a flat **in** Milan.*

5　With buildings, we can often use *at* or *in*.

*We had lunch **at/in** Luigi's restaurant.*
*She works **at/in** the post office.*

We normally prefer *at* when we think of the building quite generally as a place where something happens.

*'Where were you last night?'　'I was **at** the cinema.'*
*My brother is **at** university.*

But we use *in* when we think of the building itself. Compare:

*We stayed **at** the Queens Hotel.*　　|　*There are fifty bedrooms **in** the Queens Hotel.*

6　With addresses, we use *at* when we give the house number; in British English, we use *in* when we just give the name of the street.

*I live **at** 42 East Street.*　　|　*I live **in** East Street.*

We use *on* for the number of the floor eg *I live in a flat **on** the first floor/second floor etc.*

EXERCISE 165A

Complete the sentences using the prepositions *at*, *in* or *on*. Sometimes more than
one answer is possible.

Example:

What have you got *in* your pocket?

1 There's some tea ____ the shelf ____ the cupboard.
2 Does your train stop ____ Lyon?
3 My friend works ____ a chemist's ____ the town centre.
4 Turin is ____ the north of Italy, ____ the River Po.
5 Shall we meet ____ the coach station?
6 'Is Ken ____ the living room?'   'No, he's ____ the garden.'
7 They're staying ____ the Metropole Hotel while they are ____ Brighton.
8 Rio de Janeiro is ____ the south-east coast of Brazil.
9 There's a chemist's ____ the corner ____ the end of the street.
10 We had lunch ____ Mario's cafe ____ Main Road ____ our way home.

166   Place and movement: *in, into, out of, on, onto, off, inside, outside*

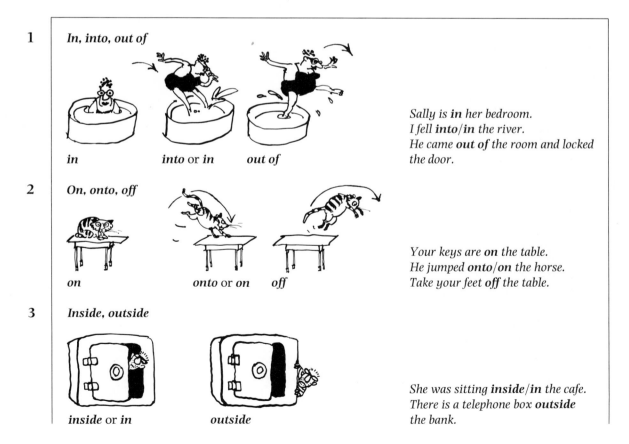

1   **In, into, out of**

in   *into* or *in*   *out of*

Sally is **in** her bedroom.
I fell **into**/**in** the river.
He came **out of** the room and locked
the door.

2   **On, onto, off**

on   *onto* or *on*   *off*

Your keys are **on** the table.
He jumped **onto**/**on** the horse.
Take your feet **off** the table.

3   **Inside, outside**

inside or *in*   *outside*

She was sitting **inside**/**in** the cafe.
There is a telephone box **outside**
the bank.

4 | Note that we use *in* with cars, but *on* with public transport eg buses, trains.

I usually go to work in my car.
Did you come to school on the bus?

We say *get in(to)/out of* a car, but *get on(to)/off* a bus, train, etc.

She got into her car and drove away.
Two policemen got on the train at Oxford.

For *by car/train* etc, see 175.

EXERCISE 166A

Complete each sentence using the most suitable preposition in the box. Sometimes more than one answer is possible.

Example:

There was an envelope lying *on* the floor.

| in   into   out of   on   onto   off   inside   outside |

1 Ken fell ____ the ladder when he was changing the light bulb.
2 Andrew normally goes to school ____ the bus.
3 When I was ____ my hotel room, I started to take my clothes ____ my suitcase.
4 There's a bus stop right ____ our house.
5 Sally came ____ the house, got ____ her motorbike and rode away.
6 My car broke down this morning so I went to work ____ a taxi.
7 The cat jumped ____ the roof of the car and looked down at the dog.
8 Annie jumped ____ the diving board ____ the swimming pool.
9 Robert came ____ the telephone box and got ____ his car.

167   Place and movement: *above, below, over, under, underneath, on top of*

1 | *Above* and *over* can both mean 'higher than'; *below* and *under* can both mean 'lower than':

a | *Over* and *under* describe a direct vertical relationship.

Ⓐ
|
Ⓑ

A is over B.
B is under A.

The nurse leaned over the sick child.
I pushed the letter under the door.

b We use *above* and *below* when one thing is not directly over or under another thing.

*A is **above** B.*
*B is **below** A.*

*We stayed at a hotel **above** the lake.*
*From the top of the hill we could see a house **below** us in the valley.*

c We use *over* to mean 'covering' and *under* to mean 'covered by'.

*He put his hand **over** his face.*
*What are you wearing **under** your coat?*

d We use *over* to mean 'across' (see also 168.5).

*We walked **over** the fields to the village.*

2 We can use *underneath* instead of *under*.

*What are you wearing **underneath** your coat?*

3 We use *on top of* to mean that one thing is 'over and touching' another thing.

*The magazine is **on top of** the fridge.*

EXERCISE 167A

Choose the correct preposition.

Example:

I found some money on the floor *under/~~below~~* the sofa.

1 The house was on a hill *above/over* the village.
2 The cat was sitting *below/under* the kitchen table.
3 On our way to the village we drove *above/over* a small bridge.
4 There are some old shoes *above/on top of* the wardrobe.
5 He sat down *below/under* an apple tree.
6 She was wearing a long dress *below/underneath* her raincoat.

168 Other prepositions of place and movement

1   *In front of, behind*

in front of   **behind**

*I'll meet you **in front of** the post office.*
*There is someone hiding **behind** that tree.*

2   *Opposite, between*

opposite   **between**

*The bank is **opposite** the cinema.*
*There is a coach service **between** Sydney and Melbourne.*

3   *Near, next to, by, beside*

near   **next to**

*They live **near** the sea.*
*The police station is **next to** the cinema.*

By and *beside* both mean 'at the side of'.
*Come and sit **by**/**beside** me.*

4   *Along, across, through*

along   **across**   **through**

*They walked **along** the street looking in all the shop windows.*
*A small bridge goes **across** the river.*
*We drove **through** the city.*

5   ***Across, over***

We use both *across* and *over* to mean 'on the other side of' or 'to the other side of'.

*The cafe is just **across**/**over** the road.*   *A small bridge goes **across**/**over** the river.*

We prefer *over* for movement to the other side of something high.
*He climbed **over** the wall.* (Not: . . . ~~across the wall.~~)

6   ***Up, down***

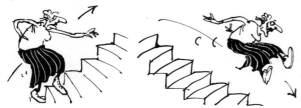

up   **down**

*She went **up** the stairs. Then she came **down** again.*

7   ***Past, (a)round***

past

*He just walked **past** me without saying anything.*

We use *round* for position or movement in a circle or in a curve.

round   **round**

*They were all sitting **round** the table.*
*I live just **round** the corner.*

We also use *round* to mean 'into all parts of' or 'all over (a place)'.
*We walked **round** the town centre.*

We can use *around* instead of *round* eg *We walked **around** the town centre.*

257

8 | *From, to, towards*

We flew from Paris to Madrid.
Who is that woman walking towards us?

9 | *Get to, arrive at/in*

We say *arrive in/at* (a place), but *get to* (a place).

She arrived in/got to Paris last night.

We say *arrive in* a country or town, but *arrive at* with other places.

She arrived in France/Paris last night.
She arrived at the hotel just after 10 o'clock.

10 | When we talk about movement, we do not use a preposition before *home*.

I went home after school.

To talk about position, we say *at home*.

I was at home last night.

EXERCISE 168A

Complete the sentences using the most suitable prepositions in the box. Sometimes
more than one answer is possible.

through	across	up	down	in	~~round~~	between	along	to	opposite	
in front of	next to	from	at	towards	behind	over	past			

Example:
What's that you've tied *round* your waist?

1 I was sitting ____ the driver in the back seat of the car.
2 A tall man was sitting ____ me at the cinema and I couldn't see much of the film.
3 There is a shoe shop ____ the chemist's and the library.
4 We walked ____ the stairs to the top floor, then we walked ____ to the bottom again.
5 What time did you arrive ____ work yesterday?
6 Who was the first person to swim ____ the Atlantic?
7 There was a woman sitting ____ the driver ____ the front passenger seat of the car.
8 We're flying ____ Paris ____ Amsterdam tomorrow. We arrive ____ Amsterdam at 6.00.
9 I got ____ the cinema late and missed the beginning of the film.
10 There's a post office right ____ my office. You can see it from my window.
11 The burglars got into the building by climbing ____ a window.
12 We were driving ____ the road looking for a petrol station for about half an hour.
13 We walked ____ the bridge to the other side of the river.
14 The dog jumped ____ the wall into someone's garden.
15 When the bus came I put out my hand, but it just went ____ me without stopping.
16 We couldn't see the man's face because he was standing with his back ____ us.

169 Time: *at, in, on*

1

We use *at, in* and *on* in these ways:

at + a time of the day	***at** 2 o'clock* ***at** 6.30* ***at** midnight* ***at** noon* (= 12 o'clock in the daytime) ***at** lunchtime*
in + a part of the day But we say *at night*.	***in** the morning* ***in** the afternoon* ***in** the evening*
on + a day	***on** Monday* ***on** Wednesday* ***on** Saturday* ***on** Christmas day*
on + a day + a part of the day	***on** Monday morning* ***on** Wednesday evening* ***on** Saturday night*
on + a date	***on** 4th July* ***on** 1st January*
at + weekends	***at** the weekend* ***at** weekends*
at + public holiday periods	***at** Christmas* ***at** Easter*
in + longer periods eg months, seasons, years etc.	***in** July* ***in** the summer* ***in** 1968* ***in** the 19th century*

2

We do not use *at, on* or *in* before *next, last, this, every, all, each, some, any* and *one*.

*We're leaving **next Monday**.*
*I'll see you **this evening**.*
*They play tennis **every weekend**.*

We do not use *at, on* or *in* before *tomorrow* and *yesterday*.

*What are you doing **tomorrow evening**?*

3

We normally leave out *at* when we ask *(At) what time . . .?*

***What time** are you leaving?*

4

We also use *in* to talk about a period of time in the future.

*I'll be finished **in half an hour**.* (= half an hour from now)
*We're meeting **in two weeks**.* (= two weeks from now)

Note the expression *in . . . 's/' time*.

*We're meeting **in a week's time**.*

We also use *in* to say how long something takes.

*I can walk from my house to the town centre **in twenty minutes**.* (= it takes me twenty minutes to do this)

EXERCISE 169A

Add *at, on* or *in* where necessary.

Example:

Can you meet me *at* 2 o'clock ⸗ next Saturday afternoon?

1 Kate doesn't normally work ____ weekends, but she had to work ____ last Saturday.
2 We're leaving ____ tomorrow morning, but we'll be back ____ three weeks' time.
3 Did she send you a card ____ your birthday?
4 ____ what time does the meeting start ____ Monday?
5 I can normally get home from work ____ about half an hour ____ Friday evenings.
6 They went on holiday to Spain ____ Easter and then again ____ the summer.
7 The bridge was built ____ the 16th century.
8 Do you enjoy driving ____ night?
9 I'm taking my driving test ____ 4.30 ____ July 3rd.
10 He was born ____ 1900 and died ____ 1972.
11 We'd better leave ____ a few minutes or we'll miss our train.

170   *On time* and *in time*

1	*On time* means 'at exactly the right time'. *The 1 o'clock train arrived **on time**.* (= it arrived at 1 o'clock) *Please try to be **on time** for the meeting tomorrow.* (= be there at the right time; don't be late)
2	*In time* means 'early enough'. *We arrived at the station **in time** to catch the train.* (= early enough to catch it) *I won't be home **in time** for dinner tonight.* (= early enough for dinner)

EXERCISE 170A

Complete the sentences using *on time* or *in time*.

Example:

I didn't arrive *in time* to see her before she left.

1 The bus service is terrible; the buses are never ____.
2 I hope my car will be repaired ____ for the weekend.
3 She's very punctual. She always arrives ____.
4 She didn't arrive ____ to say goodbye to him.
5 I don't think I'll be home ____ to see the film on TV this evening.

171 *At the end* and *in the end*

1   *At the end* means 'at the point where something stops'.

*We're going on holiday **at the end** of this week.*
***At the end** of the film I felt very sad.*

2   *In the end* means 'finally' or 'after some time'.

*We couldn't decide what to do yesterday evening. **In the end** we decided to stay at home.*
*At first, I didn't like him, but **in the end** we became good friends.*

EXERCISE 171A

Complete the sentences using *at the end* or *in the end*.

Example:

We were going to walk home, but *in the end* we decided to take a taxi.

1 I hated school at first, but ____ I quite enjoyed it.
2 They're going to Italy ____ of next week.
3 At first, he didn't want to come with us on holiday, but ____ he changed his mind.
4 I looked everywhere for my wallet and ____ I found it in my jacket.
5 She's starting work ____ of August.
6 We were all exhausted ____ of the journey.

172 Time: *in, during, for, while*

1   **In and during**

a   We can use both *during* and *in* to refer to a period of time, often with the same meaning.

*We were in Rome **during**/**in** the summer.*
*It rained **during**/**in** the night.*

b   We prefer *during* to say that something continues all through a period.

*We were in Rome **during** the whole of the summer.* (Not: ~~... in the whole of the summer.~~)

c   We use *during*, not *in*, to refer to an activity eg a visit or a meal (rather than a period of time).

*We visited the Colosseum **during** our visit to Rome.* (Not: ~~... in our visit to Rome.~~)
***During** lunch I explained my plans.* (Not: ~~In lunch ...~~)

2   **During, for and while**

a   *During* says when something happens; *for* says how long something continues.
Compare:

*It rained **during** the morning.*	*It rained **for** three hours.*
*We were in Rome **during** the summer.*	*We were in Rome **for** ten days.*

b | *While* has the same meaning as *during*. We use *during* + noun; but *while* + clause. Compare:

> | *during* + noun | | *while* + clause |

I met Sue **during my holidays**.
It started to rain **during the picnic**.

I met Sue **while I was on holiday**.
It started to rain **while they were having a picnic**.

EXERCISE 172A

Complete the sentences using *during, in, for* or *while*. Sometimes more than one answer is possible.

Example:

Someone broke into their flat *while* they were away on holiday.

1 Some people were talking in the cinema ____ the film.
2 We've been waiting ____ almost an hour.

3 Something woke me up ____ the night.
4 I was on holiday ____ two weeks ____ the spring.
5 Sarah started to feel ill ____ the meal.
6 They stopped work ____ half an hour ____ the afternoon.
7 We visited some interesting places ____ we were in London.
8 I'll be in France ____ the whole of September.

Note

–For *for, since, ago* and *before* see 174.

173   Time: *by, until, from, to/until, before, after*

1 | **By and *until***

We use *until* (or *till*) to mean 'up to the time when'; we use *by* to mean 'not later than'. Compare:

I'll stay **until** Sunday lunchtime. (= up to Sunday lunchtime)
He'll be out **till** 11 o'clock. (= up to 11)

I'll have to leave **by** Sunday lunchtime. (= not later than Sunday lunchtime)
He'll be home **by** 11 o'clock. (= not later than 11)

2 | ***From ... to/until***

The shop opens **from** 8.30 **to** 5.30 every day.
I'll be on holiday **from** Monday **until/till** Friday next week.

3 | ***Before* and *after***

I'll be home **before** 6 o'clock.
After dinner we went for a walk.

EXERCISE 173A

Complete the sentences using *by, until, from* or *to*. Sometimes more than one answer is possible.

Example:

The film starts at 8.10, so we must be at the cinema *by* 8.00 at the latest.

1 I waited ____ half past eight ____ nine o'clock, but she didn't come.
2 They hope to finish the job ____ Thursday next week.
3 He normally works ____ Monday ____ Friday.
4 How many more weeks are there ____ your holiday?
5 If you want a ticket for the concert, let me know ____ next Wednesday at the latest.
6 We won't start the meeting ____ everyone is here.

174   *For, since, ago* and *before*

1   We use *for* with a period of time to say how long something continues in the past, present or future.

*We were in Rome **for ten days** last August.*
*They usually go on holiday **for two weeks** every summer.*
*I'll be in Manchester **for the next three days**.*

2   We often use *for* and *since* with the present perfect to talk about things that have continued over a period. Compare:

*I've been waiting **for two hours**.*	*I've been waiting **since 1 o'clock**.*
*I've known her **for six months**.*	*I've known her **since April**.*
We use *for* when we mention the length of the period eg **two hours**, **six months**.	We use *since* when we mention the starting point of the period eg **1 o'clock**, **April**.

3   *Ago* is an adverb meaning 'before now'.

*It's 10 o'clock now. Sue left two hours **ago**.* (= Sue left at 8 o'clock.)

Ago comes after an expression of time.

*She left **a few minutes ago**.*
***Six months ago** they moved to Manchester.*

Note the question *How long ago . . .?* eg **How long ago** did she leave?

We use *ago* with a past tense, not the present perfect. For example, we cannot say ~~She has left a few minutes ago~~.

4   Compare *ago* and *for*:

*I went to New York two weeks **ago**.*	*I went to New York **for** two weeks.*
(= two weeks before now)	(= I spent two weeks there)

263

5 Compare *ago* and *before*:

ago = 'before now'; *before* = 'before a past time'

*John left school three years **ago**; Jane had already left school three years **before**.*

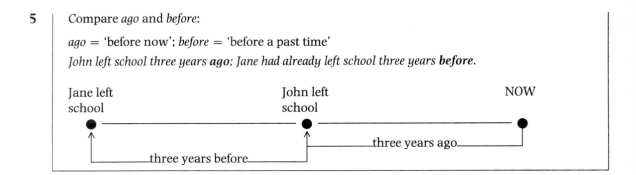

EXERCISE 174A

Complete the sentences using *for, since, ago* and *before.*

Example:

Tina moved away from Newcastle five years *ago* and she hasn't been back there *since* **then.**

1 My grandparents visited Edinburgh ____ two weeks in 1980. They had been there five years ____, so it wasn't completely new to them.
2 My brother has been interested in music ____ quite a long time. He was given his first guitar 20 years ____.
3 John worked in a travel agency ____ six months in 1985. He already had some experience of the tourist industry because he had worked in a Tourist Information office in London two years ____.
4 Patricia started working as a journalist with a newspaper in Madrid ten years ____. She's been working for the same newspaper ever ____ then.

Note

–For *for* and *since*, see also 11.

175 Means of transport: *by, on, in*

1 We use *by* + noun to say how we travel.

> *by car   by bus   by coach   by bicycle   by motorbike*
> *by train   by Underground/Tube   by tram   by plane*
> *by boat/ship   by road   by rail   by air   by sea*

*I usually go to work **by car**.*
*They travelled to Paris **by rail**.*

But we say *on foot* (= walking).

*Does he usually go to school **on foot**?*

264

2 | When we use *my/a/the* etc before *car/bus/train* etc, we cannot use *by*. We use *in* with cars and *on* with bicycles, motorbikes and public transport eg buses, trains.

*I usually go to work **in my car**.* (Not: ~~… by my car.~~)
*They went for a ride **on a motorbike**.* (Not: ~~… by a motorbike.~~)
*Did you go to London **on the train**?* (Not: ~~… by the train?~~)

EXERCISE 175A

Complete the sentences using *by, on* or *in*.

Example:

I'm not going to Rome *on* my motorbike. I've decided to go *by* train instead.

1   Annie usually goes to school ____ her bicycle, but sometimes she goes ____ bus.
2   The journey takes 10 minutes ____ bus and about 25 minutes ____ foot.
3   Robert didn't come to work ____ his car yesterday morning. His car had broken down and he had to come ____ taxi.
4   Did you travel right across London ____ the Underground?
5   We've decided to travel to New York ____ sea rather than go ____ air.

176   *Like, as* and *as if*

1 | *Like* **and** *as*

a | We can use *like* and *as* to say that things are similar:

Like

*My sister is quite **like** me.*
*He eats **like** a pig!*
*This steak is very tough. It's **like** eating leather.*

In this use *like* is a preposition; we use it before a noun eg *like a pig*, a pronoun eg *like me*, or an *-ing* form eg *like eating*.

As

*Your hair looks nice **as** it is now.*
*Nobody else can sing **as** she can.*

In this use, *as* is a conjunction; we use it before a clause, with a subject and a verb eg *as it is, as she can*.

In an informal style, we often use *like* as a conjunction instead of *as*.

*Nobody can sing **like** she can.*

Some people think that *like* used in this way is not 'correct'.

b   We use *as* as a preposition to talk about someone's job or the function of a thing.

*I once worked **as** a bus driver.*
*Please don't use my shoe **as** a hammer.*

Compare *as* and *like*:

*He works **as** a waiter.* (He really is a waiter.) *She uses the living room **as** her office.* (It really is her office.)	*He looks **like** a pop singer.* (He is not really a pop singer.) *My children treat our house **like** a hotel.* (It is not really a hotel.)

c   We can use *like* to give examples.

*She enjoys some water sports, **like** sailing and windsurfing.*

2   *As if*

a   We use *as if* before a subject + verb to say how someone or something seems.

*You look **as if** you're tired.*
*It looks **as if** it's going to stop raining.*

We sometimes use *as if* + a past tense to talk about the present.

*My brother sometimes behaves **as if** he **was** my father.*

The sentence does not refer to the past here; we use the past (*he **was** my father*) because the idea is 'unreal' (in fact *he **is** not my father*).

We often use *were* instead of *was* after *as if* to express 'unreal' ideas, especially in a more formal style.

*My brother sometimes behaves **as if** he **were** my father.*

b   We can use *as though* instead of *as if*.

*You look **as though** you're tired.*
*My brother sometimes behaves **as though** he were my father.*

c   In an informal style, *like* is sometimes used instead of *as if/though*.

*It looks **like** it's going to stop raining.*

EXERCISE 176A

Complete the sentences using *like* or *as*. Sometimes either word is possible.

Example:

Sarah looks a lot *like* her brother.

1 I worked ____ a shop assistant for six weeks last summer.
2 Their garden is in a terrible mess. It looks ____ a jungle.
3 I prefer bright colours, ____ yellow and red.
4 When you've finished, put everything back ____ it was before.
5 This tea is very weak. It's ____ drinking warm water.
6 Stop behaving ____ a fool.
7 Nobody else can make me laugh quite ____ she can.

EXERCISE 176B

Make sentences about the people in the pictures using the words in the boxes.

He/She/It looks	as if ____
They look	

it's going to rain   they've been running
~~she's just seen a ghost~~   he's going to fall
they've been arguing   she's just had some good news

Example:

She looks as if she's just seen a ghost.

EXERCISE 176C

Complete each sentence in **A** using *as if* and the most suitable idea from **B**. Use the verbs in brackets in the past tense.

Example:

1 *I'm over 16, but my parents sometimes treat me as if I was/were a child.*

A

1 I'm over 16, but my parents sometimes treat me ____
2 He's only a receptionist, but he acts ____
3 They're quite rich, but they behave ____
4 He's only got a cold, but he acts ____
5 I've never met her before, but she behaves ____

B

(own) the hotel
(know) me
(be) dying
(be) poor
~~(be) a child~~

177   *With* (= having) and *in* (= wearing)

1 | We can use *with* to say what someone or something has.

*He is a tall man **with** brown hair.* (= he has brown hair)
*London is a large city **with** a population of over 9 million.* (= it has a population of over 9 million)

2 | We can use *in* to say what someone is wearing.

*He often goes to work **in** his jeans.* (= wearing his jeans)
*Who's that woman **in** the black dress?* (= wearing the black dress)

EXERCISE 177A

Complete the sentences using *with* or *in*.

Example:

My suitcase is the brown one *with* the blue stripe down the side.

1 We're looking for a flat ＿＿ three bedrooms.
2 Who's that man over there ＿＿ the green sweater?
3 The police are looking for a short man ＿＿ black curly hair and brown eyes.
4 She's a lively woman ＿＿ a great sense of humour.
5 A fat man ＿＿ a dark blue suit came out of the bank ＿＿ a black briefcase.

178   Adjective + preposition

After many adjectives we use particular prepositions. For example, we say *afraid of,*
interested in and *bored with.*
Here are some common examples of these adjective + preposition combinations:

- *excited about   worried about   nervous about*
  angry about   annoyed about   furious about

I'm **excited about** starting my new job next week.
Are you **worried about** your exam?
What are you looking so **angry about**?

- *good at   bad at   clever at   hopeless at*

I'm not very **good at** mathematics.
You're not **bad at** tennis.

- *surprised at/by   shocked at/by   astonished at/by   amazed at/by*

We were **surprised at/by** the news.

- *famous for   well known for   responsible for*

France is **famous for** its food and wine.
Who is **responsible for** breaking this window?

- *different from/to*

He's very **different from/to** his sister.

- *interested in*

I'm quite **interested in** art.

- *afraid of   frightened of   scared of   proud of   full of*
  ashamed of   jealous of   envious of   suspicious of   short of
  aware of   conscious of   capable of   fond of   tired of

*Are you **afraid of** spiders?*
*I'm very **proud of** you.*
*Are you **jealous of** his success?*
*He's very **fond of** her.*
*My homework was **full of** mistakes.*
*I'm a bit **short of** money. Can you lend me some?*
*I'm **tired of** doing the same things every day.*

■ *nice/kind/good/friendly/polite/rude/stupid of someone*

*It was very **nice of** you to help. Thank you.*

■ *keen on*

*She's not very **keen on** tennis.*

■ *engaged to   married to   similar to*

*Marianne is **engaged to** Alan.*
*Your camera is **similar to** mine.*

■ *nice/kind/good/friendly/polite/rude to someone*

*He's always very **nice to** me.*

■ *pleased with   bored with   disappointed with   happy with*

*You look very **pleased with** yourself.*
*He's **bored with** his job.*
*I was **disappointed with** my exam results.*

■ *angry/annoyed/furious with someone for (doing) something*

*Are you **angry with** me **for** being late?*

EXERCISE 178A

Complete the sentences using the words in the box. Sometimes two answers are possible.

Example:

I'm getting bored *with* my present job.

| of | by | with | on | about | in | from | for | at | to |

1 They're very proud ____ their children.
2 My sister has just got engaged ____ her boyfriend.
3 Are you worried ____ your driving test?
4 I'm very bad ____ remembering names.
5 Sydney in Australia is famous ____ **its Opera** House.
6 She's quite capable ____ doing the job.
7 We're getting really excited ____ our holiday.

8 Are you interested ____ playing tennis tomorrow?

9 He's not very keen ____ football.

10 It was very kind ____ them to give us a lift to the station.

11 We were very disappointed ____ the film.

12 Were you afraid ____ the dark when you were a child?

13 I was shocked ____ the news of the accident.

14 This letter is full ____ typing mistakes.

15 We'll have to hurry. We're a bit short ____ time.

16 I'm not very good ____ drawing.

17 My grandparents are very fond ____ their old cat.

18 Cricket is quite different ____ baseball.

19 Their flat is quite similar ____ ours.

20 She was very angry ____ me ____ losing her key.

Note

–After some of the above adjectives other prepositions are possible eg *frightened **by***, *annoyed **at**, disappointed **in***. For more information, see a good dictionary.

179   Noun + preposition

After many nouns we use particular prepositions. For example, we say *(a) reason for, (an) example of, (an) increase in.*
Here are some common examples of these noun + preposition combinations:

■ *difference between*

*There are a lot of **differences between** living in the country and living in a city.*

■ *reason for   demand for   need for*

*What was the **reason for** the accident?*
*There is a **need for** more houses in this area.*

■ *increase/decrease in   rise/fall in*

*There has been an **increase in** the price of petrol.*

■ *difficulty in doing something*

*Does he have much **difficulty in** doing his schoolwork?*

But note: *difficulty with something*
*Does he have much **difficulty with** his schoolwork?*

■ *example of   cause of   picture/photograph of*

*This building is an **example of** good modern architecture.*
*What was the **cause of** the accident?*
*Have you got a **photograph of** your family?*

■ *answer to   solution to   reply to   invitation to*
   reaction to

*Have you had an **answer to** your letter?*
*We must find a **solution to** the problem.*
*Did you get an **invitation to** the party?*

■ *attitude to/towards*

*What's your **attitude to/towards** this idea?*

■ *relationship with*

*Simon has a very good **relationship with** his sister.*

But note: *relationship between*

*The **relationship between** Simon and his sister is very good.*

EXERCISE 179A

Complete the sentences using the words in the box. In one sentence two answers
are possible.

Example:

I've had an invitation *to* a wedding next month.

towards of between for in with to

1 I have a good relationship ____ my boss.
2 He refused to give me an answer ____ my question.
3 What are the main differences ____ the two countries?
4 It's difficult to find a solution ____ the problem.
5 Smoking is one of the causes ____ heart disease.
6 Has there been an increase ____ unemployment recently?
7 The government want to improve the relationship ____ the police and the general public.
8 He is very shy and has great difficulty ____ making friends.
9 She hasn't got a very good attitude ____ her school work.
10 There is no need ____ you to shout. I can hear you.
11 Nobody knows the reason ____ his decision.
12 The artist drew a picture ____ my mother.

Note

–After some of the above nouns other prepositions are possible. For more
information, see a good dictionary.

180   Preposition + noun

We use particular prepositions before many nouns. For example, we say *on television* and *by mistake*.
Here are some common examples of these preposition + noun combinations:

- *by mistake   by accident   by chance*

*I put salt in my coffee **by mistake**.*

- We say: (to pay) *by cheque/by credit card*, but (to pay) *in cash* or (to pay) *cash*.

*I paid **by cheque**, not **in cash**.*

- (a book/film/painting etc) *by someone*

*I'm reading a book **by** James Joyce.* (= written by James Joyce)

- (to go/come) *for a drink/a meal/a walk/a swim*

*Would you like to go **for a drink**?*

- (to have something) *for breakfast/lunch/dinner*

*We had spaghetti **for lunch**.*

- We say *for example*.

*I'd like to go somewhere warm on holiday, **for example** Greece or Turkey.*

- (to be/fall) *in love with* someone/something

*Jimmy is **in love with** Angela.*

- *in* someone's *opinion*

***In my opinion** you should phone the police.*

- (to be/go/come) *on holiday/a journey/a trip/business*

*Robert isn't working this week. He's **on holiday**.*
But note: (go/come) *for a holiday*
*I'd like to go to Jamaica **for a holiday**.*

- *on television/the radio*

*What's **on television** this evening?*

EXERCISE 180A

Complete the sentences using the words in the box.

Example:

In my opinion you're wrong.

by   with   in   on   for

1 We're going to Italy ____ a short holiday in May.
2 Robert has gone away ____ holiday for two weeks.
3 The book, *Gone With the Wind*, was written ____ Margaret Mitchell.
4 I didn't mean to do that; I did it ____ mistake.
5 I could pay you ____ cheque or ____ cash. Which would you prefer?
6 We heard the news ____ the radio last night.
7 I hadn't arranged to meet her; I met her quite ____ chance on the train to London.
8 Lynne and Bruno are very much ____ love ____ each other.

Note

–For more information about preposition + noun combinations, see a good dictionary.

181   Verb + preposition

After many verbs we use particular prepositions. For example, we say *believe in* and *concentrate on.*
Here are some common examples of these verb + preposition combinations:

■ *apologize to* someone *for* (doing) something

I **apologized to** her **for** being late.

■ *apply for*

Are you going to **apply for** the job?

■ *believe in*

Do you **believe in** ghosts?

■ *belong to*

Does this book **belong to** you?

■ *care about* (= think someone/something is important)

He doesn't **care about** me.

But: *care for* (= look after; nurse)
*She's very good at **caring for** sick animals.*

Also: *care for* (= like)
*Would you **care for** a drink?*

■ *take care of* (= look after)
*Could you **take care of** the baby while I go out shopping?*

■ *complain to* (someone) *about* (something)
*We **complained to** our neighbours **about** the noise.*

■ *concentrate on*
***Concentrate on** the road when you're driving.*

■ *crash into   run into   drive into   bump into*
*The car in front stopped suddenly and we **crashed into** it.*

■ *depend on*
*'Are you going to the beach tomorrow?'   'It **depends on** the weather.'*

■ *die of*
*She **died of** a heart attack.*

■ *dream about* (while asleep)
*I **dreamt about** Sue last night.*

But: *dream of* (= imagine)
*When I was younger I **dreamt of** being a famous pop-singer.*

Also: *dream of* (= consider)
*I wouldn't **dream of** changing my job.*

■ *hear about* (= be told about)
*Have you **heard about** Jimmy? He broke his leg in a skiing accident.*

But: *hear from* (= receive news from)
*'Have you **heard from** Sue recently?'   'Yes, she wrote to me last week.'*

Also: *hear of* (= know that someone/something exists)
*Have you **heard of** a disco called The Dance Factory?*

■ *laugh at   smile at*
*Who's that girl **smiling at** you?*

- *listen to*

*Would you like to **listen to** some music?*

- *look at* (= use the eyes)

***Look at** this photograph.*

But: *look for* (= try to find)
*Can you help me, please? I'm **looking for** West Street.*

Also: *look after* (= take care of)
*Could you **look after** the baby while I go out shopping?*

- *rely on*

*You can **rely on** me to help you.*

- *search for*

*The police **searched for** the missing child.*

- *shout at* (eg when you are angry)

*She was very angry and started **shouting at** us.*

- *speak to   talk to*

*I **spoke to** Sue this morning.*

- *suffer from*

*He **suffers from** asthma.*

- *think about* (= use the mind)

*You look sad. What are you **thinking about**?*

But: *think of/about* (= consider)
*I'm **thinking of/about** changing my job.*

Also: *think of* (= have as an opinion about)
*'What did you **think of** the film?'   'I enjoyed it.'*

Also: *think of* (= bring to the mind)
*I can't **think of** any reason why the accident happened.*

- *wait for*

*How long have you been **waiting for** the bus?*

- *write to*

*I'll **write to** you soon.*

EXERCISE 181A

Complete the sentences using the words in the box.

Example:

I was worried and found it difficult to concentrate *on* my work.

| for   from   after   to   of   on   at   about   in   into |

1 He became furious and started shouting
   ____ me.
2 Who does this jacket belong ____?
3 Selfish people only care ____ themselves.
4 He complained ____ the children ____ the
   mess they'd made.
5 You can't rely ____ the buses; they never
   come on time.
6 She apologized ____ me ____ losing her
   temper.
7 I've written ____ the company and applied
   ____ the job.
8 Mrs Woods suffers ____ bronchitis.
9 Stop smoking or you'll die ____ lung cancer.
10 We're thinking ____ going to the cinema.
11 Think carefully ____ what I said.

12 I remember his face, but I can't think ____
   his name.
13 'We went to the concert.'   'What did you
   think ____ it?'
14 'Do you know Paul Morris?'   'No, I've
   never heard ____ him.'
15 Excuse me, We're looking ____ the sports
   centre. Could you tell us how to get there?
16 Thank you for looking ____ my mother
   while she was ill.
17 I don't believe ____ horoscopes.
18 She dreams ____ being rich and famous.
19 I dreamt ____ my grandmother last night.
20 She searched through her bag ____ a pen.
21 We're depending ____ you to help us.
22 The car went out of control and crashed
   ____ the back of a bus.

Note

–For more information about verb + preposition combinations, see a good dictionary.

182   Verb + object + preposition

> After some verbs we use an object followed by particular prepositions. For example,
> we say *borrow* something *from* someone.
> Here are some common examples of these verb + object + preposition combinations:
>
> ■ *accuse* someone *of* (doing) something
>
> *The police **accused** the man **of** murder.*
>
> ■ *blame* someone/something *for* something
>
> *They **blamed** George **for** the accident.*
>
> But: *blame* something *on* someone/something
> *They **blamed** the accident **on** George.*

- *borrow* something *from* someone

I **borrowed** some money **from** my mother.

- *congratulate* someone *on* (doing) something

Did you **congratulate** Sue **on** passing her exam?

- *explain* something *to* someone

I **explained** the problem **to** the police.

- *invite* someone *to* something

Sue has **invited** us **to** her party.

- *remind* someone *about* something (= tell someone not to forget)

Don't forget to **remind** Kate **about** the meeting.
But: *remind* someone *of* something/someone (= cause someone to remember)
This song **reminds** me **of** the first time we met.

- *tell* someone *about* something

Did they **tell** you **about** their holiday?

- *warn* someone *about* something/someone

His boss has **warned** him **about** being late for work.

EXERCISE 182A

Complete the sentences using the words in the box.

Example:

They blamed the accident *on* the driver of the lorry.

| from   on   to   about   of   for |

1 Don't blame other people ___ your own mistakes.
2 You remind me ___ someone I knew years ago.
3 Will you remind Peter ___ the party next Saturday?
4 I must congratulate you ___ passing your driving test.
5 I borrowed the umbrella ___ a friend of mine.
6 The woman accused me ___ trying to steal her bag.
7 Have they invited many people ___ their wedding?
8 We've warned him ___ swimming in that part of the river.

Note
–For more information about verb + object + preposition combinations, see a good dictionary.

183   Review of prepositions

EXERCISE 183A

Complete the description of the scene in the picture using the words in the box. Use each word only once.

behind	in front of	outside	inside	up	down
on	onto	off	into	out of	along	across	at
round	towards	~~between~~	near	past	next to	opposite

There is a cafe *between* a supermarket and a post office. A woman is coming ___1___ the supermarket. Some people are sitting ___2___ the cafe. ___3___ the post office is a bank. A man is getting ___4___ a bus ___5___ the bank. ___6___ the bus there is a girl getting ___7___ a motorbike. An old man is going ___8___ some steps ___9___ the post office; a young woman is coming ___10___ the steps. Another woman is walking ___11___ the road ___12___ the bank. Some children and a dog are running ___13___ the street ___14___ the cafe. A car is waiting ___15___ some traffic lights ___16___ the supermarket. Some people are crossing the road ___17___ the car. There is a telephone box ___18___ the corner of the street ___19___ the supermarket. A young man is walking ___20___ the corner.

EXERCISE 183B

Complete the sentences using the words in the box. Sometimes more than one answer is possible.

Example:

We're going away *on* holiday *for* two weeks *in* July.

> at   in   on   since   for   from   of   to
> during   between   about   with   under

1 We're meeting ____ the clock tower ____ North Street ____ 8 o'clock this evening.
2 I went shopping ____ town ____ Friday afternoon.
3 We're thinking ____ going ____ the concert ____ Saturday. Are you interested ____ coming?
4 She's been studying ____ the University ____ Manchester ____ the past three years.
5 He had great difficulty ____ finding a job when he was living ____ the north of England.
6 They live ____ 148 Dyke Road. Their flat is ____ the second floor.
7 He fell asleep ____ the film ____ the cinema last night.
8 ____ my opinion they show too many old films ____ TV.
9 They went away ____ holiday ____ the end of last week.
10 They've been staying ____ the International Hotel ____ Oxford Street ____ they arrived ____ England.
11 He's suffered ____ bad headaches ____ he had the accident.
12 At first I didn't want to go swimming in the river, but ____ the end I changed my mind.
13 My brother worked ____ a tourist guide ____ London ____ three months ____ the summer.
14 I found an old photograph ____ the floor ____ the bed ____ my room.
15 When she was a child, she dreamt ____ being a famous dancer.
16 I'm not very good ____ making decisions.
17 You can depend ____ him to arrive ____ time; he's never late.
18 We've arranged to meet ____ a cafe ____ a drink ____ 9 o'clock this evening.
19 Do you have a good relationship ____ your sister?
20 There is no need ____ you to worry ____ me. I'll be all right.
21 You're very different ____ your mother, but quite similar ____ your father.
22 They're looking ____ a house ____ four bedrooms and a garden.
23 The police accused the woman ____ stealing the money.
24 'Do you know a pop band called Running Heads?' 'No, I've never heard ____ them.'
25 Newcastle is a large, commercial and industrial city ____ a population of about 300,000. It is ____ the north-east of England, ____ the River Tyne.
26 Is there very much difference ____ the two word processors?
27 I've always wanted my parents to be proud ____ me.
28 People are angry ____ the increase ____ food prices.
29 Did you complain ____ the hotel manager ____ the food?
30 My parents first went ____ Greece ____ a short holiday ____ 1980.

184 Indirect objects with or without *to* and *for*

1 Some verbs eg *give, buy* can have two objects: a direct object and an indirect object. Normally, the indirect object refers to a person and comes first.

> verb + indirect object + direct object

*I'll give **Sally the money**.*
*Richard bought **me some flowers**.*

2 We can also use the structure:

> verb + direct object + *to/for* + indirect object

*I'll give **the money to Sally**.*
*Richard bought **some flowers for me**.*

We use this structure, for example when we want to give special emphasis to the indirect object.

*I'll give the money to **Sally**, not Peter.*

a Some common verbs which we use in this structure with *to*:

> bring give lend offer owe pass pay post
> promise read recommend sell send show take
> teach tell throw write

*They're going to offer **the job to Sue**.*
*He showed **the letter to a friend**.*

b Some common verbs which we use in this structure with *for*:

> bring build buy change choose cook do fetch
> find fix get keep make order prepare save

*She bought **some books for her brother**.*
*I'll cook **a meal for you**.*

3 When the direct object is a pronoun eg *them, it*, we normally put this first eg *She gave **them** to her brother.* (Instead of: *She gave her brother **them**.*)

EXERCISE 184A

Rephrase the sentences without using *to* or *for*.

Example:

Give this message to Martin.
Give Martin this message.
I'll make some coffee for you.
I'll make you some coffee.

1 Have you sent the letter to your brother?
2 I'll get a present for Sally.
3 Have you told the news to your parents?
4 I bought some stamps for you.
5 She lent her car to Peter.
6 I kept a seat for you.
7 He's prepared a meal for us.
8 Will you give this message to Mrs Woods?

EXERCISE 184B

Put the parts of the sentence into the correct order.

Example:

Sarah | I | my new camera | lent | .
I lent Sarah my new camera.
to your mother | have | the money | given | you | ?
Have you given the money to your mother?

1 they | the job | me | didn't offer | .
2 for her son | she | a book | bought | .
3 the salt | pass | can | me | you | ?
4 you | this package | will | to your
   parents | take | ?
5 a taxi | ordered | they | us | have | .
6 he | to all | showed | the photographs |
   his friends | .

185   Phrasal verbs: introduction

1   Phrasal verbs are verbs which change their meaning in some way by adding 'particles' eg *down, away, on, in, up, after, off, across.*

*Please **sit down.***
*I'll **throw away** the rubbish.*
*Could you **turn on** the TV?*

2   In some cases, the meaning of a phrasal verb is a combination of the meanings of its separate parts.

Come in.

Sit down.

3   In other cases, the phrasal verb has a different meaning to the meanings of its separate parts.

*He's **given up** smoking.* (= He's stopped smoking.)
*Sue **takes after** her mother.* (= Sue looks like or is like her mother.)
***Looking after** a baby is hard work.* (= Taking care of a baby is hard work.)

EXERCISE 185A

Complete the sentences using the correct form of the phrasal verbs below.
Use each phrasal verb only once.

Example:

It was lucky that nobody was killed when the bomb *went off*.

speak up (= speak louder)	*fill in* (= complete)
come across (= find by chance)	*keep on* (= continue)
turn down (= refuse)	*go up* (= increase)
~~*go off*~~ (= explode)	*hold up* (= delay)

1 Could you _____ this application form, please?
2 They just _____ making a noise even though I'd asked them to stop.
3 The price of coffee has _____ again.
4 We can't hear you very well. Could you _____ a bit, please?
5 The coach was _____ by the heavy traffic and didn't arrive in London until 8.00.
6 Unfortunately, your request for a pay rise has been _____.
7 He _____ some old photographs when he was cleaning the attic.

186   Types of phrasal verbs

Phrasal verbs are formed by adding 'particles' eg *away, up, down, out, off, after, in, on* to verbs.

I'll **throw away** the rubbish.   He's **given up** smoking.

There are four basic types of phrasal verbs:

Type 1

These phrasal verbs do not take an object.

> verb + particle

Sit down.
Look out! (= take care)
We **set off** on our journey. (= started)

Type 2

These phrasal verbs take an object. When the object is a noun, it can go after or before the particle.

verb + particle + object		verb + object + particle

I'll **throw away** the rubbish.	I'll **throw** the rubbish **away**.
Take off your shoes.	**Take** your shoes **off**.

But when the object is a pronoun eg *it, them,* it can only go before the particle, not after it.
I'll **throw** it **away.** (Not: ~~I'll **throw away** it.~~)
Take them **off.** (Not: ~~**Take off** them.~~)

Type 3

These phrasal verbs take an object, but we cannot separate the verb from the particle.

> verb + particle + object

Sue **takes after** her mother. (Not: ~~Sue **takes** her mother **after.**~~)
Looking after a baby is hard work. (Not: ~~**Looking** a baby **after** is hard work.~~)

Type 4

These phrasal verbs have three parts: a verb + particle + preposition eg *look forward to.* We cannot separate the verb from the other parts.

> verb + particle + preposition + object

I'm **looking forward to** my holiday.
You go now and I'll **catch up with** you later.
You shouldn't **go back on** your promises.

EXERCISE 186A

Complete the sentences using the correct form of the (Type 1) phrasal verbs in the box. Use each phrasal verb only once.

Example:

My car *broke down* on my way home and I had to phone a garage.

> break out   take off   ~~break down~~   grow up
> get up

1 Our plane ____ from New York at 6 o'clock yesterday evening.
2 My younger sister wants to be a doctor when she ____ .
3 A fire ____ in the offices of the ABC cinema last night.
4 Do you like ____ early in the mornings?

EXERCISE 186B

Complete the sentences using the (Type 2) phrasal verbs in brackets. Sometimes two answers are possible.

Example:

Could you | the light? (switch on)
Could you switch on the light?/Could you switch the light on?

1 Would you like to | this jacket? (try on)
2 I don't like you smoking. I wish you'd | it. (give up)
3 He's going to | his beard. (shave off)
4 I have to speak to Mr Mason. I'd better | him. (ring up)
5 That music is rather loud. Would you | it? (turn down)

EXERCISE 186C

Replace the words in italics with the correct form of the (Type 3) phrasal verbs in the box.

Example:

We've *examined* the problem very carefully.
We've *gone into* the problem very carefully.

> get over   ~~go into~~   run into
> come into   look after

1 Who is going to *take care of* the children while you go to the pub?
2 Although she had very good medical care, it took her a long time to *recover from* her illness.
3 Jane *inherited* a great deal of money when her grandmother died.
4 I *met* an old friend *by chance* in town yesterday afternoon.

EXERCISE 186D

Replace the words in italics with the correct form of one of the (Type 4) phrasal verbs in the box.

> get rid of   put up with   come up with
> ~~go back on~~   look back on

Example:

You shouldn't *break* a promise.
You shouldn't *go back on* a promise.

1 Have you *thrown away* your old typewriter?
2 We must try to *find* a solution to the problem.
3 When you *remember* the past, it's easy to see the mistakes you've made.
4 I don't think I can *tolerate* this awful weather much longer.

EXERCISE 186E

Replace the noun in *italics* with a pronoun. (Note that sometimes you will have to change the word order.)

Examples:

Could you look after *the children?*
Could you look after them?
I'll turn off *the TV.*
I'll turn it off.

1 He's going to give up *his job.*
2 I've thrown away *the ticket.*
3 He's looking after *his sick mother.*
4 Are you looking forward to *the party?*
5 Can you fill in *the form?*
6 She takes after *her father.*
7 He can't do without *his car.*

187   Pronunciation of endings -(e)s and -ed

Compare 'voiced' and 'unvoiced' sounds:

VOICED

With a voiced sound you can feel vibration.

UNVOICED

With an unvoiced sound you can feel no vibration.

1 | **Pronunciation of -(e)s ending**

The rules for pronouncing the -(e)s ending are the same for noun plurals (eg *books*, *churches*), the possessive *'s/s'* (eg *Ken's, my parents'*) and the 3rd person singular of verbs in the present simple (eg *he plays, she watches*).

The -(e)s ending has three pronunciations:

a | -(e)s is pronounced /ɪz/ after these sounds /tʃ/, /ʃ/, /s/, /z/, /dʒ/, /ʒ/.

/tʃ/	/ʃ/	/s/
watches /wɒtʃɪz/	*washes* /wɒʃɪz/	*kisses* /kɪsɪz/
churches /tʃɜːtʃɪz/	*wishes* /wɪʃɪz/	*Chris's* /krɪsɪz/

/z/	/dʒ/	/ʒ/
loses /luːzɪz/	*bridges* /brɪdʒɪz/	*garages* /gærɑːʒɪz/
realizes /rɪəlaɪzɪz/	*George's* /dʒɔːdʒɪz/	

b | -(e)s is pronounced /s/ after unvoiced sounds (except those in **a**).

stops /stɒps/	*my parents'* /peərənts/	*books* /bʊks/
hopes /həʊps/	*waits* /weɪts/	*Mick's* /mɪks/
laughs /lɑːfs/	*months* /mʌnθs/	
wife's /waɪfs/	*maths* /mæθs/	

c | -(e)s is pronounced /z/ after voiced sounds (except those in **a**).

plays /pleɪz/	*cars* /kɑː(r)z/	*Ken's* /kenz/	*dogs* /dɒgz/
wives /waɪvz/	*ends* /endz/	*clothes* /kləʊðz/	*trees* /triːz/

2 | **Pronunciation of -ed ending**

The -ed ending is used to form the past tense and past participle of regular verbs (eg *played, watched*).

The -ed ending has three pronunciations:

a | -ed is pronounced /ɪd/ after the sounds /t/ and /d/.

/t/	/d/
waited /weɪtɪd/	*ended* /endɪd/
started /stɑːtɪd/	*needed* /niːdɪd/

b | -ed is pronounced /t/ after unvoiced sounds (except /t/).

stopped /stɒpt/	*looked* /lʊkt/	*watched* /wɒtʃt/
hoped /həʊpt/	*worked* /wɜːkt/	*touched* /tʌtʃt/
washed /wɒʃt/	*kissed* /kɪst/	*laughed* /lɑːft/
wished /wɪʃt/	*danced* /dɑːnst/	*coughed* /kɒft/

c | -ed is pronounced /d/ after voiced sounds (except /d/).

played /pleɪd/	*opened* /əʊpənd/	*lived* /lɪvd/	*filled* /fɪld/
showed /ʃəʊd/	*raised* /reɪzd/	*agreed* /əˈgriːd/	*used* /juːzd/

EXERCISE 187A

Put these words into three groups according to the pronunciation of the -(e)s endings.

opens	waits	washes	Mick's	cars
stops	teaches	Sally's	misses	drives
dishes	Alice's	watches	admits	shows
books	Bert's	studies	brings	hopes

1	2	3
/ɪz/	/s/	/z/
washes	waits	opens

EXERCISE 187B

Put these words into three groups according to the pronunciation of the -ed endings.

passed	failed	painted	loved	finished
ended	hoped	opened	planned	invented
danced	studied	worked	waited	
lived	watched	remembered	admitted	

1	2	3
/ɪd/	/t/	/d/
painted	passed	failed

188   Spelling of endings -(e)s, -ing, -ed, -er, -est, -ly

Nouns, verbs, adjectives and adverbs can take the following endings:

Noun + -(e)s (plural)	books
Verb + -(e)s (3rd person singular present simple)	works watches
Verb + -ing (present participle or gerund)	working watching
Verb + -ed (past tense or past participle)	worked watched
Adjective + -er (comparative) Adjective + -est (superlative)	slower slowest
Adjective + -ly (adverb)	slowly

When we add these endings, there are sometimes changes in spelling:

1   **Adding -e before -s**

a   If a word ends in -ch, -sh, -s, -x or -z, we add -e before -s.

watch	watches
dish	dishes
bus	buses
mix	mixes
fizz	fizzes

b   The nouns tomato, potato, echo, hero, negro and the verbs do and go also add -e before -s.

tomato	tomatoes
potato	potatoes
do	does
go	goes

2 | **Nouns ending in -f(e)**

Some nouns ending in -f or -fe drop the -f/-fe and add -ves in the plural eg *half, thief, leaf, loaf, self, shelf, wolf, knife, wife, life.*

half	*halves*
thief	*thieves*
knife	*knives*
wife	*wives*
life	*lives*

3 | **Dropping -e**

a | If a word ends in one -e, we normally drop the -e before -ing, -ed, -er and est.

Exception: *be/being*

live	*living*
dance	*danced*
late	*later*
large	*largest*

b | Verbs ending in -ee do not drop -e before -ing.

see	*seeing*
agree	*agreeing*

c | Adjectives ending in -e do not drop -e before the adverb ending in -ly.

extreme	*extremely*
polite	*politely*

d | But adjectives ending in -le change the -le to -ly for the adverb.

Exceptions: *true/truly, whole/wholly*

simple	*simply*
terrible	*terribly*

4 | **Changing -y to -i**

a | If a word ends in a consonant + -y, we change the -y to -ie before -s.

city	*cities*
study	*studies*

b | If a word ends in a consonant + -y, we change the -y to -i before -ed, -er, -est and -ly.

study	*studied*
happy	*happier*
heavy	*heaviest*
easy	*easily*

c | We do not change -y to -i before -ing.

study	*studying*
hurry	*hurrying*

d | We do not change -y to -i after a vowel.

Exceptions: *day/daily, pay/paid, say/said, lay/laid*

play	*plays*
enjoy	*enjoyed*
grey	*greyer*

5 | **Changing -ie to -y**

If a word ends in -ie, we change the -ie to -y before -ing.

die	*dying*
lie	*lying*

6 | Doubling final consonants

a	If a one-syllable word ends in one vowel + one consonant, we double the final consonant before -*ing*, -*ed*, -*er* and -*est*.	sit — *sitting* stop — *stopped* big — *bigger* hot — *hottest*
b	But we do not double -*y*, -*w* or -*x* at the end of words.	play — *playing* slow — *slower* mix — *mixed*
c	If a word of two or more syllables ends in one vowel + one consonant, we double the final consonant only if the final syllable is stressed.	begin — *beginning* (be'gin) prefer — *preferred* (pre'fer) admit — *admitted* (ad'mit)
	If the final syllable is not stressed, the final consonant is not doubled.	open — *opening* ('open) listen — *listened* ('listen)
	Exception: In British English, we double -*l* at the end of a word even if the final syllable is not stressed.	travel — *travelling* ('travel) cancel — *cancelled* ('cancel)

EXERCISE 188A

Add the -*s*/-*es* ending to these words; put the words into the correct groups: 1, 2, 3 or 4.

> wait   shelf   copy   catch   buzz   plate
> worry   miss   run   pay   admit   wife
> finish   fly   knife   spy   disco   tomato
> teach   marry

1	2	3	4
+-s	+-es	-y̸+-ies	f̸/f̸e̸+-ves
waits	catches	copies	shelves

EXERCISE 188B

Add the -*ing* endings to these words; put the words into the correct groups: 1, 2, 3 or 4.

> stop   die   dry   come   play   knit   show
> fix   make   tie   offer   visit   travel   write
> plan   marry   shop   behave   stay   admit
> leave

1	2	3	4
+-ing	e̸+-ing	i̸e̸+-ying	×2+-ing
drying	coming	dying	stopping

EXERCISE 188C

Add the *-ed* endings to these words; put the words into the correct groups: 1, 2, 3 or 4.

> ~~apply~~   ~~rob~~   ~~wash~~   ~~arrive~~   trap   pull
> move   empty   drop   carry   discover
> phone   pray   hope   travel   study
> show   admit   save

1
$+$-*ed*
washed

2
$\not e +$-*ed*
arrived

3
$\not y +$-*ied*
applied

4
$\times 2 +$-*ed*
robbed

EXERCISE 188D

Add the *-er* and *-est* endings to these words; put the words into the correct groups: 1, 2, 3 or 4.

> ~~happy~~   ~~big~~   ~~high~~   ~~nice~~   wet   late
> busy   slow   simple   short   wide   fat
> easy   thin   cheap   white   red   black
> funny

1
$+$-*er*/-*est*
higher – highest

2
$\not e +$-*er*/-*est*
nicer – nicest

3
$\not y +$-*ier*/-*iest*
happier – happiest

4
$\times 2 +$-*er*/-*est*
bigger – biggest

EXERCISE 188E

Add the *-ly* endings to these words; put the words into the correct groups: 1, 2 or 3.

> late   happy   gentle   hopeful   real   horrible   idle
> quick   beautiful   lucky   dry   sudden   definite
> polite   heavy   probable   temporary

1
$+$-*ly*
lately

2
-*l*$\not e +$-*ly*
gently

3
-*y*$\not +$-*ily*
happily

189 Contractions

1   'Contractions' are short forms such as *I'm* (= *I am*), *you've* (= *you have*), *isn't*
    (= *is not*) and *don't* (= *do not*).

    We often use contractions in spoken English, and in informal written English eg in
    letters to friends.

    When we write contractions, we put an apostrophe (') in place of the letter or letters
    which we leave out.

    I'm (= *I am*; ' = *a*)   **you've** (= *you have*; ' = *ha*)
    isn't (= *is not*; ' = *o*)   **don't** (= *do not*; ' = *o*)

2   Here are the most common contractions:

    I'm /aɪm/ (= *I am*)
    I've /aɪv/ (= *I have*)
    I'll /aɪl/ (= *I will*)
    I'd /aɪd/ (= *I had* or *I would*)

    you're /jʊə(r)/ (= *you are*)
    you've /juːv/ (= *you have*)
    you'll /juːl/ (= *you will*)
    you'd /juːd/ (= *you had* or *you would*)

    he's /hiːz/ (= *he is* or *he has*)
    he'll /hiːl/ (= *he will*)
    he'd /hiːd/ (= *he had* or *he would*)

    she's /ʃiːz/ (= *she is* or *she has*)
    she'll /ʃiːl/ (= *she will*)
    she'd /ʃiːd/ (= *she had* or *she would*)

    it's /ɪts/ (= *it is* or *it has*)
    it'll /'ɪtl/ (= *it will*)
    it'd /ɪtəd/ (= *it had* or *it would*)

    we're /wɪə(r)/ (= *we are*)
    we've /wiːv/ (= *we have*)
    we'll /wiːl/ (= *we will*)
    we'd /wiːd/ (= *we had* or *we would*)

    they're /ðeə(r)/ (= *they are*)
    they've /ðeɪv/ (= *they have*)
    they'll /ðeɪl/ (= *they will*)
    they'd /ðeɪd/ (= *they had* or *they would*)

    let's /lets/ (= *let us*)

    isn't /'ɪznt/ (= *is not*)
    aren't /ɑːnt/ (= *are not*)
    wasn't /'wɒznt/ (= *was not*)
    weren't /wɜːnt/ (= *were not*)
    don't /dəʊnt/ (= *do not*)
    doesn't /'dʌznt/ (= *does not*)
    didn't /'dɪdnt/ (= *did not*)
    haven't /'hævnt/ (= *have not*)
    hasn't /'hæznt/ (= *has not*)
    hadn't /'hædnt/ (= *had not*)
    can't /kɑːnt/ (= *cannot*)
    couldn't /'kʊdnt/ (= *could not*)
    won't /wəʊnt/ (= *will not*)
    wouldn't /'wʊdnt/ (= *would not*)
    shan't /ʃɑːnt/ (= *shall not*)
    shouldn't /'ʃʊdnt/ (= *should not*)
    oughtn't /'ɔːtnt/ (= *ought not*)
    mustn't /'mʌsnt/ (= *must not*)
    needn't /niːdnt/ (= *need not*)
    mightn't /maɪtnt/ (= *might not*)
    daren't /deənt/ (= *dare not*)

    Note that:
    's can be *is* or *has*

    She's a student. (= *She is a student.*)
    She's got two brothers. (= *She has got two brothers.*)

    'd can be *had* or *would*

    I'd seen the film before. (= *I had seen the film before.*)
    I'd like a coffee. (= *I would like a coffee.*)

    am not is contracted to *aren't* /ɑːnt/ in questions eg **Aren't** *I right?*

Note also that sometimes two possible negative contractions are possible. For example, we can say *she **isn't*** or *she**'s** **not**, you **aren't** or you**'re** **not**, he **won't** or he**'ll** **not**.*

3   We most often use short forms after a personal pronoun eg *I'm, you've* or in the negatives eg *isn't, don't*. But sometimes we can use a short form (especially *'s*) after a noun.

Maria's *a student.* (= *Maria is a student.*)
*My **father's** got a new car.* (= *My father has got a new car.*)

We can also use a short form after a question word eg *what, where who*, and after *there, here, that* and *now*.

What's *the time?* (= *What is the time?*)   **There'll** *be trouble.* (= *There will be trouble.*)
Where's *Peter gone?* (= *Where has Peter gone?*)   **That's** *right.* (= *That is right.*)

4   We cannot use the affirmative short forms *'s, 've*, etc at the end of a sentence (because a verb at the end of a sentence is stressed).

*Do you know who she **is**?* (Not: ~~*Do you know who she's?*~~)
*'Have you finished?'   'Yes, I **have**.'* (Not: ~~*'Yes, I've.'*~~)

But we can use the negatives *isn't, haven't*, etc at the end of a sentence.

*'Is she English?'   'No, she **isn't**.'*
*You've finished, but I **haven't**.*

Note

–In 'non-standard' English (English which is not considered 'correct') *ain't* /eɪnt/ is often used as a short form of *am not, are not, is not* and *have not, has not* eg *I **ain't** hungry.* (= *I am not hungry.*)
–Do not confuse *it's* (= *it is* or *it has*) and *its* (the possessive form of *it*) eg *The cat ate **its** food.*

190 Irregular verbs

Verbs can be regular or irregular:

1   **Regular verbs**

Regular verbs (eg *work, play, move*) add *-ed* in the past tense and past participle.

INFINITIVE FORM	PAST TENSE	PAST PARTICIPLE
work	work**ed**	work**ed**
play	play**ed**	play**ed**
move	mov**ed**	mov**ed**

2   **Irregular verbs**

Irregular verbs do not add *-ed* in the past tense and past participle:

a   Some irregular verbs have the same form in the infinitive, the past tense and the past participle.

INFINITIVE FORM	PAST TENSE	PAST PARTICIPLE	INFINITIVE FORM	PAST TENSE	PAST PARTICIPLE
bet	bet	bet	put	put	put
burst	burst	burst	read /riːd/	read /red/	read /red/
cost	cost	cost	set	set	set
cut	cut	cut	shut	shut	shut
hit	hit	hit	split	split	split
hurt	hurt	hurt	spread	spread	spread
let	let	let			

b   Other irregular verbs are the same in two of the three forms.

INFINITIVE FORM	PAST TENSE	PAST PARTICIPLE	INFINITIVE FORM	PAST TENSE	PAST PARTICIPLE
beat	beat	beaten	fight	fought	fought
become	became	become	find	found	found
bend	bent	bent	get	got	got
bleed	bled	bled	hang	hung	hung
breed	bred	bred	have	had	had
bring	brought	brought	hear	heard	heard
build	built	built	hold	held	held
burn	burnt*	burnt*	keep	kept	kept
buy	bought	bought	lay	laid	laid
catch	caught	caught	lead	led	led
come	came	come	lean	lent*	lent*
creep	crept	crept	learn	learnt*	learnt*
deal	dealt	dealt	leap	leapt*	leapt*
dig	dug	dug	leave	left	left
dream	dreamt*	dreamt*	lend	lent	lent
feed	fed	fed	light	lit	lit
feel	felt	felt	lose	lost	lost

INFINITIVE FORM	PAST TENSE	PAST PARTICIPLE	INFINITIVE FORM	PAST TENSE	PAST PARTICIPLE
make	made	made	stand	stood	stood
mean	meant	meant	stick	stuck	stuck
meet	met	met	sting	stung	stung
pay	paid	paid	strike	struck	struck
run	ran	run	sweep	swept	swept
say	said	said	swing	swung	swung
sell	sold	sold	teach	taught	taught
send	sent	sent	tell	told	told
			think	thought	thought
shine	shone	shone	understand	understood	understood
shoot	shot	shot	win	won	won
sit	sat	sat	wind	wound	wound
sleep	slept	slept			
smell	smelt*	smelt*			
speed	sped	sped			
spell	spelt*	spelt*			
spend	spent	spent			
spill	spilt*	spilt*			
spit	spat	spat			
spoil	spoilt*	spoilt*			

*These can also be regular: *burned, dreamed, leaned, leaped, learned, smelled, spelled, spilled, spoiled.*

c   Other irregular verbs are different in all three forms.

INFINITIVE FORM	PAST TENSE	PAST PARTICIPLE	INFINITIVE FORM	PAST TENSE	PAST PARTICIPLE
be	was/were	been	ring	rang	rung
begin	began	begun	rise	rose	risen
bite	bit	bitten	see	saw	seen
blow	blew	blown	sew	sewed	sewn*
break	broke	broken	shake	shook	shaken
choose	chose	chosen	show	showed	shown
do	did	done	shrink	shrank	shrunk
draw	drew	drawn	sing	sang	sung
drink	drank	drunk	sink	sank	sunk
drive	drove	driven	speak	spoke	spoken
eat	ate	eaten	spring	sprang	sprung
fall	fell	fallen	steal	stole	stolen
fly	flew	flown	stink	stank	stunk
forbid	forbade	forbidden	swear	swore	sworn
forget	forgot	forgotten	swim	swam	swum
forgive	forgave	forgiven	take	took	taken
freeze	froze	frozen	tear	tore	torn
give	gave	given	throw	threw	thrown
go	went	gone	wake	woke	woken
grow	grew	grown	wear	wore	worn
hide	hid	hidden	write	wrote	written
know	knew	known			
lie	lay	lain			
mistake	mistook	mistaken			
ride	rode	ridden			

*This can also be regular: *sewed.*

Appendix: American English

The grammatical differences between British and American English are not very great. The main differences are as follows:

a   Americans very often use the past simple to announce 'news' in cases where British people use the present perfect (see 6.3).

AMERICAN ENGLISH	BRITISH ENGLISH
*Did you **hear** the news?*	*Have you **heard** the news?*
*My sister **had** a baby!*	*My sister **has had** a baby!*

Americans often use the past simple with *just, already* and *yet* in cases where British people use the present perfect (see 8).

AMERICAN ENGLISH	BRITISH ENGLISH
*He **just went** out.*	*He**'s just gone** out.*
*I **already had** breakfast.*	*I**'ve already had** breakfast.*
*Did you **write** the letter yet?*	*Have you **written** the letter yet?*

b   Americans often use *have*, with *do* and *does* in negatives and questions, in cases where British people use *have got* (see 33).

AMERICAN ENGLISH	BRITISH ENGLISH
*I **have** a car.*	*I**'ve got** a car.*
*He **doesn't have** a job.*	*He **hasn't got** a job.*
*Do you **have** a pen?*	*Have you **got** a pen?*

c   American English has two past participle forms of *get: gotten* and *got*; British English has only one: *got* (see 190.2).

AMERICAN ENGLISH	BRITISH ENGLISH
*I've **gotten/got** a ticket.*	*I've **got** a ticket.*

d   Americans often use the infinitive without *to* after verbs like *suggest, insist, recommend*, etc (see 55.1).

*I **suggested** (that) he **see** the doctor.*
*They **insisted** (that) she **take** the money.*

This structure is also used in British English, especially in a more formal style.

e   There are differences in the use of some prepositions. For example:

AMERICAN ENGLISH	BRITISH ENGLISH
on the weekend/weekends	*at the weekend/weekends* (see 169.1)
*Monday **through** Friday*	*Monday **to** Friday* (see 173.2)
*different **from/than****	*different **from/to*** (see 178)
*stay home/stay **at** home*	*stay **at** home* (see 168.10)
*write somebody/write **to** somebody*	*write **to** somebody* (see 181)

* Although some American speakers think that *different than* is not 'correct'.

f   In American English, *-l* is not normally doubled at the end of a word if the syllable is not stressed (see 188.6c).

AMERICAN ENGLISH	BRITISH ENGLISH
'traveled	*'travelled*

g   The verbs *burn, dream, lean, leap, learn, smell, spell, spill* and *spoil* are normally regular in American English eg *burned, dreamed, leaned, leaped, learned*, etc (see 190.2b).

Glossary

This glossary explains the grammatical terms used in the book.

active: see **passive**

adjective a word such as *red, old, beautiful*, which is used to describe a noun eg *a red car, an old man*, or a pronoun eg *It's red. He's old.*

adverb a word which modifies a verb, an adjective, another adverb, or a sentence, and answers questions such as how? when? or where? eg *She works slowly. He's very old. I'll see you tomorrow. Come here.*

affirmative the opposite of **negative** eg *I know* is **affirmative**, *I don't know* is **negative**.

agent In passive sentences, the agent is the person or thing that the action is done by eg *The radio was invented by Marconi.*

apostrophe the sign (') eg *my friend's car*

article The articles are *a/an* and *the*. See also **definite article** and **indefinite article**.

auxiliary verb a verb such as *be, have* and *do* when it is used to help make verb forms, the passive, etc eg *We are waiting, I have finished, You don't know. It was stolen.* See also **modal auxiliary verb**.

clause a group of words, normally with a subject and a verb eg *I went out* and *it stopped raining*. A sentence is made of one or more clauses eg *I went out when it stopped raining*. See also **main clause**.

comparative eg *older, slower, more intelligent* are the comparative forms of *old, slow, intelligent*

compound a word formed from two or more parts eg *toothbrush (tooth + brush), something (some + thing)*

conditional a sentence or clause with *if* (or a word with a similar meaning) eg *If I see Martin, I'll give him your message. If I knew the answer, I'd tell you.* Note that **conditional** is also used for a structure with *would* (or *should* with *I* and *we*) eg *He would come. I would/should like some coffee.*

conjunction a word which is used to join two clauses eg *and, but, when, if*

consonant: see **vowel**

continuous a verb form with *be* + *-ing* eg *I'm working* (present continuous), *I was working* (past continuous, *I've been working* (present perfect continuous). See also **simple**.

contraction a short form eg *I'm* (= I am), *They've* (= They have), *don't* (= do not)

countable noun *book, egg* and *girl* are examples of countable nouns. Countable nouns are the names of separate things, people, etc which we can count; they have singular and plural forms, and they can be used with *a/an* and numbers eg *a book, two books; an egg, six eggs; one girl, three girls.* See also **uncountable noun**.

defining relative clause a relative clause that tells us which person or thing the speaker means eg *I spoke to the man who works in the post office.* (*Who works in the post office* tells us which man.) See also **non-defining relative clause**.

definite article *the*

demonstrative adjective/pronoun The demonstrative adjectives/pronouns are *this, that, these, those.*

direct object In *I gave John the book*, the **direct object** is *the book*, and the **indirect object** is *John*.

direct speech: see **reported speech**

exclamation word(s) expressing a sudden strong feeling eg *Stop! How incredible!*

exclamation mark the mark (!) written at the end of an exclamation

expression a group of words used together eg *have a bath.*

first person (1st person): see **person**

formal We use **formal** language when we want to show respect eg in business letters and in polite conversations with strangers. We use **informal** language in friendly, everyday conversations and in letters to friends.

full verb an ordinary verb (eg *work, look, run*), not an auxiliary verb (*be, have, do*) or a modal auxiliary verb (*can, must, may*, etc)

genitive: see **possessive 's**

gerund an *-ing* form which is used like a noun eg *Walking is good for you.*

gradable adjective *good* and *large* are **gradable** adjectives: things can be more or less good or large. *Dead* is a **non-gradable** adjective: we do not normally say that something is more or less dead (it is either dead or it is not).

hyphen a short line (-) that joins words eg *tin-opener*

imperative Imperatives have exactly the same form as the infinitive without *to* eg *wait, be, have*. We use the imperative to give orders, make offers, etc eg *Wait here. Be quiet, Have some more tea.*

indefinite article *a/an*

indefinite pronoun eg *something, anyone*

indirect object: see **direct object**

indirect question a question beginning with a phrase like *Do you know . . .?* or *Could you tell me . . .?* eg *Do you know where Ken is?*

infinitive In *I can drive* and *You must come*, the forms *drive* and *come* are the **infinitive without to**. In *I'd like to drive* and *You have to come*, the forms *to drive* and *to come* are the **to infinitive**.

informal: see **formal**

-ing form the form of a verb ending in *-ing* eg *working, running*. See also **gerund** and **present participle**.

intonation the speaker's voice going up (rising intonation) and going down (falling intonation)

irregular: see **regular**

main clause In the sentence *I phoned Maria when I got home*, the **main clause** is *I phoned Maria*; the other clause *when I got home* is a **subordinate clause**. A main clause can stand alone as a sentence, but a subordinate clause cannot.

modal auxiliary verb (or modal verb) The modal auxiliary verbs are *can, could, may, might, will, would, shall, should, ought (to), must, need* and *dare*.

modify to change the meaning of something

negative: see **affirmative**

non-defining relative clause a relative clause that does not tell us which person or thing the speaker means, but which adds information about a person or thing already identified eg *Mrs Higgins, **who is 48**, has just had a baby*. (*Who is 48* does not tell us which person; we already know that it is *Mrs Higgins*.) See also **defining relative clause**.

noun a word that is the name of a person, thing, etc eg *student, girl, car, bedroom*

object: see **direct object** and **subject**

participle: see **present participle** and **past participle**

passive In *I told Peter*, the verb *told* is **active**. In *Peter was told*, the verb *was told* is **passive**.

past participle a verb form like *broken, seen, cleaned*, which can be used to help form perfect tenses eg *I've cleaned my room* (present perfect), the passive eg *The room has been cleaned*, etc. The past participle of regular verbs end in *-ed* eg *cleaned, worked*. Irregular verbs have different past participle forms eg *break* → *broken*. *see* → *seen* (see 190).

perfect a verb form with *have* + past participle eg *I have worked* (present perfect simple), *I had worked* (past perfect simple)

person the way in which we show the speaker (**1st person**), the person spoken to (**2nd person**), and the people or things spoken about (**3rd person**) eg 1st person = *I, we*, 2nd person = *you*, 3rd person = *he, she, it, they*

phrasal verb a verb + particle (adverb or preposition) eg *get up, switch on, throw away*, or verb + particle + preposition eg *look forward to, go back on*

phrase a group of words which are used together eg *a red car* (noun phrase), *would have been* (verb phrase)

plural a form which is used for more than one. *Car* and *he/she* are **singular**, *cars* and *they* are **plural**.

possessive adjective The possessive adjectives are *my, your, his, her, its, our, their*.

possessive pronoun The possessive pronouns are *mine, yours, his, hers, ours, theirs*.

possessive 's (genitive) the form of a noun made with *'s or s'* eg *John's, my parents'*

preposition eg *in, on, of, at, for*

present participle a verb form such as *working, worrying, playing*, which can be used to help make continuous tenses eg *I was **working*** (past continuous), or as an adjective eg *a **worrying** problem*, or as an adverb *I hurt my leg **playing** tennis*.

progressive: see **continuous**

pronoun a word such as *she, they, them, mine*, which is used in place of a noun or noun phrase

question tag an expression like *isn't it?* or *have you?* put at the end of a sentence eg *It's cold, **isn't it?***

question word The question words are *what, where, who, whose, when, why, which, how*.

quotation mark When we quote speech, we can use single quotation marks ('), or double quotation marks (" ") eg *"Goodbye," he said,/'Goodbye,' he said*.

reflexive pronoun The reflexive pronouns are *myself, yourself, himself, herself, itself, ourselves, yourselves, themselves*.

regular a **regular** form follows the same rules as most others; an **irregular** form does not eg *cars, books, rooms* are regular plurals (ending in *-s*), but *men, children* are irregular plurals.

relative clause: see **defining relative clause**, **non-defining relative clause** and **relative pronoun**

relative pronoun In *I spoke to the man who works in the post office*, the word *who* is a relative pronoun. We can use *who, that, which, whose, whom, what* as relative pronouns.

reply question short questions which are used to reply to statements eg *'I'm leaving now.'* *'Are you?'*

reported speech In *He said, I'm cold*, the clause *I'm cold* is **direct speech**. In *He said he was cold*, the clause *he was cold* is **reported speech**.

second person (2nd person): see **person**

sentence a group of words that form a statement, a question, an order, or an exclamation. A sentence normally has one or more clauses. A written sentence begins with a capital letter (eg *A, F, Y*) and ends with a full stop (.), a question mark (?), or an exclamation mark (!).

short answer an answer made with a subject and an auxiliary verb eg *Yes, I am, No, she hasn't*

simple a verb form that is not continuous eg *I work* (present simple), *I worked* (past simple), *I've worked* (present perfect simple). See also **continuous**.

singular: see **plural**

statement a sentence which gives information eg *I'm a student. They went to the cinema.*

stress the way in which we say some words or parts of words with more force than others. In the word *forget*, the stress is on the second syllable *for'get*.

subject a noun or pronoun that comes before the verb in an affirmative sentence eg ***John** went to London.*

superlative eg *oldest, slowest, most intelligent* are the superlative forms of *old, slow, intelligent*

syllable eg *remember* has three syllables re-mem-ber

tag: see **question tag**

tense a verb form which shows the time of an action or state eg *is working* (present), *worked* (past).

third person (3rd person): see **person**

to **infinitive**: see **infinitive**

uncountable: see **countable**

verb a word like *work, play, go, be*. See also **full verb, auxiliary verb** and **modal auxiliary verb.**

voiced sound With a **voiced sound** eg /d/, /b/, /n/, you can feel vibration. With an **unvoiced sound** eg /p/, /k/, /t/, you can feel no vibration.

vowel: The letters *a, e, i, o, u,* are **vowels**. The other letters eg *b, c, d, f, g, h,* are **consonants**.

***wh-* question** a question beginning with a question word eg ***What** are you doing? **Where** did she go? **When** can we start?*

***yes/no* question** a question which can be answered with *Yes* or *No* eg *Are you working? Did she go out? Can we start now?*

Index

Index numbers refer to units, not pages.